CHINA since 1

CHINA SINCE 1911

Richard T. Phillips

First published 1996 by
MACMILLAN PRESS LTD
Houndmills, Basingstoke, Hampshire RG21 6XS
and London
Companies and representatives
throughout the world

ISBN 0–333–63879–4 hardcover
ISBN 0–333–63880–8 paperback

A catalogue record for this book is available
from the British Library.

10   9   8   7   6   5   4   3   2   1
05 04 03 02 01 00 99 98 97 96

Printed in Malaysia

Contents

Acknowledgements

For anyone attempting to write a general history of any kind, the greatest debt must be to the innumerable scholars who have explored aspects of that history through their writings and teaching. For this history of China, some of these scholars have been my teachers in the flesh, in particular Martin Bernal, Denis Twitchett, the late John Fairbank and Roy Hofheinz, but most I know only through the printed word. To them all I offer my thanks, for their collection of information and for their pursuit of understanding through interpretation and analysis of that information. I cannot acknowledge them all personally and can only hint at my debt in the Selective Bibliography that closes this book. I can only hope that my assimilation of their knowledge will be within a framework that does not detract from their scholarly standards.

Institutionally I offer thanks to the University of Auckland, which has provided periods of research leave. Two of these were spent at, respectively, the Research School of Pacific Studies at the Australian National University and the Centre for Modern Chinese Studies at the University of Oxford. I thank their directors for the hospitality provided and their university libraries for access to sources. Josie Underhill and Patrice Hicks typed parts of earlier versions of the manuscript, for which much gratitude. To my students at all levels, I owe my continuing enthusiasm for teaching about China and my realisation that even the best textbook is of limited use without the immediacy of talking and thinking about China.

I dedicate this book to the memory of my late mother, Dr Grace Phillips, who agonised and cajoled so that her 10-year-old son might learn to write those ten-line essays beloved of British primary school teachers, little dreaming that one day he would write something a thousand times longer.

RICHARD T. PHILLIPS

ix

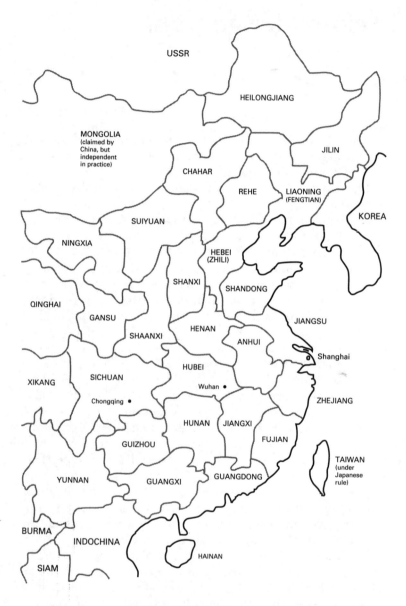

**Provinces of Eastern China
in the Mid-Republican Era, c. 1928**

Romanisation and Abbreviations

This book uses the *pinyin* system for Chinese personal names throughout, treating all personal names as being read in Mandarin Chinese, with surname first, given name second. This results in the following forms for names of individuals linked to the Nationalist Party who are often known by other romanisations:

Jiang Jieshi = Chiang Kai-shek	Jiang Jingguo = Chiang Ching-kuo
Kong Xiangxi = H.H. Kung	Li Denghui = Lee Teng-hui
Song Ziwen = T.V. Soong	Sun Yixian = Sun Yat-sen

Chinese city and province names are also rendered in *pinyin*, except for the terms Tibet (not Xizang), Manchuria (not Dongbei), Macau (not Aomen), Kowloon (not Jiulong) and Hong Kong (not Xianggang). Two Tibetan places, Lhasa and Aksai Chin, have been left in the forms that are standard in Western atlases. The place-name, Mukden, is noted in the text with its *pinyin* equivalent, Fengtian, since to call it by its present name of Shenyang would confuse readers who have heard of the Mukden incident (September 1931) from histories of Japan.

Abbreviations have been kept to the minimum, despite their frequent use in Chinese publications for English readers. The following appear:

APC   Agricultural Producer Cooperative
CCP   Chinese Communist Party
CI   Communist International (Comintern)
CPPCC Chinese People's Political Consultative Conference
GMD   Guomindang (Chinese Nationalist Party)

NRA   National Revolutionary Army
PLA   People's Liberation Army
PRC   People's Republic of China
SEZ   Special Economic Zone

1 Introduction

The purpose of this book is to outline the history of China since the abdication of the last Qing emperor in early 1912. That abdication spelt the end of rule by a system of hereditary monarchy, which had emerged by the start of China's recorded history some 3000 years before. Although the forms of government around the monarch or emperor had changed markedly through that long period, the basic principle of control at the top belonging to a royal house remained unchallenged, even while actual royal families were deposed as dynasties fell to be replaced by others. The disappearance of a hereditary emperor belonging to a named dynasty not only left a huge hole at the centre of Chinese political life but also deeply affected developments which were already occurring in the social, cultural and economic life of China. The collapse of the political system which had been made legitimate by traditional Chinese values left the Chinese searching for new ways to organise their society and for new values to legitimise their innovations, a process which proved both time-consuming and divisive, as will be detailed in the remainder of this text.

The collapse of the Qing dynasty in 1911 and 1912 was caused by strains imposed upon it by both internal and external pressures, which will be outlined in brief below, in order to provide a background to the remainder of the book. The dynasty's replacement by an attempt at a republican parliamentary democracy was specifically related to the extensive challenges posed by foreigners from beyond continental East Asia. These foreigners from the United States of America (USA), Japan and the nations of Europe did not in general acknowledge the superiority of Chinese culture, as had most previous invaders of China. Although all these nations were keen to gain the maximum number of concessions and privileges in China, no one country at that time was keen to conquer China as a whole and to move its capital to Chinese territory, thereby coming under

1

the direct influence of Chinese culture. Hence the events of 1911 and 1912 represented a clean break with the dynastic changes which had previously occurred in China. In these the existing dynasty had always been overwhelmed by either domestic or foreign opponents, who did not, and in fact could not, conceive of an alternative political form beyond hereditary monarchy based in a capital city located in an area of China populated by Chinese-speaking inhabitants, even if another capital might be temporarily maintained elsewhere in the case of foreign invaders.

The lowlands of present-day China form the most easterly part of the temperate zone of the Eurasian landmass and it was in this area that Chinese civilisation arose. Although archaeological evidence can reveal human or proto-human habitation in the Chinese area for several hundreds of thousands of years, a fully developed Chinese civilisation can be securely dated to the middle of the second millennium BC when the Shang dynasty began to flourish in north China, with a complex writing system in use, with extensive towns and with unsurpassed working of bronze for ritual and other purposes. Although some aspects of the civilisation may have drawn on contacts with other parts of Asia, the majority arose within the context of China, as the indigenous population sought to resolve the problems of survival. The leaders of the Shang dynasty and its successor, the Zhou, perceived their area of civilisation to be surrounded on all sides by less-cultured barbarians.

During the Zhou dynasty (c.1122–256 BC) the Chinese discovered iron, and the area under the influence of Chinese civilisation expanded to include central China along the Yangzi River and even parts of south China. At this point the key features of Chinese civilisation included intensive grain-based agriculture in settled permanent communities, a strong focus at least among the elite upon the family and its appropriate rituals including ancestor worship, a strongly hierarchic society relying upon heredity and male dominance, and the use of character-based writing systems blending pictures and sound-based elements.

It was during the Zhou dynasty that the most important philosophers of traditional China were active, including Confucius. The major focus of their deliberations was the creation and maintenance of an acceptable society, both in terms of individual morality and of governmental approach. There was little intellectual interest in religious matters involving the spirit world or gods, beyond the exploration of the concept of the Mandate of Heaven. This clearly religious term had been used by the Zhou to justify its overthrow of the Shang, but came to be defined by philosophers in the later Zhou period as a more general political principle whereby bad rulers could and should be overthrown, with evidence for Heaven's disapproval of the ruler's behaviour being revealed by unusual natural events, such as earthquakes and unpredicted eclipses. The new ruler's legitimacy would be justified by winning the Mandate, which meant in practice winning the race to become the new ruler by defeating all rivals.

The concept of the shifting Mandate of Heaven allowed the Chinese to pass through a whole series of ruling dynasties without any blood links between the ruling houses and even to accept that foreigners might rule China if they could win the Mandate. The first long-lasting dynasty to rule all of lowland China with a centralised administrative system was the Han (202 BC – 220 AD) and the majority (94 per cent) Chinese-speaking part of the population of modern China is referred to as the Han Chinese as a result. During the Han there had been continual problems with the pastoral peoples along the Inner Asian frontiers of China, who had access to horses and were generally more martial in their culture. After the fall of the Han the first wave of Inner Asian attacks gradually penetrated ever more deeply into China, creating foreign dynasties in the north. Chinese rule was reasserted in the late sixth century, but later two further waves of Inner Asian attacks occurred, culminating in the conquest of all of China by the Mongol or Yuan dynasty (1276–1368) and the Manchu or Qing dynasty (1644–1912), with the Han Chinese Ming dynasty (1368–1644) in between.

Although the Mandate of Heaven concept focused upon the morality and behaviour of the ruler as the crucial factor in causing dynastic achievement, modern historians have sought to analyse the pattern of dynastic rise and fall, the so-called dynastic cycle, in a wider framework, while acknowledging the importance of the ruler's leadership qualities. The successful challenger for imperial power had to create an administrative and military machine that could deliver effective results, but after a few generations the ability of the centre to ensure administrative honesty and military vigilance became eroded, as emperors brought up in the closed environment of the palace became disinterested in the detail of their ruling. Corruption spread within the system, that is, the excessive presence of private wealth-seeking in the public sector. Tax revenue, which had been efficiently collected at the start of the dynasty, now did not meet the needs of the dynasty, which often indulged in expensive building projects at the whim of emperors.

Military success at the start of the dynasty often meant the expansion of the frontiers of controlled territory into hostile non-Han regions, with increasing maintenance costs as resistance built up. Within the Han areas regional power-holders tried to erode the ability of the centre to control finance and appointments in their areas, and every success in this respect encouraged others to do likewise. A successful dynasty ensured peace within the country and this allowed the population to expand, putting pressure upon many aspects of the economy but especially upon food supplies in years of poor weather. In addition every sign of internal weakness was taken as an opportunity for those on the edges of China to demand more concessions or to raid more deeply into Chinese territory. Such external attacks only encouraged more popular anger with a government that could not provide adequate defence. Ultimately the combination of problems would bring such widespread discontent with the existing dynasty that new aspirants hoping to wield a more effective dynastic power would arise, either inside or outside China or both.

Such a perceived cyclical pattern in relation to the holding of central political power does not mean that there were no differences at all between dynasties nor that there was absence of change over a longer time period than that of a dynasty. Modern historians have been very keen to point to changes, such as in agricultural technology, in the composition of the elites from whom the imperial officials were chosen, or in the commercialisation and urbanisation of society, to illustrate the variations over time and the increasing complexity of Chinese society.

Historians are also clear that the Ming and Qing dynasties faced more demanding challenges than previous dynasties because of an unprecedented rise in the population under their control. Whereas the Chinese population had oscillated for more than a thousand years around the 60 million figure achieved in the Han dynasty, for reasons that are not fully understood the population doubled during the Ming dynasty to somewhere in the 120–150 million range and then trebled to somewhere in the 400–500 million range by the end of the Qing dynasty. Such increases, although small in percentage growth rate terms per year (c.0.5 per cent), imposed immense burdens upon the administrative ability of the government to provide services for the population. The Qing dynasty did not increase the small number (c.20 000) of centrally appointed officials to match the population rise and thus officials away from the capital were forced to rely increasingly upon locally recruited clerks of doubtful worth to collect taxes and assist in the delivery of government services.

During the eighteenth century at the time of the peak effectiveness of the Qing dynasty China reached one of the high points in its entire history. This was experienced not only in the quality of life within China but also in the ability of the central government to project its power geographically, either by direct rule as in parts of Mongolia, Tibet and Turkestan or by military action in, and subsequent payment of tribute by, non-administered areas, such as Nepal after the 1790s. This mid-Qing geographical heritage has been of vital importance to the definition of the territory of modern China because modern Chinese governments have aspired to regain the whole of the Qing-administered territory, however limited the real level of Qing control might have been. The wider tribute-offering zone has never been seriously regarded by modern Chinese leaders as fully part of China, although there is a wish to maintain influence in this region for security reasons.

By the early nineteenth century the Qing dynasty had passed its peak as China experienced a wave of rebellions which were suppressed only with difficulty, the first major one being the White Lotus rebellion of 1796–1804. The government was obliged to allow local areas to organise their own military forces to restore order because the central forces proved inadequate, a trend that was greatly accelerated in the suppression of the Taiping rebellion (1851–64), which saw regional armies financed from local taxes as the new mainstay of the dynasty. These rebellions had arisen on the basis of traditional factors, such as rural hardship, corruption, ethnic rivalries and religious calls for popular action in evil times. Many of the rebels sought to increase the appeal of their actions by stressing the foreignness (non-Han-ness) of the Manchu ruling elite, an ironic situation because the Manchus had made strong efforts to court the Chinese elite by upholding Chinese values and preserving China's heritage.

The internal problems of the Qing dynasty were matched by difficulties on the frontiers of the imperial domain, as could have been expected in any dynastic decline, but the form and location of these difficulties differed from all previous cases. All previous dynasties had faced their major external threat from the horsemen of Inner Asia, but with the widespread availability of firearms and artillery the military advantages of the Inner Asian fighters had largely been lost. The new enemy on the Inner Asian side of China was the tsarist Russian state, with its desire to expand from its main base in Europe towards the Pacific Ocean. At first the existence of an expansionist Russia had been of assistance to the stability of the Inner Asian borders of China, since it restricted the mobility of the traditional Inner Asian enemies of China, but by the mid-nineteenth century Russia had begun to impinge directly upon areas which the dynasty regarded as its territory.

In the nineteenth century foreigners began to pose a serious military threat from a new direction, along the Chinese coast. Although the Chinese had considerable experience of pirate activity and of overseas trade along the coast, the nineteenth-century experience was different, in that the foreigners, from Europe and the USA, were prepared to launch limited military actions in order to change the trading arrangements along the coast to their advantage. In addition these foreigners and the Japanese were willing to act along the coast to seek clear definitions of the boundaries of China, not merely over islands such as Taiwan, but also over continental areas such as Korea, Vietnam and Burma. Nevertheless the European nations which had fought to conquer and populate all the other temperate zones of the globe did not choose to colonise East Asia, preferring rather an indirect control through unequal treaties mostly imposed in the 60 years after the British victory over China in 1842. In part this choice arose from the realisation that no one European country could hope to rule China by itself and that the alternative of a division of China among the powers would provoke more conflict among the powers than the division was worth to each power.

Foreign attacks from the Chinese coast resulted in two occupations of the Imperial capital, Beijing, in 1860 and 1900, thereby revealing the military inadequacy of the Imperial forces. Efforts to rectify this military inadequacy automatically required access to Western military knowledge. The attempts after 1860 focused on the acquisition of new equipment, including the construction of arsenals, which in turn promoted some limited industrial activity in China. This movement, known as self-strengthening, assumed that the basic fabric of Chinese society and culture was sound and that Western knowledge would play only a very limited role.

Defeat by Japan in 1894–5 and the second occupation of Beijing in 1900 provoked a much stronger demand for change. At one extreme were the revolutionaries, groups of plotters who since 1895 had been calling for the overthrow of the Qing dynasty and its replacement by a republic modelled on Western political institutions. Less extreme were those reformers who sought a constitutional monarchy for China, that is, the retention of the Qing dynasty with its structure amended to incorporate some Western institutions. The government's major response to 1895 was the beginning of a new centrally funded army modelled on Western training, with Yuan Shikai as the principal organiser. The government's response after 1900 was to begin to restructure the bureaucracy with a much wider range of duties for government, such as promotion of commerce and education. The military programme was also expanded with the creation of New Army units, most vigorously in north China around the capital where a six-division Beiyang Army was developed. Then after Japan's defeat of Russia in 1905, the government began to develop its own constitutional reform programme, creating provincial assemblies in 1909 with the final goal of a national parliamentary system in place by 1917.

The collapse of the Qing dynasty can thus be traced to two separate sets of issues, those relating to problems which a declining dynasty would normally have faced and those which were new because of the new challenge posed by the foreign powers. In some cases the two overlapped, as in the large indemnities imposed by the victorious foreigners, which required the raising of further taxes from the already discontented taxpayers facing the decay of public works and the erosion of official honesty. Historians have argued that the Qing dynasty made a vigorous effort to act more effectively between 1901 and 1908 in the face of its difficulties. This effort ultimately failed because the dynasty lacked the resources to finance its programme adequately, because the reforms required the strengthening of central government at a time when the regions were asserting their power, and above all because after 1908 the ruling royal family lacked well-established leaders willing to take political risks. The dynasty was led by an inexperienced Regent after the death of the Guangxu Emperor and of the Empress Dowager Cixi in 1908 and he was much more concerned to preserve his own position within the Manchu hierarchy than to tolerate any acceleration of reform plans which might increase the role of Han Chinese in the Imperial government.

The first month of the 1911 Revolution which toppled the dynasty drew its principal actors from the provincial elites and the provincial units of the New Army, who rallied to the anti-Qing cause in 1911. Their discontent with the Qing arose from conflicts over the role of the new provincial assemblies, over the composition of the new cabinet of 1911 and especially over the question of the control of the railways planned for China. Although illegal revolutionary parties had been active for sixteen years promoting revolution, their organisations and finances were not strong in 1911 and they were unable to dominate the flow of events. The most famous of the revolutionary parties was the Tongmenghui, the Revolutionary Alliance, established in 1905 in Tokyo, with Sun Yixian as its leader. Despite the organisational weaknesses of the revolutionary parties the decision to create a republic out of the collapse of the Qing owed much to the propaganda of the revolutionaries, as did the widespread appeal of the attack upon the Qing as non-Han, which provided the main unifying factor for those in revolt.

The revolution began on October 10 in the triple city of Wuhan in central China where the Yangzi and Han rivers meet. Wuchang to the south of the Yangzi was the provincial capital, while to the north of the Yangzi were Hanyang and Hankou, a treaty port opened to foreign trade after 1860. New Army units in this area had been considerably infiltrated by revolutionary sympathisers, but the opportunity for action occurred after troops from the Wuhan area had been sent west in September to Sichuan province to quell unrest there over railway nationalisation. Revolutionary organisers among the remaining troops decided to prepare to rise in the expectation of support from revolutionaries based in Shanghai, but the unintended explosion of a bomb being prepared by the plotters threatened to ruin the whole undertaking. Faced with police repression, the plotters were forced to act at once, without a clear leadership structure in place. After a false start on 9 October, military success was achieved in Wuchang from the evening of 10 October, with the top Qing officials fleeing the city. Lacking a clear local leader with wider revolutionary credentials, the rebels turned to the most senior military officer present whom they could persuade to join their undertaking, one Li Yuanhong. Li was not an active revolutionary and was known to have reported suspected revolutionaries to the Qing authorities. Nevertheless he was now thrust into prominence quite fortuitously, later becoming president of China. Under Li's leadership the independence of Wuhan from the Qing was proclaimed, with support from the provincial assembly and the local chamber of commerce. The rebels were extremely worried that the foreign powers would intervene in the anti-Qing process and hence quickly announced that all existing treaties between the Qing and the foreigners and all the privileges granted therein would be respected.

Thus the pattern for an anti-Manchu independence movement was established. The Manchus were attacked as a group that was ready to betray China to foreign interests rather than lose their own special privileges. The anti-Manchu cause could win support from a wide range of social groups – the local educated elites seeking greater power under the constitutional reforms, the military seeing the ineptness of the Qing defence of China, the small bourgeois class desiring protection from foreign competition, and even the mass of the population which had preserved anti-Qing feelings through the activities of rebellious secret societies long predating revolutionary activity. Nevertheless anti-Manchu feeling could not be turned immediately into general anti-foreign action, because the foreigners presented too great a threat to the success of the anti-Qing movement. Hence the irony that the revolutionary victors of 1911 had to allow all foreign rights to remain. By focusing on the issue of Manchu political power, the leaders at Wuhan and subsequent centres also restricted any wider attempt at social or economic revolution, even though Sun Yixian in his revolutionary propaganda had called for a commitment to improve people's livelihood, in addition to his calls for national leadership by the Han majority and for people's rights.

Thus the revolution of 1911 represented only the first step in the re-creation of Chinese society. The political attack on the Qing became the basis for the rejection of the dynastic system, but much else needed to change before China could emerge again as a strong nation able to resist external pressure and to provide stable living conditions for all its population. The Chinese Communists later viewed the 1911 Revolution as the first stage of the bourgeois-democratic revolution in China. Although the role of the bourgeoisie as leaders in the revolution needs to be questioned vigorously, the sense that this was the start of a larger process of change is clearly useful.

2 The Early Republic

The Wuchang uprising of 10 October 1911 provided a direct impetus for declarations of independence which spread through thirteen provinces within a month, stretching from Shanxi in the north to the whole of South China. The declarations were based upon a rejection of the Qing dynasty as a Manchu imposition and were announced in most cases by the provincial assemblies or the New Army units or both. The takeover of power was generally quick and relatively bloodless, a sign that the Qing dynasty had outlived its support. The direct involvement of the overseas revolutionary parties was limited except in Shanghai and Guangdong, but in the absence of a clearly acceptable candidate for a Chinese emperor to replace the Qing, all the rebelling provinces readily grasped at the republican formula as another basis for their actions. Coordination between the rebels was urged in telegrams from the leaders in Wuchang and Shanghai in November. In early December at Wuchang, delegates from the rebel provinces had outlined a new government structure, while Nanjing, captured on 2 December, emerged as the seat of the provisional government. Most of the provincial representatives from seventeen provinces had reached there by the latter part of December.

The desired form for the new government was that of an elected legislative system whose representatives would choose the president who would designate the cabinet. In the period before general elections, the provincial delegates would act as the legislative assembly. In the December outline the definition of the relationship between president and cabinet was none too clear. Over the coming months the exact form of this relationship was to become a source of major political tension, because a strong executive presidency could overrule the cabinet, which the revolutionary politicians hoped to dominate, while a weak symbolic presidency would not suit the political style of the available candidates. Sun Yixian returned to China on 25 December 1911, and was appointed provisional president on 29 December, as a famous revolutionary leader and also as a compromise candidate to resolve the squabbling among the representatives of the independent provinces. Sun was sworn in on 1 January 1912, thereafter regarded as the start of the Republican calendar. The provincial representatives voted the next day for a strong presidential system, whereby presidential decrees did not require the countersignature of the relevant cabinet minister, although the president was required to gain assembly approval for his cabinet appointments.

Meanwhile the Qing dynasty, surprised at the rapidly deteriorating situation, had little choice but to recall Yuan Shikai, the military bureaucrat who had created the Beiyang Army. This army, based in North China, was the best part of the modernised army developed in the late Qing period, but it proved reluctant to move into battle while Yuan remained in retirement. Yuan's price for re-emergence was high. He only agreed to serve actively when offered the position of prime minister in early November, having turned down earlier lower offers, although he had to prove his worth by persuading his military subordinates to counterattack against rebel-held Hankou, which was retaken on 2 November. Yuan insisted that the Qing dynasty move towards a more meaningful form of constitutional monarchy and received a free hand in his negotiations with the rebels. Yuan, as the most senior and militarily the best-placed bureaucrat in China, now had the opportunity to pursue his own career while bringing about a reconciliation between the two sides. While sternly rooting out republican sympathisers from the northern army, he conducted both public diplomacy with the southern rebels on behalf of the dynasty and secret talks to discuss a possible turn to the republic by himself and his forces with the presidency as a reward. Talks had begun as early as 11 November and were held in earnest in December after an unconditional truce at Wuhan from 1 December.

Politics in 1912

January 1912 witnessed further clever politicking by Yuan as he sought to ensure that the collapse of the Qing dynasty should also bring the enhancement of his own power. He reacted very cautiously to Sun Yixian's offer on 1 January to hand over the presidency to Yuan, while Yuan arranged for his military subordinates to telegraph the imperial court on 2 January with their total opposition to a republic. Once an agreement had been reached in secret with the revolutionaries, however, Yuan began to pressure the court for an abdication. The court nobles met for six conferences from 17 January, but only gave way after another telegram from military leaders, this time insisting on a republic. Yuan was empowered by the court to negotiate abdication terms and on 12 February the edict of abdication was issued, which instructed Yuan to organise the provisional republican government. By the terms of abdication agreed by both Yuan and the Nanjing leaders, the Emperor was permitted to keep his titles, his properties and an annual pension of 4 million taels, an agreement that was upheld for almost thirteen years.

The Nanjing provisional government now attempted to restrict the power of Yuan Shikai, whilst granting him his formal reward as provisional president, but was only partly successful before its amalgamation with the leaders in Beijing. The Nanjing leadership carried a vote to make Nanjing the national capital, after threatening the assembly at Nanjing with the use of the military police, and a nine-man delegation went north to escort Yuan to Nanjing for his inauguration. The response in the north was a mutiny in Beijing on 29 February, which spread to Tianjin and severely damaged Baoding. Japanese troops were immediately sent to reinforce the foreign quarter in Beijing and Yuan was able to plead that in the circumstances the change of capital was unsuitable. Suspicion remains that Yuan plotted the mutiny, but it seems more likely that he stood to lose by encouraging any indiscipline amongst his troops and that therefore the mutiny was a response by subordinate military men who opposed the removal of a northern capital. The foreigners too were known to prefer Yuan to remain as a firm leader in North China, where their legations allowed access to government in Beijing protected by military rights gained after the Boxer uprising of 1900.

Yuan was sworn in as provisional president in Beijing on 10 March without knowing what constitution he was swearing to

uphold, since Sun was only to proclaim the provisional constitution the next day. The constitution, while continuing the
interim power of the existing provisionally appointed assembly,
called for elections within ten months to create two chambers,
a senate by provinces and a house of representatives by population distribution. The president's powers were extensive, but
were restricted by the need for assembly approval for war, peace
and treaties and for the appointment of diplomatic envoys and
of cabinet ministers, who were to co-sign all laws before enactment. A cabinet was appointed after considerable negotiation,
with Tang Shaoyi as premier and with ten ministers, all with
overseas training, approximately balanced between the revolutionaries and Yuan's confidants, although the major posts of
army, foreign affairs and civil affairs ministers went to Yuan's
side. Tang was regarded as an acceptable compromise candidate, because he had served with Yuan since 1885, but had
joined the revolutionary side in 1912 when he had been officially serving as Yuan's negotiator. With the cabinet decided,
Sun Yixian formally relinquished his position on 1 April and
thereafter the Nanjing assembly adjourned its operations to
move to Beijing, where its membership was almost trebled by
Yuan calling for more members from each province to be appointed in accordance with the provisional constitution.

Politics during the remainder of 1912 centred on two areas,
the struggle by Yuan Shikai to increase presidential power and
the efforts by the revolutionaries to resist Yuan and to build a
post-revolutionary political party to take advantage of the parliament due in early 1913. Conflicts between Yuan and his cabinet
arose over the question of how to fund the central government through foreign loans, which were seen as necessary given
the financial disruption in China, and over who should initiate
policy. Premier Tang finally resigned in June when his pro-
revolutionary candidate for the governorship of Zhili province
around Beijing was ordered back by Yuan to Nanjing to dis-
band troops, without the necessary countersignature from the
premier. Tang's revolutionary colleagues also tendered their
resignations, which were officially accepted in mid-July, after
Yuan had proposed Lu Zhengxiang, a non-partisan diplomat,
as premier. The assembly, threatened by force, voted Lu's acceptance, but within a day began impeachment proceedings

against him for neglect of duty and rejected his cabinet team. Lu pleaded illness and Zhao Bingjun, minister of civil affairs and a major figure in the creation of China's modern police force, became acting premier, until formally endorsed in 24 September. Zhao was very close to Yuan, but had agreed to join the Tongmenghui, the Revolutionary Alliance, in March 1912. His cabinet became acceptable to the revolutionaries when most of its members joined the revolutionaries' new party, the Guomindang, set up in August 1912. On 25 September an eight-point agreement was announced among Yuan, Sun Yixian, Huang Xing and Li Yuanhong, implying a public front of unity among the different factions in China, as the new republic sought formal recognition by the foreign powers and the solution of diplomatic problems in Tibet and Mongolia.

One important effect of declaring a republic was the legally permitted appearance of political parties which had been banned under the Qing. Over 300 party names are known for 1911 and 1912. The majority of the Tongmenghui members of various factions responded warmly to the decision in January 1912 to form an overt political party. At its congress in March Sun was elected as its president and a new party constitution was drawn up, stressing consolidation of the republic and the promotion of social welfare. Nevertheless some members preferred to organise their own parties, partly in resistance to the choice of Sun as leader. Those who had favoured constitutional reform before the revolution also moved to create their own parties, the most important becoming the Republican Party, seen as supporting Yuan, and the Democratic Party, soon led by Liang Qichao, the long-term reformist opponent of the Tongmenghui. Among other parties formed was a Chinese Socialist Party, whose study groups rapidly burgeoned in the cities, reading socialist works including parts of the 'Communist Manifesto' in translation.

In the interest of fighting the forthcoming election, whose electoral law was announced in August 1912, the Tongmenghui leaders, in particular Song Jiaoren, discussed the possibility of expanding the party's chances through amalgamation with other smaller parties. The first negotiations were with the United Republican Party, which agreed to a merger, subject to the dropping of the name Tongmenghui and the removal of the principle of social welfare. After some resistance over the name, the merger plans were completed during August in Beijing, and on 25 August the founding meeting of the Guomindang or Nationalist Party was held, combining the Tongmenghui and four smaller parties. The new party dropped some of the Tongmenghui planks, including the call for international equality for China, equal rights for men and women and the equalisation of land rights. The new party chose Sun Yixian as head of its executive committee, but he delegated the task to Song Jiaoren. Sun's followers suggested in later years that Sun had disagreed with the formation of the Nationalist party and had withheld his support, but he is known to have encouraged ex-Tongmenghui members to work for the new party and to have raised funds for it among overseas Chinese, although he did also offer some support to the Chinese Socialist Party in the latter part of 1912.

Politics in 1913

The elections at the end of 1912 and the start of 1913 established the Nationalist Party as the leading party, under its principal organiser, Song Jiaoren. Basic voting was open to adult males with two-year residence qualifications and either elementary schooling or property holdings of $500 or direct tax payments of $2 per year, resulting in an electoral eligibility for 20 to 25 per cent of all adult males, with actual voting rates varying from 33 to 80 per cent in different places. The basic voters selected colleges of electors (c. 30 000 in all) who chose the 596 lower-house representatives by constituencies and the members of the provincial assemblies, which in turn selected the 274 upper-house senators by provinces. The Nationalists, who had campaigned for local self-government and provincial autonomy, won 269 lower seats and 123 in the Senate, by far the largest single party figure, even winning seats where the provincial governor was opposed to the Nationalists, implying a relatively incorrupt election process. As the scale of the Nationalist success became clear in January 1913, Song Jiaoren began to speak out in criticism of the central government. Rumours began of moving the parliament away from Beijing and Yuan's influence, and of the possibility that the parliament might not confirm Yuan as full president once the permanent constitution had been drawn up. As Song boarded a train to travel to Beijing on 20 March to attend the parliamentary opening and probably to become premier, he was gunned down, dying two days later of his wounds. When the assassin was captured, the evidence pointed to the existing premier, Zhao Bingjun, and his secretary as the instigators. It was even revealed that in January Yuan had met the Shanghai-based hirer of the actual assassin.

The murder of Song, even if not directly ordered by Yuan, was a symptom of major problems which beset Yuan as he endeavoured to fulfil his own ambitions as provisional president. The 1911 Revolution had resulted in a severe loss of power by the central government, for as the provinces and even some sub-provincial units declared independence they usually appointed local leaders as local officials, to replace the centrally appointed local bureaucrats, who under Qing rules had not been allowed to be locals. The provinces faced soaring military costs as up to 1 million troops were recruited during the months of the revolution, but suffered loss of revenue for reasons including the increased autonomy of sub-provincial units, the revolutionary hints about lower taxation and the increased political power of the local elite. The latter now dominated the provincial assemblies and were keen to pay less tax. The result was straitened financial circumstances for the provinces, which therefore refused to remit any money to the centre. Since a major reason for provincial support of the revolution was to attain local leadership over reform, the provinces were also reluctant to see political interference by the centre in either appointments or policy and began to implement their own programmes. The most radical was in Guangdong under Tongmenghui leader, Hu Hanmin, with efforts towards sexual equality, universal education and financial reform.

Yuan regarded the devolution of administrative authority as weakening the power of the country and sought to re-establish the centre's strength, relying on his presidential mandate, the favour of the foreign powers and the quality of his staff, both civil and military. He attempted to appoint provincial officials and to divide provincial leadership between a civil and a military governor, but met with little success up to 1913, except near Beijing.

Yuan's major worry was fiscal, because he had lost provincial revenues, and the major central revenue – the customs taxes on international trade – was earmarked to repay foreign loans and debts. He survived through 1912 with small loans from abroad, but it was clear that he would need access to greater financial resources, which forced him into negotiations for a large reorganisation loan from the consortium of foreign banks, which received the backing of the governments of Britain, France, Germany, Russia, Japan and the USA. Although admitting in private that China's credit was sufficient for loans on the existing basis, the bankers insisted upon the earmarking of salt taxes for repayments, under foreign inspectors, and upon the appointment of foreign supervisors to oversee the use of the funds. Negotiations over these impositions dragged out for fourteen months, but finally in April 1913 Yuan was ready to sign, although he knew that the parliament would never agree. So he persuaded the foreigners to accept his signature as sufficient authority, despite its implication of foreign connivance in the undermining of a constitutional process which had been modelled on the West.

The Reorganisation Loan was nominally for £25 million, but after deductions for the bankers, for the clearance of old debts and for possible indemnities for 1911 Revolution foreign losses, less than half the money was actually available to Yuan's government, at a long-term cost of almost £68 million over 47 years. The US banks withdrew from the loan talks after the inauguration of President Wilson in March 1913, who argued that the loans impinged on China's integrity, but these banks agreed privately not to threaten the nearly completed talks by offering any independent loans of their own.

The assassination of Song Jiaoren and the Reorganisation Loan indicated to the Nationalists how far Yuan would be prepared to go to achieve greater power, even at the cost of selling out to the foreigners as the Qing had done and of subverting the constitution he had sworn to uphold. Sun Yixian and other Nationalist leaders began to consider a military challenge to Yuan, which they were to name as the Second Revolution, but militarily they could not match Yuan. Yuan had placed northern troops in Hubei at the invitation of Li Yuanhong, who feared Nationalist plottings. Yuan had also taken over the Shanghai arsenal after a local uprising. With his troops well-trained and with funds in hand, Yuan financed the creation of the Progressive Party to combine all anti-Nationalist politicians, and in June he ordered the dismissal, first, of the most annoying Nationalist governor, Li Liejun, in Jiangxi, and then of others in Guangdong and Anhui. Li, after accepting his dismissal quietly, reacted promptly to the introduction of northern troops into Jiangxi by declaring independence on 12 July. Nanjing turned to the Nationalists on 15 July, but although declarations of sympathy came from Anhui, Sichuan, Hunan, Guangdong and Fujian, the main fighting occurred in Jiangxi and Jiangsu, where Yuan's forces were fully victorious by 1 September. The Nationalists had not used the defence of provincial rights as a rallying cry nor sought popular mobilisation in their resistance to Yuan, while he had been able to argue the need for national unity to isolate the Nationalists.

The failure of military resistance against Yuan left the way open for the formal inauguration of Yuan as president and his further rejection of constitutional restraints on his power. Although Yuan's political strength came ultimately from his relations with the Beiyang modern army, his formally legitimate authority could only derive from the parliament, and the major foreign powers, except the USA, were only willing to accord full recognition to Republican China after the completion of the presidential election. The Second Revolution had led to calls for all Nationalist parliamentarians to leave Beijing for the south, but these calls had only been heeded by a minority of members, thereby allowing Yuan a quorum in the parliament for the presidential election, provided that he could persuade those present to vote for him.

Normal constitutional procedure would have required the completion and acceptance of the full constitution by the parliament, to be followed by elections under the new rules enacted, but Yuan urged on his supporters to demand the separate presentation and enactment of the presidential election laws before the rest of the constitution. As a result these sections of the constitution were ready on 6 October 1913 and the parliament began the election, with the building surrounded by secret police disguised as Yuan supporters who refused to let the members out without a pro-Yuan vote, which was gained on the third ballot. Full recognition was now accorded to the republic, especially after the newly secure president signed an agreement with Russia accepting Russian activity in Outer Mongolia.

Although it had confirmed Yuan as president, the parliament still had to produce the rest of the constitution and, despite Yuan's pressure, designated a cabinet and not a presidential system. With the parliament opposed to him over the constitution and over his conciliatory foreign policy, including new concessions to Japan for damages at Nanjing during its recapture at the end of the Second Revolution, Yuan moved on 4 November to dissolve the Nationalist Party. He dismissed from Parliament both the currently registered members and those who had at some stage been registered, thereby leaving the Parliament without a quorum. Parliament's fate was to be discussed by a new body, the Political Conference, appointed by Yuan, which resulted in the formal dissolution of Parliament in January 1914.

Politics in 1914

During 1914 Yuan proceeded to consolidate his own authority and to increase central control over the provinces, in the process rejecting the remaining representative institutions of the late Qing period. In the aftermath of the Second Revolution, Yuan was able to introduce his troops into over two-thirds of the Han-majority provinces of China, with the remaining third in the south cowed into submission. He began the restoration of central appointment over local officials, by insisting upon the replacement of many officials who had taken office under local initiative during the revolutionary changeover in 1911. In the spring of 1914 he published regulations to increase the powers of civil governors and to reduce those of military governors, especially over appointments and taxation. At the same time provincial assemblies were abolished and sub-provincial assembly members were dismissed, thereby removing the possibility of the articulation of local elite opinions and grievances through Western-style institutions.

At the centre, Yuan's creation – the Political Conference – established a Constitutional Conference, which met under an ex-Nationalist chairman to revise the constitution to suit Yuan's presidential ambitions. The constitution of 1 May 1914 extended the president's powers very widely, to include senior appointments without any other institutional consent needed and the issuance of government regulations in both ordinary times and emergencies. Several of the Chinese terms used had distinctly imperial overtones, including that used for Yuan's principal assistant, the secretary of state, a post awarded to his very old friend, Xu Shichang. A consultative council was set up, which soon took over legislative duties at Yuan's behest, and which revised the presidential election laws, to allow for ten-year renewable terms, for the cancellation of elections if circumstances required, and for the existing president to nominate the candidates, up to three in number, for the next election.

Although open opposition to Yuan was quelled, not all his plans could be carried through because of the opposition of the military leaders, whom Yuan had formerly promoted through his Beiyang Army. Even as provisional president in 1912 and 1913, Yuan had suggested various plans to reorganise the provincial structure of China and in particular to create new military regions independent of the old provincial units. In May and June 1914, he reorganised the leadership of the military, by creating the headquarters of the Commander-in-chief, where the power of the army minister, Duan Qirui, could be diluted by Yuan's appointees and by promulgating the replacement of the 22 provinces by 89 districts, which would have been far weaker in their ability to resist the centre. Such a shift of power was rejected by the existing provincial leaders, but Yuan was able to discontinue the office of military governor, while reappointing most ex-military governors and some civil governors as 26 *jiangjun* or generals.

This setback to Yuan's reorganisation plans and his awareness that the Beiyang Army senior officers were no longer his obedient tools led Yuan to begin the organisation in October 1914 of a model army corps, independent of the army ministry and drawn at first from high-grade officer material. Four brigades were trained in the first six months and Yuan's aim seems to have been the creation of ten divisions of central troops, drawing on these officers. In August 1915 a special government conference even discussed the use of this new army

as the centre's main force and the demotion of Beiyang troops
to provincial police duties. By then it was clear that Yuan had
become distrustful of his own earlier creation, the Beiyang Army,
which he could no longer control adequately. His plans to super-
sede it caused resentment within the Beiyang Army leadership,
which found expression in opposition to the consolidation of
Yuan's monarchy plans in 1916.

One important result of the growing power of the centre
during 1914 was a return to budgetary self-sufficiency by August, through the extraction of more revenue from the provinces and the retrenchment of expenditures. This balance was
to be vital, given the outbreak of the First World War, which
prevented further foreign loans to the Chinese government for
three years.

China and the War in Europe

The outbreak of a major European war posed the major question of how the Chinese government should react, especially
given the existing foreign concessions in China and the likelihood of naval warfare in the Pacific. With Yuan pro-British and
very close to Jordan (the British Minister in Beijing) and with
many of the Beiyang Army officers certain of German victory
after their German military training, the obvious course was to
declare neutrality and to urge the foreign powers to forbid
belligerent activity in the treaty ports. Such a course was not
welcome to Japan, which reckoned that the European war presented a unique opportunity to advance in China.

Immediately the war began in Europe, the Japanese government sought to persuade Britain that Japan should enter the
war under the Anglo-Japanese alliance arrangements. Britain
tried to dissuade Japan, suspecting that Japan's intentions concerned China, rather than any European commitment, but Japan
insisted, declaring war on Germany on 23 August after issuing
an ultimatum requiring Germany to hand over Qingdao, the
German port on the south Shandong coast taken in 1897. The
ultimatum stated that the port should be handed to Japan with
a view to its eventual restoration to China, but over the next
months this suggestion was dropped from the Japanese approach

because, as Japan argued, the Germans had rejected the ultimatum. Japanese troops with a token British contingent landed in Shandong in September and captured Qingdao by November, fighting across Chinese territory which Yuan Shikai was forced to declare a belligerency zone. Once fighting ceased, China wished to revoke the war-zone permission, but Japan insisted on stationing troops in the area, on replacing Chinese railway guards by Japanese soldiers and on taking over the customs service, resulting in anti-Japanese public meetings in Shandong by December.

The situation with Japan came to a head in January 1915, when the Chinese official announcement of the end of the Shandong war zone provoked the presentation of Japan's Twenty-One Demands, which Hioki, the Japanese minister in Beijing, had been under orders to hand in at a suitable moment. The demands represented months of bureaucratic negotiations within Japan to produce a document which would both clarify the existing Japanese position in China and seek to extend that position. The demands were in five groups, with the fifth group officially listed as *desiderata*. The first four groups covered Japanese demands over Shandong, Manchuria, the iron industry in the Yangzi valley and the status of Fujian, demands which the Japanese could have expected to be acceptable to China and the other foreign powers, given China's weaknesses. Group Five, with its demands for Japanese advisers throughout the Chinese government and Japan as sole supplier of foreign armaments to the Chinese army, was quite unacceptable.

Japan, under Foreign Minister Kato, handled the negotiations very poorly, requiring absolute secrecy from the Chinese and providing the increasingly apprehensive Western powers with incomplete copies of the demands. Chinese diplomacy was masterful, with careful leaking of the demands to win international sympathy and clever delaying tactics by insisting on clause-by-clause negotiation and by use of counter-proposals. Finally Japanese patience was exhausted and an ultimatum was presented on 7 May, requiring Chinese acceptance of the first four groups of demands. Yuan agreed at this point, despite the opposition of his army minister, the leading Beiyang general Duan Qirui, and the public outcry against Japan, including a boycott of Japanese goods. The treaty was signed on 25 May, and 7 May, the day of the ultimatum, became known as 'national humiliation day'. The other foreign powers, as part of their rejection of Japan's excessively aggressive diplomatic approach, agreed that they would not avail themselves of the extra rights which Japan had gained and which could theoretically be shared amongst all the powers by the most-favoured-nation clauses of earlier treaties.

Yuan Shikai's Monarchy Project

The resolution of the diplomatic crisis with Japan allowed Yuan to proceed with his restoration of the monarchy in China, although he did not appear at first to be openly sponsoring the monarchical government. Yuan seems to have decided that the republican system, even under the new presidential rules, could never generate sufficient power and legitimacy for the centre and that a return to monarchy would accord with the general will of the population, to whom republicanism was strange. The transformation of Yuan into the legitimate emperor would also tend to remove his image as a military dictator, which was seen as an impediment to possible US loans, and the whole process was encouraged by various Beijing politicians, including Yuan's son, Yuan Keding.

Yuan's plans would undoubtedly require cooperation from abroad and most importantly he sounded out the Japanese, who replied vaguely but generally encouragingly. He also invited the leading US constitutional law expert, Goodnow, to provide his opinions, which firmly favoured a monarchy over a republic for a country such as China. Within a week of Goodnow's memorandum, a Peace Planning Society was formed to agitate publicly for monarchy and during the autumn of 1915 the Political Conference made arrangements which culminated in a unanimous ballot by almost 2000 Yuan-appointed representatives in favour of a monarchy. Yuan at first declined the offer of being emperor, in a display of traditional modesty, but accepted on 12 December, naming the forthcoming imperial era as *hongxian* – glorious constitution.

Yuan's monarchy was faced with opposition from the moment of its announcement. The Japanese had already turned firmly against a monarchy by October 1915 and informed Yuan accordingly. The Japanese leaders had disliked Yuan on a personal basis since his strongly anti-Japanese activities in Korea in the 1880s, but now added new fears that domestic opposition to Yuan would provoke turmoil in China to the detriment of Japanese interests, as well as realising that Yuan was being deliberately slow in implementing the May 1915 treaty. The Japanese threatened to use Sun Yixian against Yuan, since Sun had been in exile in Japan since 1913, but Sun and the small Chinese Revolutionary Party whose members had sworn personal loyalty to Sun were hardly a serious threat, especially after Sun's fawningly pro-Japanese stance during the Twenty-One Demands period had damaged his nationalistic reputation.

The major internal resistance to Yuan was organised by Cai E, one of Yuan's supporters back in 1913, who slipped out of Beijing to return to Yunnan in the south-west, where he had been military governor in 1911. Cai had no particular liking for parliamentary rule, but was determined that monarchy should not be restored, a view that was shared by Cai's colleagues in the Progressive Party, notably Liang Qichao, the great constitutional reformer of imperial times. Under Cai, Yunnan sent an ultimatum to Yuan to abandon his monarchy and when no reply was forthcoming, independence was declared on 25 December 1915. A Yunnanese army marched into Guizhou province, leading to another declaration of independence in later January. The Yunnanese army which marched northwards into Sichuan was met with strong military resistance, although it was not fully defeated, despite the numerical superiority of the defending pro-Yuan troops, and hence no further declarations of independence occurred at this time.

Yuan's political demise was not caused principally by the immediate opposition from the south-west and Japan, but more importantly by the withdrawal of support by Yuan's former colleagues in the Beiyang Army, even after he had abandoned his monarchical scheme. In particular the support from Feng Guozhang in central China was only lukewarm. Yuan announced the postponement of the coronation on 23 February 1916 and turned to his other senior general, Duan Qirui, for help. Duan was then in disgrace for his opposition to the acceptance of the Twenty-One Demands. He opposed plans for a monarchy

and therefore pleaded illness. Yuan continued to try to isolate
the rebels in Yunnan, but efforts to secure Guangxi by new
military appointments saw that province declare independence
on 15 March, while a cease-fire in Sichuan resulted from local
agreements.

A petition began to circulate among the nominally pro-Yuan
provinces calling for an end to the monarchy to prevent further
unrest and Yuan, realising the failure of his scheme, announced
the end of the monarchy on 22 March by a return to the presidency. Duan Qirui now agreed to serve Yuan militarily on condition that parliament was recalled and that he had full control
over the army. By late April Duan was secretary of state with a
policy of peace talks with the south.

The provincial response to the abandonment of monarchy
was shocking for Yuan. Feng Guozhang announced that mere
abandonment would not satisfy the south and in early April
Guangdong and Zhejiang both declared independence to join
the southern rebels demanding the total retirement of Yuan.
Finally a separate southern government was established in early
May and Feng Guozhang sponsored an unsuccessful conference of central provinces to propose the temporary retention
of Yuan until parliament could be reconvened. Even this idea
was unacceptable to the south where two more provinces declared independence in late May. The country was heading
for political chaos and Yuan's dreams of retaining power without a monarchy seemed hopeless.

The Death of Yuan Shikai and its Aftermath

Just as the confused situation was moving towards its climax,
Yuan died of natural causes on 6 June 1916, thereby allowing
the various participants to produce a compromise to restore
the republican system in its 1913 form including the re-
establishment of provincial assemblies. The immediate result
in Beijing was the appointment of Li Yuanhong, the vice-
president, as the president, on the basis of Yuan Shikai's will
and Yuan's constitution of 1914. The southerners did not object
to Li as president but insisted that he should be appointed
according to the cabinet-style constitution of 1913 or the

provisional constitution of 1912. The south intimated that it would dissolve its separate government once a cabinet had been approved by parliament.

Power in the north was divided between Duan Qirui, who was acting as premier and army minister and was a confirmed republican, and Feng Guozhang whose monarchical sympathies were well-known, even though he had opposed Yuan as monarch. At Yuan's death Feng and the staunchly pro-Qing general, Zhang Xun, whose troops still retained the Manchu-style *queue* or pigtail, plotted for a possible Qing restoration, but were dissuaded by emissaries from Duan. Zhang Xun also organised a conference of twelve provinces on 9 June for the consolidation of the Beiyang group, proposing a programme which included new parliamentary elections and opposition to participation in government by violent radicals, meaning ex-members of the Nationalist Party.

At the end of June a revolt of the Chinese navy organised through the efforts of Sun Yixian's Chinese Revolutionary Party pressured Feng Guozhang to persuade Duan Qirui to accede to southern requests over the recalling of parliament and the restoration of the 1912 constitution. The southern independents under the urgings of Liang Qichao now announced the end of their government and acceptance of Duan as premier. Parliament was reconvened on 1 August and despite Nationalist efforts to push Duan aside into the weak vice-presidential slot and to have 1912 premier Tang Shaoyi return as premier, the parliament finally voted in Duan as premier and Feng Guozhang as vice-president, thereby giving central roles to the two chief heirs of Yuan Shikai's military power.

Thus, three months after Yuan's death a semblance of unity had been restored to China, but the reality was otherwise. All the eastern provinces of China from Manchuria down to Guangdong except Zhejiang formed themselves into a league of thirteen provinces in September, with the intention of preserving the Beijing government and rejecting any Nationalist governors, while the inland provinces had begun to operate once again in disregard of the central government. Within the thirteen provinces the rivalry between Feng Guozhang and Duan Qirui and between their aspiring subordinates became more and more pronounced, until it was to erupt in open warfare in 1920 after Feng Guozhang's death. As the politicians at the centre became more open in their cynical manipulation of the parliamentary system, so the respect for the centre decayed and the most important criterion for local power became naked military strength, a situation usually regarded as 'the warlord era', which will be the subject of the next chapter.

Parliament and the First World War

Nevertheless there are some features of central politics in 1916–18 which can usefully be discussed here, since they bear upon issues raised in the Yuan presidency, most notably the roles of parliament, premier and president and the question of China's involvement in the European War which was to expand to a world war in 1917. The reconvened parliamentary members regrouped themselves into a large number of new organisations, but the general outlines of rivalry between the ex-Nationalists and the ex-Progressives remained, resulting in severe friction over constitution drafting. Parliamentarians appealed to provincial military leaders to support their respective positions, thereby bringing military threats into the parliamentary process. Relations between President Li Yuanhong and Premier Duan Qirui were strained because Duan tried to bypass the president as much as possible, while relations between Duan and his own cabinet were soured by the overbearing actions of the cabinet secretary, Xu Shuzheng, a representative of Duan's military faction. By early 1917 Beiyang's provincial leaders were meeting to discuss ways to bring order into the Beijing political situation, implying some direct action on the president and parliament.

The issue of the First World War provided the catalyst for an amazing set of events in 1917, which temporarily resolved the Beijing political situation by enhancing the power of Premier Duan Qirui. Although Chinese labourers had been hired by France for shipment in July 1916 and a major British recruitment of Chinese labour for duty in France had begun in January 1917, the Chinese government officially maintained neutrality in the European war. International pressure for a change came after the German announcement of unrestricted submarine warfare on 31 January 1917 and the subsequent severance of relations with Germany by the USA, which called on other nations to join its protest. Reinsch, the US minister in Beijing, urged a Chinese response, suggesting – without official clearance from Washington – that the USA would provide adequate means to help China. The implication was that US loans would become available. The Chinese delivered a protest to the German minister on 9 February, but after it was clear that no US funds would be forthcoming, another month of discussion elapsed before diplomatic relations were severed, because this was seen as a major step towards a full war declaration.

Premier Duan wished to declare war, because he wanted a Chinese seat in the peace conference and foresaw financial advantages in joining the war, without any likelihood of actual military commitment. Opponents of Duan, including President Li, argued that a German victory was still probable, that any financial or military aid would be channelled to the benefit of Duan alone for possible use in civil wars in China and that the impact of professed Allied war aims was unclear as far as China was concerned. These latter suspicions were well-justified, because in February and March 1917 Japan signed secret agreements with Britain, Russia, France and Italy, guaranteeing Japan's position in Shandong. These agreements allowed Japan to shift from opposition to support of Chinese involvement in the war, because China could not now gain from the peace conference over the Shandong issue.

Although the Parliament had firmly supported a war declaration in early March, Duan's use of threats and physical abuse against members meant that by mid-May the Parliament refused to pass the war-participation bill while Duan was premier. Duan's military supporters urged the president to dissolve the Parliament, but he replied by dismissing Duan, who then joined his military allies in threatening Beijing and declaring independence. Zhang Xun, the organiser of the Beiyang meetings in 1916, offered to mediate and his troops were allowed to pass through Tianjin to Beijing by Duan's military. Zhang apparently reached some understanding with Duan, which included forcing the president to dissolve the Parliament, which was done on 12 June, but when Zhang proceeded to his next step, the restoration of the Qing dynasty on 1 July, Duan

immediately declared war on Zhang. Zhang's Qing restoration
was given support by a number of older Chinese figures, including Kang Youwei, the leader of the 1898 reform effort under
the Qing, but militarily the restoration was doomed within a
few days, as Duan's forces retook the capital.

With the Parliament officially dissolved and President Li in
disgrace for allowing events to reach a Qing restoration, Duan
now had a free hand to carry out his policies at the capital,
including the declaration of war against Germany on 16 August 1917. The war declaration revealed that China was can-
celling German and Austro-Hungarian treaty rights in China
and debt obligations under the Boxer Protocol of 1901 and
that the other powers were allowing a five-year moratorium on
Boxer payments. The former meant the first major break in
the solid structure of special privileges held by the foreign powers
and their nationals, although the allies insisted that the German and Austro-Hungarian concessions in treaty ports be placed
under provisional arrangements, not returned completely to
Chinese administration. The latter meant that from 1917 China
virtually ceased to remit overseas any further payments on the
Boxer indemnity, because post-war negotiations with the powers led to commutation of most remaining payments to serve
projects within China. China also expected a seat at the peace
conference and later warned the USA and Japan that China
would not be bound by any private agreements about China
between other countries, a reference to the negotiations which
produced the Lansing–Ishii agreement of November 1917,
whereby the USA recognised the special neighbourly interests
of Japan in East Asia.

Consolidation of Duan's power at the capital required funding, the reconstruction of the Parliament and attacks upon his
provincial enemies. Funding proved relatively easy, since the
new Japanese government under Terauchi had moved from
the 1915 confrontational style of the Twenty-One Demands to
a policy of winning support by economic means, using the huge
surpluses Japan had acquired in its export trade to serve the
warring Europeans. The loans, totalling up to 200 million yen,
were mainly negotiated secretly through Terauchi's close friend
Nishihara and were mostly unsecured. This meant that they
were not automatically repayable out of foreign-controlled salt

and customs taxes, an issue which hindered foreign loan negotiations after the First World War and the fall of Duan's government. Although some of the loans mentioned specific economic
projects, in practice the money fed into Duan's general expenses and in return Duan was willing to sign a military and
naval cooperation agreement with Japan, which confirmed Japan's gains from 1915.

Duan's parliamentary manoeuvrings required the creation of
a new parliament which would be pliant to his will. By claiming that Zhang Xun's Qing restoration had produced a second anti-Qing revolution, Duan argued for a new provisional
national assembly to draw up new electoral rules and to rede-
sign the parliament, as in 1911–12. Over the objections of five
southern provinces, where many of the 1913 parliamentarians
had gathered after the June 1917 dissolution, Duan created
his provisional assembly in late 1917. He held his elections,
notorious for their corruption, in mid-1918 and formed a parliament of 470 members, three-quarters of whom were drawn
from Duan's party, the Anfu Club, named after its headquarters in Anfu Lane in Beijing. Since July 1917, Duan had continued his wranglings with the president, now the major military
figure, Feng Guozhang, after Li's disgrace. Therefore Duan was
delighted to have the new parliament appoint the weaker Xu
Shichang as president from 10 October 1918, on the grounds
that Yuan Shikai's original five-year term (1913–18) had been
completed.

Duan's plans for reducing his provincial enemies took two
forms: the employment of existing Beiyang forces for the defeat of the south, and the creation of a new army with Japanese help, called the War Participation Army (later the Border
Defence Army), which could be used later to quell his rivals in
the Beiyang group. Duan's attack against the south began with
the movement of troops into Hunan in July 1917 and open
war began there in October 1917 culminating in a northern
victory under General Wu Peifu the following April. Duan's
open enmity to the southern provinces and his manipulation
of the parliamentary situation brought the southern provinces
together under the title of 'protectors of the constitution', with
Sun Yixian elected as grand marshal in charge on 3 September 1917. Although finally winning in Hunan, Duan was less

successful in Sichuan and Sichuan joined with the southern provinces in early 1918. Soon after, the southern government structure was reorganised to reflect the military strengths of its participants and Sun Yixian resigned from the seven-man executive which was officially created in May 1918.

Thus at the end of the First World War China was clearly divided into a larger northern section and a smaller, but un-defeated, southern alliance·which claimed to represent a more revolutionary heritage and a firmer faith in the value of the immediately post-1911 political institutions. Within both areas there was considerable rivalry among the nominal provincial supporters of each government and there were many sub-pro-vincial areas which could not with any accuracy be described as obedient to either government. With its house thus divided China faced the peace conference and the return of European political and economic power to East Asia. Instead of taking political advantage of the European war China had been held back by its own divisiveness, and the aspirations of the 1911 revolutionaries to build a stronger China without the Qing dynasty seemed to have been dashed.

Wider Trends in Society in the 1910s

The preceding outline political history of the failure of the republican system to create a unified and stronger China pro-vides a background for a wider discussion of trends and issues in the 1910s. The most obvious feature of the 1911 revolution was its limitation to the realm of central political institutions: there were no immediate fundamental changes in the social structure, the distribution of wealth, the methods of lower administration or in economic activities, such as one usually associates with the term 'revolution'. Although the original call for a republic rather than a constitutional monarchy had come from the secret revolutionary organisations based overseas, the events of the revolutionary months in 1911 handed power over to the existing provincial social leaders and their military al-lies without major effective intervention by the revolutionary parties. Power thus fell to the younger members of the Confu-cian-educated elite which dominated the provincial assemblies and who provided much of the army officer corps because of the upgraded evaluation of a military career since the Sino-Japanese war of 1894–5.

Paradoxically the political basis for the prestige of Confucian education had been weakened by the abolition of the state Confucian examinations in 1905 and destroyed by the revolution. Although Confucianism as a personal philosophy could survive without the imperial system, so much of what passed as Confucian social practice, especially among the elite, had been sustained only by imperial support, which accepted Confucian learning as proof of superiority. The disappearance of the emperor at the same time as the growing adoption of foreign ways in many fields created an unstable situation, where local power-holders, newly enhanced in strength by the weakness of the centre after the revolution, were in fact no longer bolstered in their legitimacy for power by the traditional ideological support from the centre. They could not expect to retain power merely from central respect for Confucian learning, but would have to compete for power through the new republican institutions against those at the centre seeking greater concentration of power and against those in the provinces who saw the breakdown of the old system as a chance for redefining power relationships in terms of coercive military power. In the event republican institutions were too new and too shallowly implanted in the political culture of China for the provincial civil powerholders to survive, and power shifted first to the centre and then to the warlords.

Although the 1911 Revolution only removed the dynastic system with no immediate results to strengthen China, as many pre-1911 critics of the revolutionaries had warned, yet that removal was to be irreversible, as two attempts at monarchical restoration showed. Enough of the old order had been undermined to prevent its viable reestablishment, not because the common people rejected imperial symbolism, there is little evidence that they did, but because the China-wide victors of post-1911 politics could not accept restriction of their power by permanently enhancing any power-holder at Beijing with imperial prestige. The end of the imperial institution, with its claim to universal kingship, not only reflected China's weakness in a multipolar world but also made possible a more extensive

experimentation in politics and culture which sought to overcome that weakness. Although the Qing dynasty had been destroyed in part by traditional rebel activity, as in anti-Manchu
secret societies, the destruction of the whole dynastic structure
was a more formidable and more modern achievement, which
forced new adjustments at the top of society, even while underlying continuities at the village level remained. Even these
lower level continuities came to be gradually disrupted, because
the imperial order, whatever its shortcomings, had been committed to the maintenance of viable conditions for subsistence
agriculture and assumed that peasants would revolt if deprived
of these conditions for too long. The new governments, beset
with foreign pressures and elite demands for modernisation,
neglected basic agricultural stability and came to regard peasant unrest as illegitimate, even while imposing higher taxes on
peasants or backing harsher treatment of tenants.

The political leaders after 1911 were committed to the preservation of their own power and to the strengthening of China
against the threat of the foreign powers, but the methods for
gaining this strength were various. From the viewpoint of the
centre what was necessary was firm central control overriding
regional power, but the provinces could equally well argue that
the centre was too beholden to foreign pressure and that therefore national strength would best be built on the basis of provincial development. This argument might have seemed more
persuasive if more provinces had actually created development
programmes. Since the intention was to match foreign strength
eventually, another dilemma occurred over the acquisition of
new skills in government; should this be done with the help of
foreign advisers or should China wait until sufficient Chinese
had been trained overseas? Some foreign supervisors had been
forced upon the central government by loan negotiators and
many foreign staff were employed in the customs and postal
services, but the early Republic did turn voluntarily to further
foreign advisers in both civil and military spheres. Although
understandable in the short term, this policy opened the government to even more charges of selling out, from its nationalistic critics, just as did the equally contentious issue of funding
the central government from foreign loans.

Although China adopted the model of republicanism as being

a source of strength in other countries, there was only a very limited sense in which the liberal principles behind the Westernised forms were either supported or understood by most of the Chinese elite. Western liberal beliefs in the supreme value of the rights of the individual and the legitimacy of different interests within society were submerged beneath the need for consensus and collective purpose, which resulted from China's strained international position and the traditional reluctance to view open dissent as anything but disruptive and socially unpalatable. Hence participatory institutions which were effective in raising national strength overseas failed to produce in China the gains which their original proponents had envisaged. Therefore many were tempted to explore again more traditional methods of power-sharing, raising personalised factions above Westernised political parties and allying civil prestige with military force. Even that most Westernised republican, Sun Yixian, beguiled by the image of himself as the most important force for development in China, was willing to turn to a Chinese Revolutionary Party run like an over-centralised traditional secret society and to parley for his own presence in a militaristic government without serious regard for its representativeness.

Instability over the political development in the 1910s provided the context for activities by two groups in Chinese society – the bourgeoisie and the intellectuals – who both sought to advance their own schemes for development. Although the Chinese bourgeoisie was small in 1911, in view of the limited modern economy in China's cities, the years of the early republic allowed a great expansion of its position, especially during and immediately after the First World War, when most foreign competition was withdrawn. Although the late Qing only reluctantly accepted the organising of chambers of commerce and professional associations, those bodies were active after 1911 in temporarily organising city governments and in bringing opinions to the national government, which responded by such helpful measures as the issuance of standard silver coinage in 1914, the necessary first stage in bringing order to China's tangled currency. The impact of the First World War allowed China to regain a near-balance on its overseas trade account, after three decades of excess imports, and to begin the rapid expansion of modern light industry estimated at 13.8 per cent per annum growth in 1912 to 1920, with textiles in the lead. Most of the expansion occurred in the treaty ports where foreign presence kept overt disorder at bay. Shanghai, for example, more than doubled its population between 1910 and 1920. There is also evidence for a wider distribution of increased economic activity in handicrafts and other traditional fields, mostly made possible by the productivity of agriculture in a decade of kindly climatic conditions. This spurt of economic activity was to continue for almost two years after the end of the First World War, but then foundered in the wake of full international competition and increased internal disorder in China, thereby terminating what has been called the 'golden age of Chinese capitalism'.

For the intellectual leaders of China the collapse of the imperial system provoked widespread rethinking on the nature of Chinese society and the role that Chinese traditions and Western innovations should play in the future of the country. The intellectuals sought to decide what required preservation in order to ensure that being Chinese had a real meaning. Some argued that the Confucian social order was the irreplaceable core of Chinese life which would survive any conquest and a few went as far as urging the creation of a formalised Confucian religion drawing on Christian models. Most realised that the survival of a Chinese polity was even more necessary, thereby fully adopting the Western idea of the clearly delineated nation-state in preference to older Chinese ideas about a Chinese cultural area with imprecise frontiers. Nevertheless, even within a growing nationalistic commitment to a geographic China, it was possible to differ over what should be the goal of cultural development within the defended borders. Many argued that there was a national essence worthy of preservation and propagation from among the host of traditions in China, while others, such as Liang Qichao, argued for certain traits of national character, which must be retained while pushing forward. Such positions, initially strongly supported, came under attack from those who despaired of the operation of any viable representative government without a long period of cultural education which would require the replacement of Chinese values by those of the West. The failure of the republican experiment had convinced these thinkers that the conventions of Chinese society, especially as codified in Confucian behaviour rules, stunted the development of the individual and made impossible any practice of democracy within China. Their remedy of cultural re-education implied that the short-term problems of the political sphere would have to be accepted unchallenged while the youth of China were prepared for participation in a better future.

The stress on education as a way to social betterment was a traditional one within China, but it was to receive a provocatively iconoclastic twist, especially through the actions of two men, Cai Yuanpei and Chen Duxiu, both European-trained. As a minister of education in the first part of 1912, Cai was able to issue a call for a new approach to achieve a republican education and to hold a conference of the late Qing provincial education associations to discuss the necessary changes in education, including the standardisation of a national language to allow the development of vernacular writing programmes to replace the archaic classical writing curriculum. Their role thus centrally recognised, the provincial education associations went on to form a national federation and to hold annual meetings of progressive educators. After Yuan Shikai's death they came to promote a reform movement based on 'new education' for democracy and individual development. Cai became Chancellor of Beijing University in December 1916 and by appointing new staff converted it from a centre for training government officials into an academic centre where he promoted freedom of expression and research, although the government required this freedom not to be extended into political activism.

Chen Duxiu founded the magazine *Youth* (but very soon retitled *New Youth*) in Shanghai in September 1915 for the propagation of his ideas on change. His call was to the young of China as the vital force to achieve the regeneration of the country and his approach was bitterly opposed to all aspects of traditional China. He argued that China must Westernise under the influence of Mr Sai (Science) and Mr De (Democracy), in order to regain its strength in a modern world. His magazine published translations of Western literature and thought and articles about education and culture, but very little directly on politics. *New Youth* circulated among the students in the urban centres of China, sparking off debates and the formation of study societies, including one in Hunan organised by a young teacher, Mao Zedong, in April 1918. Although created by Chen Duxiu, *New Youth* soon gathered editorial help from other radical intellectuals, including Li Dazhao, librarian at Beijing University, who, while supporting *New Youth*'s desire for a new culture, also contributed to magazines with a more political outlook.

One major issue raised in *New Youth* was literary reform, with the crucial impetus coming from Hu Shi, a student of John Dewey, the American pragmatist. As mentioned above, language reform in education had been in the air in 1912. On the literary scene novels in *baihua*, vernacular style, had been produced for centuries, but the orthodox literary criticism within China regarded such writings as inferior, stating that true literature had to be written in *wenyan*, classical style, based on pre-imperial grammar. In the late Qing period many had advocated the use of *baihua* for writings to popularise new knowledge, but none had urged it as the main literary form. Hu Shi's importance arose from his argument that *baihua* writings had been the mainstream of Chinese literature for hundreds of years and that the continued imposition of *wenyan* in Ming and Qing times had prevented the full flowering of a vernacular literature which had vigorously emerged before the Ming. He therefore argued for the use of *baihua* in literary creation and for the need for *baihua* as a prerequisite for modern intellectual activity. Hu's ideas, first mooted to Chen Duxiu by letter in October 1916, appeared in January 1917's *New Youth* as 'Some tentative suggestions for the reform of Chinese literature', but Chen Duxiu took up the issue much more positively in his February 1917 call for a literary revolution. The differences between Chen and Hu related not merely to decisiveness, but more importantly to the purposes of literary change. To Hu Shi priority went to the linguistic tools, to the acceptance of the literary value of *baihua*, with little discussion of new content in the new style, whereas for Chen the issue was content, that a literary revolution should throw out the themes and the morality which pervaded the old literature, a task which would be assisted by the change in literary written style.

The success of the call for *baihua* as the medium for mainstream literature was overwhelming, not only from *New Youth*'s advocacy, but also from the general opinion of progressive educators, who ensured that *baihua* was the official style for all elementary schools texts by 1921. A new body of literature, at first in short forms such as essays and short stories, began to appear, with Japanese-trained Lu Xun as the strongest figure. This new literature with its realism and attention to social and political matters was limited in its appeal to the better-educated in the cities, whereas the older popular *baihua* literature with its love, detective and scandal themes sold much more widely. Thus although *baihua* new literature had been promoted by its apologists for its greater readability as compared with difficult classical writings, in practice this claim was not fulfilled quickly, for two reasons. First, the new written style of the Westernised intellectuals, although nominally vernacular, contained Europeanised phrasings and classical allusions, which rendered much of it as remote from daily speech patterns as the classical style; the Westernised content also proved somewhat indigestible. Second, the idea of a national vernacular style was premature, in that the *baihua*, based on Beijing speech patterns, did not directly reflect speech throughout the country, especially in the south. A programme of national language education would be necessary, before *baihua* could become a popular national medium. This programme is still going on today.

This New Culture Movement, with its literary revolution as a major component, was the expression of long-term hope by the radical fringe of China's intellectuals after the failure of the early Republican system. Events after the end of First World War in November 1918 were to transform this highly elitist movement into the basis for the political movements which would seek to remedy China's problems by an escape from the warlord impasse, which forms the subject of the next chapter.

3 Central Collapse

The failure of Western-inspired republican institutions to produce the desired strengthening and revitalising of China in the years after 1911 condemned China to a period of regional governments and continuing weakness, which could only begin to be overcome through the input of further Western ideas, particularly from the Soviet Union. Although the period of disunity under the regional military had historical precedents in periods between major imperial dynasties, notably in the tenth century, the situation in the twentieth century was different. It was not at all clear how the eventual military victor would or should construct his regime, given that the imperial model was now regarded as unacceptable. Moreover the insistence by the foreign powers that Beijing be treated as the capital, however weak its real power, created an artificial distortion both of military strategy, with Beijing as the essential goal of almost every large militarist, and of historiography. Events concerning Beijing seemed more important than developments elsewhere, especially when viewed through the archives of the foreign powers. Although the period of disunity is usually dated 1916 to 1928, it is possible to trace back intimations of local independence into the nineteenth century and overt practice to the 1911 Revolution, while many of the military figures involved continued their careers after 1928 with more formal deference to the centre but almost equal lack of obedience.

The Warlords

There were two basic requirements for the militarist rulers of regionalised China, called 'warlords' by their opponents: control of an autonomous army and control of extensive territory. The total number of warlords operating in China is indistinct. There were at least 1300 military officers of the rank of brigadier and above in China between 1912 and 1928, but although each was potentially an independent militarist, most tended to work under a few senior figures whose names feature in the historical record. The basis for most of the warlord armies had emerged since the military reforms which had been introduced in China from 1895, such as the creation of the Beiyang Army in the north and other New Army units elsewhere. In some places a few bandit leaders, such as Zhang Zuolin in the north-east, had their originally bandit forces incorporated into officially sanctioned forces. Although the suppression of the Taiping movement (1851–64) had provoked the creation of regionalised military forces, which drew support from regional taxes, the armies of the early twentieth century were not the direct descendants of those personalised armies, but the result of a central policy to form modern, largely centrally financed armies with elements of Western training and a modernised military hierarchy of command. Nevertheless, the traits of independence and financial autonomy revealed in the mid-nineteenth century have encouraged many to date the origins of militaristic regionalism to that time, a view that is acceptable in terms of the practice of warlord politics, as long as continuity in personnel and organisations is not assumed.

Methods of control of territory fell into two main categories, creating two different styles of warlord, the static and the peripatetic. The static warlord became established in one area with the expectation that this area would remain his firm base throughout the coming years of struggle. Certain areas lent themselves geographically to such an approach, such as the north-east under Zhang Zuolin and his son, Zhang Xueliang, until the Japanese invasion of 1931 or Qinghai on the northern edge of Tibet or Shanxi under Yan Xishan; but protective geography alone could not guarantee stability under a single warlord, as the continuously divided condition of Sichuan province revealed. Even a warlord with a secure and satisfactory base area could be tempted out to improve his fortunes elsewhere, especially in the case of the north-east with its access to Beijing, but most warlords moved their area of control as their situation required. An extreme case of the peripatetic warlord was the so-called Christian General, Feng Yuxiang, whose activities between 1916 and 1928 ranged from southern Sichuan to Beijing and on to Gansu in the northwest, as he combined with different allies and readjusted his expectations according to battlefield and political fortune. The senior generals linked to the two major north and central China groupings, the Zhili and Anhui cliques, moved less far in total than Feng, but shifted frequently between provinces as the balance of power altered, resulting in no provincial continuity of authority for the majority of China's population.

Since the use of force was more overtly the final source of power during the warlord period, all the warlords sought to increase the size of their armies and consequently had to augment the income necessary to feed and equip them, but at the same time they tried as much as possible to avoid squandering their forces. From the former cause came an increasing militarisation of society, while the latter produced much inter-warlord diplomacy and at first a reluctance to fight vigorously. Estimates for the numbers of troops in China at this period are notoriously difficult to confirm, but the likely figures seem to be over half a million in 1916, over a million in 1918, over 1.5 million in 1924 and over 2 million by 1928. Recruits for warlord armies were obtained by press-ganging and by offers of wages and plunder, which had an appeal in a densely populated countryside where land was scarce. In addition to warlord armies, local militia sprang up for local protection, after being suppressed under Yuan Shikai; these were financed by merchant or landlord groups. Banditry continued to flourish at the edges of administrative control, one of the most famous early bandit organisers being White Wolf, who kept much of Yuan's army at bay between 1912 and 1914. Casualties in the major warlord wars are also difficult to assess, but news reports, the increased duration of the wars and the greater availability of more destructive weapons after the end of the First World War all indicate a growing casualty list. For instance a few thousand casualties resulted from the five days of fighting in the Zhili–Anhui war of July 1920, whereas tens of thousands of casualties resulted from the wars of 1926 to 1928. The rising trend was to continue after nominal reunification, with the major civil war of 1930 claiming some 150 000 casualties.

Acquisition of income to finance their armies forced warlords to exploit existing tax mechanisms and to devise ways to extract further income. Although a very few top warlords, such as Duan Qirui and Zhang Zuolin, could draw on overseas funding and others spent time vainly seeking overseas support, the vast majority of warlords had to rely upon local resources. With the customs taxes collected by the foreigner and the salt tax officially under foreign management, the main legal responsibilities left were the land tax, local trade taxes (e.g. *likin*) and the issuance of paper currency, while extortion, ransom and looting provided useful additional tools, especially to an army on the move. Land-tax collection required some collaboration from local officials, who held the tax records, but the appointment of local tax farmers was also a possibility, such men being instructed to turn in specific quota from an area, without any restrictions on the actual amount collected – a ready recipe for increased tax burdens on the peasantry. The basic land-tax levels of the Qing era were no longer sufficient to meet the voracious needs of the warlords and therefore a host of surtaxes on the land tax were imposed, increasing the basic tax rate. Alternatively peasants could be compelled to raise cash crops, notably opium which could be traded profitably by the warlords. Another mechanism to increase funding was the device of taxing in advance, that is demanding advanced payment of tax for future years: at its worst in Sichuan province this had peasants nominally paying taxes up to 60 years ahead. The issuance of paper currency was equally disruptive to rural survival, because the money issued to pay for food and wages was only valid within the geographic range of the issuing army, would be resisted by ordinary people even within that area, and would become useless once that army moved on, having in effect gained goods and services for virtually nothing.

The finance generated by warlord taxation policies was devoted almost entirely to the maintenance and equipping of armies, military equipment coming in considerable measure from overseas. In 1916 China had eight functioning arsenals capable of producing weapons, but even with the addition of makeshift provincial plants over the next decade, these could not satisfy the demand for arms and ammunition. The foreign powers, emerging from the First World War in 1918, realised that their now redundant arms stockpile could find tremendous service in China's civil wars, but although this might benefit the arms dealers, it was also seen as a danger for China. Britain therefore proposed in May 1919 an arms embargo on China, a move joined by France, Japan, Italy and the USA. Each of these countries either made provisos for special cases or found it difficult in practice to prosecute gun-runners: Japan refused to include war exports to the northeast, Britain continued to supply aircraft, and Italy refused to participate until all existing contracts were fulfilled. More importantly, major arms producers, such as the Soviet Union, Norway and Czechoslovakia, were not party to the agreement, their nationals remaining free to deal in arms. Thus although the embargo remained until April 1929 in theory, in practice arms were readily available to those with money to pay, and even Britain, which policed its embargo more strictly than most, is estimated to have exported over £100 million of arms to China between 1923 and 1929.

The major concern for each warlord, after securing sufficient revenues for paying and equipping his army, was to ensure the improvement of his situation, thereby ensuring the continued loyalty of his forces and the possibility of greater power and wealth. Although the warlord armies were personal armies, in the sense that the warlord had the ultimate power to commit his men to or withhold his men from battle, whatever his political entanglements, in practice the armies did have a regular discipline and command structure, in which formal hierarchies often outweighed personalised links of loyalty. As a result seeking defections from one's rivals' lesser units became an important part of warlord strategy, because these units could be integrated intact into one's own forces as long as one could offer adequate rewards. Similarly the defeat or death of a warlord did not render his troops ineffective, but they could be used by others through their lower officers. Hence warlords were continually searching for ways to ensure the loyalty of their subordinates beyond the mere mercenary attraction of adequate pay.

Two major devices were used, one very traditional, the other old in form but partly new in content. The traditional method, used both within warlord armies and between warlord allies, was to rely on the networks of personal linking relationships, *guanxi*, which largely defined personal interactions in China.

Relationships which implied mutual solidarity included most strongly the nuclear family, teacher–student and patron–client relationships, while weaker ones included ties through marriage, sharing the same county or province of origin and having attended the same school. By stressing the importance of such relationships, a warlord could add greater strength to the otherwise temporary or fortuitous organisational connections with others, but except for nuclear family, these relationship patterns with their overlapping and sometimes conflicting demands could not permanently ensure loyalty.

The second device was to add an ideological component to the aims of the warlord, through training of the troops and through propaganda work. Although all major warlords might aspire to rule the whole of China, this goal alone was inadequate to inspire one's troops in lesser battles, so that a variety of other issues were targeted. Much of the inter-warlord debate, conducted through circular telegrams issued to the press, relied upon Confucian morality for its accusations of treachery, scandal and unworthiness. Some warlords, notoriously the illiterate Zhang Zongchang, promoted Confucianism very vigorously, even issuing new editions of the classics; in many ways this hypocritical use of Confucianism by obviously corrupt figures was the final straw contributing to the success of the intellectuals' contemporaneous attack against Confucianism as the source of public morality. The call to defend one's province could be raised much more vigorously than through *guanxi*, by arguing that each province ought to be self-governing and that development in a province should continue, even while the nation was weak. This call could lead to virtual separatism, as in Shanxi, or to support for federalism, which Hunan province promoted in the early 1920s. The most famous provincial warlord grouping, the Guangxi clique, began and ended its career by promoting stability and development in that one province, but for three years, 1926 to 1929, could not resist the opportunity to try its hand in the wider arena.

The newer elements in the ideological programme centred on nationalism, but a wide variety of Western political ideas were also tried out. It is frequently suggested that the first use of nationalism and Western organisational methods came with the Northern Expedition (1926–8) of the Nationalist Party at

the close of the warlord era, but this is inaccurate. Nationalism, especially in terms of verbally attacking the unequal treaties, was part of most warlords' approach in the 1920s and a
number of warlords such as Feng Yuxiang and Yan Xishan sought
to energise their troops with ill-digested lessons from socialism, economic planning, Christianity and other Western knowledge. The final advance of the Northern Expedition with its
commitment to end warlordism was met by fierce resistance
from northern warlords who appealed to both anti-Russian
nationalism and anti-communism for justification, citing the
Soviet aid and advice which had made the Nationalist–Communist northward advance possible.

Although the above discussion indicates the basis of warlord
control, and of warlord interaction, it does not tell us much of
the character and background of the leading warlords and their
principal subordinates. Although a few of the warlords based
on the Beiyang Army had been promoted before 1916 by normal seniority procedures, the majority were promoted because
of their personal abilities, at a time when traditional scholarly
standards for political preeminence were absent. It is therefore no surprise that many of them appear larger than life
and that each features in a host of anecdotes, revealing highly
personal ways of behaviour, such as 'Christian General' Feng
Yuxiang's hosepipe baptisms for his troops or the imperial pretensions of Zhang Zuolin in Beijing. The leading warlords were
drawn from the lower levels of society, and raised to power
either through the military hierarchy directly or through banditry first. The majority of the divisional commanders and leading
provincial military officials of the warlord era had had military
education in the military schools set up in the late Qing and
although this may not have granted the scholarly literacy of
the Qing high civil officials, totally illiterate warlords were the
exception rather than the rule. At lower levels in their armies
levels of literacy and training dropped alarmingly, with China's officer schools able to train only a small proportion of
the officers needed as militarisation spread. Although these officer
schools had been established according to national plans and
trained men to serve in a developing national army, the collapse of the centre and the ensuing administrative difficulties
often converted highly motivated young officers into cynical

manipulators whose only guiding force was self-interest, in a gradual perversion of the nation-building hopes of the late Qing military reformers.

Warlords: Their Territories and Wars

A history of the warlord period, at the military and political level, is necessarily confusing, because of the fluidity of the alliance patterns among the warlords, and requires an understanding of the geographical constraints which affected all participants.

On the Inner Asian side of China, where the climate was harsh through poor rainfall or high mountains, the areas lost all administrative direction from, and virtually all political interest in, the centre. Tibet and Mongolia declared independence from Beijing and, except for a brief incursion into Mongolia in 1919, remained free from Han Chinese troops throughout the Republican era. Outer Mongolia, which received guidance from both tsarist Russia and the Soviet Union, finally became independent of China after a plebiscite in 1945, while Tibet was only reincorporated in 1950 as an autonomous region of China.

Xinjiang also passed out of central control, but its commanding warlords were all Han Chinese, keeping the peace over the local minority peoples. Sheng Shicai who came to power there in 1933, gravitated strongly towards the Soviet Union, until controversies with the USSR in the early 1940s turned him back to the Chinese government fold in 1942. Even then the area was too remote for effective application of central power until after the Communist victory in 1949. The north-east or Manchuria, gradually unified under Zhang Zuolin by 1919 from his base in Fengtian province, might well have proved equally remote if Zhang had not felt attracted by the proximity of Beijing and by the hope of greater power, an attraction which his Japanese backers repeatedly urged him to forgo.

Moving towards the coast from these outer areas of the Qing empire one comes to a whole group of inland Han Chinese provinces which had barely been touched by modern developments in communications, such as railways and metalled roads. These areas too had very limited connections with the government in Beijing, although Shaanxi province was often controlled by men professing loyalty to major warlord cliques in coastal China. Large-scale warfare in these provinces was rendered virtually impossible by transportation problems and by the lack of the equipment more readily available near the coast. The result was a continuous warfare among small armies, none able to annihilate the others, since sufficient destructive ability was lacking. Worst hit in this respect was Sichuan, where perhaps two-thirds of all the known wars of the warlord era occurred. No warlord was able to dominate the province effectively from 1916 until 1937 – that is, until the central government was forced to evacuate into Sichuan by the Japanese invasion. Guangxi too was severely fragmented, until the rise of the Guangxi clique under Li Zongren and Bai Chongxi by 1925. Yunnan, where one of the best late Qing army programmes had developed, prided itself on its interest in constitutional central government for China, under its leader Tang Jiyao, but proved reluctant to accept any outside authority, even as late as the anti-Japanese war (1937–45), when warlord Long Yun kept the central government at arms' length despite a large-scale influx of eastern Chinese and later of Americans, all serving national purposes.

The remaining area of China, stretching from Beijing to Guangzhou, witnessed the major activities of the great warlords, whose armies were bigger and better-equipped and whose alliances, wars and political acts feature in all accounts of the period, often to the total exclusion of anybody anywhere else. This was the area where railway lines, particularly from Beijing to Hankou, and from Tianjin to Pukou (opposite Nanjing), provided the means to move troops in large numbers and to supply heavy equipment to a battlefront. The piecemeal state of the Wuchang–Guangzhou railway, which was only finished in 1936, and the mountainous border between Guangdong and Hunan preserved Guangdong in the south from serious danger of invasion from the Yangzi Valley, thereby allowing a number of lesser warlords to operate in the province and to seek some national legitimacy by tolerating members of the Nationalist Party in administrative posts from 1916. Guangdong was in greater danger from guest armies from Yunnan and Guangxi, which were not driven out until 1925, by which time the Nationalist Party had begun to organise its own very effective party army. To the north of Guangdong lay Hunan, which was regarded by the northern warlords as the key to a successful reunification effort against the south. Hunan was the site of the first north–south war of 1917–18, mentioned in the last chapter. Although the north was victorious, the division of spoils and the question of the viability of warfare against the south were two issues which gradually soured the relations amongst the generals of the Beiyang army.

Two major cliques, the Anhui and Zhili, emerged in North China from the original unity of the Beiyang Army, as it gradually split apart after the death of Yuan Shikai. This split occurred despite the initial commitment among the army leaders to preserve unity through consultation, which produced at least eight conferences of Beiyang generals between June 1916 and November 1918. The Anhui clique crystallised more quickly around the leadership of Duan Qirui, from Hefei in Anhui, with just under half its important members being Anhui provincials. Since Duan had moved from direct army command into central politics before Yuan Shikai's death, he also sought to base his power in manipulation of the central politicians, through the Anfu club of parliamentarians and the skill of his right-hand man, Xu Shuzheng, a figure widely detested, especially after arranging in June 1918 the assassination of a leading anti-Duan Beiyang general. Duan's military allies did not control the strongest of the forces available and therefore Duan was obliged to pursue his plans for a new national army with Japanese assistance, while urging his Beiyang rivals in central China to fight against the south. As a result the forces linked to the other main Beiyang general, Feng Guozhang, began to urge the reunification of north and south China by peaceful means, in opposition to Duan's conquest plans, especially after military success in Hunan resulted in the appointment of a pro-Duan governor, and not of the battlefield victor, Wu Peifu. Wu called in a public telegram for the end of civil war in August 1918, this call being promptly backed by the southern government, and after the September failure of Duan's parliament to elect Wu's superior, Cao Kun, as vice-president, as Duan had promised, all the lower Yangzi governors joined the call for peace.

The momentum for a north–south peace conference was beginning to overwhelm Premier Duan, who resigned in October

1918, and the conclusion of the First World War led to strong foreign pressure on north and south to convene a peace conference. Eventually after many exchanges of conditions, the negotiators met on 20 February 1919 on neutral ground in the International Settlement in Shanghai, but the conference came up against enormous difficulties over the parliament and demobilisation. Nevertheless, the mood for peace had allowed China to compose a national team to represent China at the Versailles peace conference to settle the world war. The departure of Duan from the premiership prior to the peace conference had not meant the end of his military plans, and in February 1919 he signed an extension of his military agreement with Japan, providing for further help in military training. As the scope of Duan's secret arrangements with Japan became clearer and the mood of national anger against Japan intensified, the southern negotiators insisted in mid-May that all secret Sino-Japanese agreements must be repudiated and their perpetrators punished, something the northerners could not accept, at which point both teams resigned. The appointment of the head of the Anfu club to lead a new northern team in August was regarded by the south as quite unacceptable and the peace conference ground to a halt.

The growing antagonism to Duan Qirui over the peace conference and his military plans welded his Beiyang opponents into a solid grouping, called the Zhili clique, named after the provincial origin of its senior leaders, Feng Guozhang and Cao Kun, and of just over half its important members. The clique became more clearly structured around Cao Kun after the death of Feng Guozhang at the end of 1919. During the first half of 1920 tension increased between Duan and the Zhili clique. In addition Duan had irritated Zhang Zuolin of the north-eastern Fengtian clique by attempts to spread his power northwards from Beijing into Mongolia. In April 1920 the Zhili and Fengtian cliques met in conference to agree on an alliance and to demand the reopening of the north–south peace conference and the transfer of Duan's Japanese-trained army to central government control. Duan refused and Wu Peifu's Zhili forces began to move north, leaving Hunan to be taken over by local forces. A further conference in June led to an ultimatum against Duan, who mobilised his forces for war, which was

declared in July. Hostilities were limited to five days and resulted in total defeat for Duan's foreign-trained forces. The
1920 Zhili–Anhui war greatly enhanced the power of the Zhili
faction which could now control eight of the main provinces,
leaving only two weak Anhui clique governors on the south-
east coast, but it also allowed its ally, the Fengtian clique, to
gain ground in Inner Mongolia.

Despite the Zhili victory in mid-1920, nominal central government leadership remained in the hands of the appointees of
the Anfu-dominated parliament as president and premier, until Zhang Zuolin of the Fengtian clique manoeuvred a new
premier into position in December 1921. This action met immediate rejection from the Zhili clique, who accused the new leaders
of treason and embezzlement. Tension mounted as Zhang
Zuolin's troops moved into Beijing and full-scale war between
the Zhili and Fengtian troops erupted in late April 1922. Severe fighting lasted a week and Fengtian troops were withdrawn
into the northeast, leaving the Zhili clique dominant in north
and central China and in Inner Mongolia. The Fengtian leaders had been in close contact with southern warlords, but in
the event these potential southern allies had not been able to
move quickly enough.

With the Fengtian clique's defeat, the Zhili clique was now
in a position to intervene in national politics unimpeded. The
first step was to force the resignation of the Anfu-appointed
President Xu Shichang in June 1922, to reappoint Li Yuanhong,
the original 1912 republican vice-president and to recall the
old parliament. Li was forced to flee Beijing in June 1923 after army officers and policemen surrounded the presidential
building demanding arrears of pay, thereby leaving the way
open for the parliament to elect Cao Kun, the Zhili leader, as
president in October 1923, after the distribution of $5000 to
each member of parliament. The election was immediately
opposed by the Fengtian clique, the remnants of the Anhui
clique and the government in Guangzhou in the south, but no
one was willing to make a military move, while their forces
were being reorganised and retrained. The election of Cao Kun
was seen as final proof of the corruptness of parliamentary politics
and it also soured the relations within the Zhili clique between
Cao with his presidential ambitions and other generals who

argued that the unification of China, being more important, would be hindered by Cao's appointment.

The next major war was occasioned by the wish of the Zhili clique to overwhelm Zhejiang province, the last area held by remnants of the Anhui clique. War broke out in September 1924, leading to the capture of Zhejiang by the Zhili general, Sun Chuanfang, but the Fengtian clique attacked from the north-east in support of Zhejiang. This attack could have been beaten back by the Zhili troops, but in late October a leading Zhili general, Feng Yuxiang, turned against his superiors and took over the capital in alliance with the north-eastern attackers. Cao Kun, the President, was imprisoned, the Zhili clique's power in the north was broken and Feng renamed his army the Guominjun, the national army. North-eastern troops entered Beijing in strength in November 1924 and Feng Yuxiang retired to the northwest, where he began to benefit from some Soviet aid. Fengtian clique troops and governors were introduced further and further into north and central China during 1925, by warfare and diplomacy, until finally driven from the Yangzi valley in October 1925 by the Zhili warlord, Sun Chuanfang.

The defeats for Fengtian clique in central China provided the opportunity for the Guominjun to move in from the northwest and to plot for the defection of a leading Fengtian general, Guo Songling, who revolted on 23 November 1925. Zhili clique troops also attacked, but Guo's revolt was quashed after a very successful start, because the Japanese would not allow his troops to move on or near their South Manchurian Railway and because they supplied assistance to Zhang Zuolin, the Fengtian leader. At this point the Zhili clique troops, under Wu Peifu, decided to join with Fengtian troops in attacking Feng Yuxiang who was seen as the betrayer of the 1924 Zhili war effort, with the result that Feng's Guominjun was again driven into difficulties in the northwest. Feng went to the USSR and returned in 1926 to ally his forces with the revolutionaries of the south. Wu Peifu continued to press his attack against his personal enemy Feng, even when Wu's own base in central China had begun to be challenged by the Nationalist Party's army on its northern expedition, which was finally to destroy the Zhili clique in 1927.

Opposition to Warlordism: The May Fourth Movement

The shifting warlord alliances and the major wars in eastern China provided little hope of a quick final solution leading to unification and development. This therefore spurred other actors in the political arena to seek other means to tackle the problems facing China, through the creation of new organisations and a broader appeal to the general population. The foreign powers too despaired of conditions in China, which prevented peaceful trade and threatened foreign lives and property through banditry and warfare, but it was often unclear how far the powers would go in promoting and sustaining China's integrity in practice, despite a number of positive statements of intent. The interplay of foreign action and domestic response forms a crucial factor for the understanding of how China emerged from the warlord era into the nominal unification under the Nationalist Party, because the strongest mass emotion that was called into political play at the time was nationalism, expressed in virulently anti-foreign ways. The essential argument of the radicals was that China could not be independent and modernised until the twin burdens of internal militarism and foreign imperialism had been removed. By firmly asserting that foreign imperialism deliberately sustained internal militarism, a claim that is open to doubt for many warlords, the radicals could use anti-foreign feelings to attack internal enemies as well.

The first outburst of anti-foreign feeling on a national scale occurred as a result of the First World War peace conference at Versailles in the first half of 1919. Although China had experienced localised anti-foreign demonstrations before, as in anti-missionary incidents through the nineteenth century, and had seen limited local boycotts of specific nations, as against the USA in 1905 over immigration issues, the geographic scope of the anti-Japanese movement in 1919 was new to China, as demonstrations and strikes occurred in urban areas all over China. The trigger for the first demonstration, on 4 May 1919 in Beijing, came from the announcement that Japan, as a result of its secret treaties of 1917, would retain control in Shandong, despite China's presence at the peace conference and the fine rhetoric of US President Wilson on self-determination. A demonstration which had been planned for 7 May,

National Humiliation Day, was quickly brought forward and
several thousand students marched through Beijing on 4 May,
urging the saving of the country. Their immediate anger was
directed towards the three most pro-Japanese members of the
Anfu government, one of whom was beaten up, another of whom
had his house burnt down. A Beijing Student Union was formed
on the following day and propaganda efforts were immediately
begun. The police response was severe and arrests grew in
number.

The May Fourth demonstration quickly called forth supportive reactions from students elsewhere in China, from most of
the press and from teachers, workers and chambers of commerce, which turned the initial demonstration into the catalyst for six weeks of strikes and anti-Japanese boycotts, at their
most intense in Shanghai. Eventually the central government
was forced to release those arrested in Beijing, to retire the
pro-Japanese ministers and not to sign the Versailles treaty.
The question arises as to why anti-Japanese activity achieved
such a size only in 1919, whereas demonstrations over the Twenty
One Demands had failed to do so. A number of reasons can
be suggested, some of which are more cogent than others.

The most obvious reason was the dashing of the heightened
expectations for an improvement of China's international position at the Versailles conference. Since war participation had
been such a major political issue in 1917 and it had been argued that China's place at the peace conference would ensure
a fair hearing, it was assumed that the conference would return former German areas in China. Many hoped the conference would achieve more for China, with the Chinese delegation
trying to remove the whole range of foreign privileges in China,
but in the context of the declared war aims of the victors, the
very least to be anticipated was the return of Shandong. In
contrast, in 1915 or 1918 the international situation was much
less sympathetic to a vigorous presentation of Chinese desires
and roused far fewer hopes of success.

The second reason was the developing commitment of students
to the renovation of Chinese society, a renovation which would
be threatened by national dismemberment by foreign powers.
In the last chapter the new role of Beijing University and the
growth of the New Culture Movement were discussed, but this

was presented in terms of a rejection of short-term politics and a concern for long-term cultural re-education. Although their teachers could understand the need for caution, the students were not to be prevented from discussing politics and from organising study groups which examined political topics, on the basis of freedom for academic debate which Cai Yuanpei had encouraged. The growing popularity of New Culture magazines among the students gave rise to a questioning of established authority, which could readily be transferred into the political sphere, if a burning issue appeared. The students came to face a major intellectual problem in that their recipe for the improvement of China required the rejection of the Chinese past and extensive Westernisation, whereas their immediate political success in 1919 came from the call to save China from the impact of overseas domination and betrayal. This paradox was not to be solved, until the later general acceptance in China of Lenin's views on imperialism, which provided a modern theory from the West which at the same time laid the blame for China's problems on the West, and not on China's weaknesses.

The third difference between 1919 and earlier years such as 1915 lay in the political and social changes which had occurred. In 1915 Yuan Shikai was presiding over a relatively united country and could apply his police and press censorship powers with some measure of success, thereby controlling the expression of anti-Japanese feeling, whereas by 1919 much of this control had been eroded. In early 1915 the merchants and industrial entrepreneurs had hardly begun to benefit from the removal of European competition, but by 1919 business was booming, with chambers of commerce and business associations ready to make their opinions known. The growth of industry had greatly raised the numbers of industrial workers, who were also able to act collectively through their guilds and increasingly through more modern-style trade unions. Hence in 1919 the students' appeal was less easily stifled in Beijing, more widely known through China and supported by urban organisations of much greater power than before.

The last possible difference, and the most controversial, concerns the impact in China of the Bolshevik revolution of November 1917 in Russia. Given the enormous long-term influence of Marxism–Leninism and of the Soviet Union in China, it has been too readily assumed that this influence began from the moment of the revolution in 1917. Careful studies have shown that the impact of Marxism in China before 1917 was negligible: in fact much more interest was expressed in European anarchism, with anarchist societies flourishing in China after 1911. The 1917 revolution, about which only very confused reports reached the Chinese press, inspired two known public responses in 1918, a telegram by Sun Yixian to Lenin and an article by Li Dazhao in *New Youth* in October 1918 on the victory of Bolshevism. Li proclaimed his faith in the new Soviet regime and thereafter supported a Marxist study group in Beijing. Nevertheless the appeal of Marxism was as a historical tool, rather than as a political weapon in the context of China, because its revolutionary message referred mainly to societies more advanced industrially than China and because nothing was known of how Lenin applied Marxist theory to a country such as Russia. The chaotic state of Russia in 1918 and 1919 did not augur well for the success of the revolution and the public in China knew more about the activities of the White Russians in Siberia and Manchuria, than they did of events in the revolutionary areas. The most important, early pro-Chinese act by the Bolshevik government was the Karakhan declaration, offering the abolition of all Russian privileges in China. This declaration was not issued until July 1919 in Moscow, well after the major events of the May Fourth upsurge, and the diplomatic isolation of Moscow meant that the declaration was only available publicly in China in March 1920, by which time Moscow was not actually ready to concede so much.

The six weeks of intense urban activity after 4 May 1919 provided a new direction for the New Culture Movement by revealing the political potential of youth in a society under threat. As a result of the May–June 1919 activities, the New Culture message reached far more widely within urban China, and some 400 magazines, mostly written in vernacular style, sprang up to cater for the new readers, who demanded information on the West and on China's situation. Even Sun Yixian, who was ambivalent about the anti-Confucian aspects of the movement, was forced to concede that the newly energised young must be harnessed. He therefore formally re-established in China the Guomindang or Nationalist Party in October 1919, bringing to an end his Chinese Revolutionary Party which had been essentially a party for overseas Chinese. He also began publication of his own magazine, *Reconstruction*, which ran Sun's 'Plans for national reconstruction' and discussed socialism.

The events of 1919 produced an acceleration in the impact of the New Culture Movement and in its politicisation. Although it is possible analytically to separate the New Culture Movement from the events of May 1919, the Chinese themselves and historians of China have come to label the years around 1919 as the May Fourth period, regarding the demonstrations as a culmination of events since about 1915 and as an inspiration for events to follow. May Fourth is now celebrated as youth day in the People's Republic, but a word of caution is necessary. Just as the famous 1898 reformer, Kang Youwei, attacked as a young upstart by the seniority-based bureaucracy, was actually 40 years old, so the age of some of the young radicals in 1919 is higher than one might expect from the term 'youth'. For example, Chen Duxiu was 40, Li Dazhao 30, Mao Zedong in Hunan 26. Such men as these were young in a society which traditionally had respected old age. Their emergence into prominence in the turbulent and progressive May Fourth era marked them out as leaders for the regeneration of China, with a political life of some 60 years ahead of them, during which time younger generations would be unable to shift them from power.

The Shandong decision at Versailles which provoked the May Fourth demonstration also disturbed the Western powers, which began to fear Japanese ambitions and to seek means to curb them. The first forum in which this could be achieved was that of the negotiations for a new consortium of foreign banks to supply loans to China, negotiations which began formally during the Versailles conference. Japan tried to insist that certain areas in Manchuria and Inner Mongolia be placed outside the consortium arrangements, because of prior Japanese interests, but the USA and Britain refused such reservations, indicating that private spheres of interest were now obsolete. Japan finally backed down and joined the consortium without reservations in mid-1920. In practice because of the harsh terms sought by the consortium banks for new loans to China, no loans were ever granted by the consortium, but its existence hindered other lenders from openly approaching China. The re-creation of the consortium of foreign banks in 1920 provoked the now more numerous and stronger Chinese modern banks to form their own consortium, which gained promises from the central government to commit surplus customs revenue to the repayment of internal government loans from the banks.

The Washington Conference

President Wilson of the USA had anticipated that the League of Nations, established by the Versailles peace conference, would provide the forum for peaceful settlement of world issues after 1919, but the US Senate failed to ratify American participation, partly because of the Shandong affair. The USA began to fear a naval arms race with Japan, which was the only clear rival to American power in the Pacific and in 1921 President Harding proposed a naval disarmament conference, to which was soon added a general conference on East Asian issues. The conference met in Washington from November 1921 to February 1922, resulting in defence and disarmament agreements between Japan and the Western powers. More importantly for China, a nine-power treaty was signed by Japan, USA, Britain, France, Portugal, the Netherlands, Italy, Belgium and China, pledging commitment to the territorial and administrative integrity of China: the term 'administrative integrity' was new to international agreements on China and implied foreign support for eventual unity in China. The treaty also provided an immediate rise in customs tariffs and the promise of negotiations on the end of foreign control of customs rates and of foreign privileges in legal cases (extraterritoriality). In a separate Sino-Japanese treaty of February 1922, Shandong was returned to China, with compensatory payments to Japan for railways in the province.

It had been hoped that the Washington settlement would provide for peaceful cooperation between powers in the eastern Pacific area, but mutual suspicions between Japan and the USA, and changing circumstances in China rendered this impossible. Despite the promises made at Washington, nationalistic Chinese, especially under advice from the USSR, regarded the Washington settlement as inimical to China's independence, because they believed the powers still treated China as a passive pawn to be manipulated at will. Therefore the Chinese were prepared to challenge the foreign presence by armed force, with some successes in the later 1920s. Even before this the Chinese had continued their anti-foreign demonstrations, such as in 1923 over the continued Japanese presence in Port Arthur and Dairen which was only sanctioned by the resented May 1915 treaty, and as in 1925 over the incident in Shanghai on 30 May, which will be discussed later. The Chinese central government also tried to insist on the renegotiation of treaties falling due for renewal in the mid-1920s and it succeeded in calling a tariff conference from October 1925 and establishing an extraterritoriality commission in January 1926, in fulfilment of Washington agreements. The three-years delay in the two last-named projects was not occasioned by China's divided state, as is often suggested, but resulted from France's tardiness in ratifying the Washington package of agreements for reasons not relating to China. The two sets of negotiations did not yield immediate concrete results, but the tariff conference did recommend tariff autonomy for 1929, before adjourning after a change of Chinese government: this recommendation formed the basis for the successful regaining of tariff autonomy after nominal reunification of China by the Nationalist Party.

The Nationalist and Communist Parties

All that remains in this chapter is to discuss the rise of the Nationalist Party and of its junior ally, the Chinese Communist Party (CCP), because these were the organisations which broke the power of the first generation of warlords and which harnessed the growing strength of urban nationalism. Just as the alliance of the two parties was achieving its first major military success in the conquest of central China by early 1927, the Nationalists turned against the Communists in a series of bloody attacks and thereafter the two parties were locked in hostility, either directly on the battlefield, 1927–36, and 1946–9 or in uneasy and often broken truce, 1937–45. The history of the 1920–27 period for both parties is intimately connected with events in and personalities from Soviet Russia, because the CCP drew its inspiration and detailed guidance from Moscow, and the Nationalists turned to the same source for aid and military advice in 1923, after being refused aid by the Western powers.

The Re-emergence of the Nationalist Party

The Nationalist Party or Guomindang, founded in 1912 and banned in 1913, was officially restarted in October 1919 by Sun Yixian and sought opportunities for political power and administrative responsibilities in south China. The south was chosen because the southern provinces had been most keen on constitution protection as a propaganda line in the years from late 1915 and therefore had found it convenient to host and humour Nationalist parliamentarians to prove southern legitimacy. In addition the top leadership of the Nationalist Party was still drawn from the pre-1911 Tongmenghui, which had been biased towards the south. Sun Yixian had been the generalissimo of the Guangzhou government between September 1917 and May 1918 and still retained personal connections with many southern warlords. The chance to return to Guangdong province came after guest armies from other south-western provinces were driven out by October 1920 by local warlord, Chen Jiongming, who invited the parliamentarians to return. Chen had been visited during 1920 by a Soviet agent Vilensky, who reported most favourably on Chen's socialist tendencies and who argued that Chen represented the best candidate for Soviet aid and for the promotion of a Chinese Communist Party. This suggestion was not followed through, because a parallel Soviet mission to northern China under Voitinsky was given preference by the Soviet authorities.

Sun Yixian and his colleagues moved to Guangzhou, where 200-odd members of the 1913 parliament elected Sun national president in April 1921, but relations between Sun and Chen Jiongming were not harmonious. Chen wished to strengthen his position in Guangdong province, whereas Sun argued vigorously for a northern expedition to begin the reconquest of China. In June 1921 Guangdong troops conquered their local enemy, Guangxi, and this encouraged Sun's wider ambitions to the north. Chen, holding most of the available military power, was able to hinder Sun's efforts, until careful manoeuvring of military forces loyal to Sun forced Chen's resignation in April 1922. Thereupon Sun mounted a northern expedition into Jiangxi province, which advanced successfully, while troops loyal to Chen reoccupied Guangzhou, finally forcing Sun to take refuge on a gunboat in Guangzhou harbour for almost two months, until Sun fled to Shanghai in August 1922. Chen's action related to irritation with Sun's ambitions and also to popular feeling that a negotiated settlement with the north was possible after restoration of the old constitution and Li Yuanhong as president by the Zhili clique in Beijing.

Sun Yixian, ousted this second time from the south, canvassed again for foreign help. He met the Soviet Agent, Sneevliet, alias Maring, in August 1922 and began to correspond with the Soviet representative in Beijing, Joffe. Sun and Joffe met in January 1923 in Shanghai and agreed that Soviet Russia could help the Nationalist Party in its reunification struggle, even though China was not ready for communism. Simultaneously troops from a number of provinces recaptured Guangzhou for Sun, their pay coming from money raised by Sun's supporters. The conquerors of Guangzhou were again warlord units over whom Sun could expect to retain little control, unless he could provide adequate funds from the taxation of Guangzhou. Chen Jiongming still remained strong in eastern Guangdong province and the northern warlords plotted to overthrow the new government. Sun had moved on 1 January 1923 to issue a Nationalist Party manifesto, modernising Sun's Three People's Principles, Nationalism, Democracy and People's Livelihood, to the needs of 1920s, but party organisation was still weak, with party membership lists either lost or inadequately maintained. Sun's weak situation was to be transformed in the next two years by the injection of Soviet aid, which was granted in accordance with very specific policy intentions in Moscow.

Russian Interest in China

The leaders of the 1917 Bolshevik revolution in Russia had two sets of reasons for interest in China, one relating to existing strategic considerations, the other to the new revolutionary requirements of the government. Russia shared a very long border with China and once Russia emerged out of the worst moments of its civil war, there was a desire to consolidate the border area and the Russian-owned Chinese Eastern Railway, passing through Manchuria to Vladivostok. Therefore whilst negotiating with Sun in the south and helping to create the CCP, Soviet representatives were also engaged in diplomatic negotiations with the Beijing warlord government, which had withdrawn recognition from the pre-Bolshevik Russian diplomats left in China after 1917 but which had not recognised the Bolshevik government. These negotiations were regularly halted over the issue of Outer Mongolia, where a Russian-backed Communist government had been installed in 1920, because China regarded Outer Mongolia as part of China. Another contentious issue was the Chinese Eastern Railway, which Soviet Russia had appeared to offer back to China in 1919, but which was then excluded from later Russian offers on the abolition of tsarist privileges and concessions. Agreement was finally reached for a Sino-Soviet treaty in 1924, just as Soviet aid was arriving in quantity in south China to facilitate the destruction of the Beijing government.

Soviet revolutionary mobilisation in China began in 1920. When Lenin had initiated the Communist International (Comintern, CI) in 1919, all attention had been directed at European affairs and the only Chinese involvement came from representatives of Chinese workers resident in Russia. By the time of the CI's second congress in mid-1920, it was clear that immediate revolution in Europe was impossible, after the failure of European insurrectionary efforts had ensured the isolation of the new Soviet government in its European context. A new strategy was therefore necessary to continue the drive towards revolution. Lenin argued that the imperialist capitalist countries could be attacked indirectly through the promotion of national independence movements in colonial areas, which would prevent the extraction of the excessive profits which made imperialism possible. China, although not formally a colony, was also a field for imperialist exploitation and could therefore be included in this approach. Nevertheless the theoretical desire for national independence movements did not provide precise practical guidance on how to achieve the most effective movement with the limited resources available to the Soviet government.

The 1920 CI Congress was presented with two possible approaches, one by the young Indian, Roy, the other usually described as Lenin's, but largely drafted by the Dutch Communist, Sneevliet, who had worked to create an Indonesian revolutionary movement. Roy suggested the creation of independent communist parties, which would pursue revolutionary social and national goals without compromising with other organisations, whereas Sneevliet, noting the weakness of the social base for a communist party in economically undeveloped colonies, urged that the local communist parties must assist the national bourgeoisie of the colonies in their national liberation struggles. The second approach would bring quicker national liberation, it was argued, but the communist parties must be careful to retain their organisational independence and to prepare the small industrial working class (proletariat) and the much larger peasantry for the transformation of the national liberation movement into a socialist revolution. The CI Congress adopted the second approach because it promised faster results for breaking Soviet Russia's isolation, but the choice placed enormous difficulties before the local organisers in identifying suitable national revolutionary partners and in judging the timing of policy shifts. It was all very well to say theoretically that the revolution had two stages, the national liberation and the social, but once the masses were aroused, they tended to demand social reforms, even when these threatened the national liberation campaign, by challenging the privileges of the national bourgeoisie.

Early Communist Activity in China

From its headquarters in Moscow and then from its Far East office in Irkutsk established in 1921, the CI began to pursue the new approach, seeking to create a Chinese Communist Party and to analyse the political scene in China. As mentioned earlier, two missions went to China in 1920, under Voitinsky to the north and Vilensky to the south. Voitinsky met leaders of the *New Youth* group, whose interest in Marxism had already been publicly stated, and he gradually persuaded them that the stricter organisational methods of Lenin were necessary for the successful prosecution of Marxist goals. Chen Duxiu, who had in 1919 begun to promote radical labour organisations, founded the Socialist Youth Corps in August 1920, and in November the magazine *Gongchandang* (Communist Party) began in Shanghai. Small groups calling themselves Communists also appeared in Beijing under Li Dazhao, in Changsha under Mao, in Guangzhou, Tianjin, Wuhan and Jinan, but the ideological understanding of the group members was often confused, with the result that the current CCP prefers to portray its official founding date as the First Congress of July 1921, rather than these earlier cells. Chinese students who had gone overseas for study in Japan or on work-study schemes to Europe also made contact with Marxists in those countries and in particular the French group was to produce major leaders for the later CCP, notably Zhou Enlai, Li Lisan and Deng Xiaoping.

The First Congress of the CCP was held in July 1921, in Shanghai at first and later near Hangzhou, with thirteen members present, representing a nominal fifty-seven members. Neither Chen Duxiu nor Li Dazhao, the most famous figures in the Party, were present, but three later leaders were – Mao Zedong and Dong Biwu, who remained in power until the 1970s, and Zhang Guotao, who was expelled in 1938, after unsuccessfully challenging Mao's leadership. Existing CCP members had already plunged into trade union work, on the Marxist principle of the leading revolutionary role of the proletariat, and this practice was endorsed by the Congress, which barely mentioned the peasants. The Congress rejected the view that the Party should be essentially a study group propagating Marxist ideology and the view that there should be no cooperation with other radical individuals, but refused to endorse the wish of the CI representative at the Congress, Sneevliet, that the new CCP should pursue cooperation with the Nationalist Party. The CCP elected Chen Duxiu as secretary-general, rather than Li Dazhao, apparently because Chen could devote himself more fully to Party work, having resigned his Beijing University post. Chen, who remained as secretary-general from 1921 to 1927, was opposed to cooperation with other parties and concerned over the dangers of militarism, opinions which soon clashed with the CI requirements for alliance with the Nationalists and the creation of a party army.

The new Party with its CI links represented the first direct application of Leninist as opposed to Marxist ideas in China, with the revolutionary vanguard of CCP members consisting of young intellectuals with urban training motivated by concerns expressed in the May Fourth Movement for national survival and regeneration. In contrast to Europe where communist parties developed from conflicts within the socialist movement, the CCP emerged in a nationalistic context with no major socialist rivals seeking to contest its power in the growing labour movement. Recent studies have indicated that it took until 1927 for Party leaders to appreciate fully the meaning of being in a Leninist party in which devotion to the party and its policies should replace all other loyalties.

The first major activities of the CCP were in the labour field, although Peng Pai worked to organise peasants in Haifeng in eastern Guangdong. The economic situation encouraged worker unrest, in that the wartime boom came to an end in 1920 and modern factories in China were pressured by the competition from Europe and Japan, resulting in lay-offs and attempts to reduce wages to retain profitability. Not all the strikes were led by the CCP, with the most vigorous one of 1922, the successful strike by Hong Kong seamen, from January to March, being led by a traditional workers' organisation. The sectors most susceptible to CCP organisation were not the textile factory workers, who tended to be female and often short-term, but the transport and mining workers. The railways in particular provided major pools of relatively skilled labour, while the miners suffered especially from the inequities of the Chinese system of contract hiring of labour through middlemen. The most famous mining strike involved the Anyuan mines in Jiangxi in September 1922 where Mao, Li Lisan and Liu Shaoqi were all active as CCP labour organisers. Strikes on the railways, although very effective in terms of publicity, always threatened the activities of warlords who needed continuous access to rail transport for their military plans. Several rail strikes were put down by force, for example in Hunan in September 1922 with ten strikers killed by troops, but the worst repression occurred in the north when Wu Peifu, who had previously declared his interest in labour reform, banned the trade union on the Beijing–Hankou railway in February 1923. The striking workers were attacked by Wu's soldiers, with thirty-five deaths. The union was destroyed and other warlords took the opportunity to close trade unions elsewhere in China.

The 1923 warlord attack on the labour movement forced a crucial reappraisal by CCP leaders, who came to realise that the labour movement could not flourish without some political protection, which could only be provided by an alliance with a permissive government. The only obvious candidate was the Guangzhou regime under the Nationalist Party. Hence the CCP, which at its Second Congress in July 1922 had again rejected an alliance with the Nationalists, turned reluctantly in 1923 to accept such an alliance. It thereby aligned itself with the CI policy which had been urged all along by Sneevliet, who in August 1922 had ordered the Party to obey CI directives on an alliance. The CCP shift was fully endorsed by the Third Congress of June 1923, which affirmed the central role of the Nationalist Party in the national revolutionary movement and offered CCP support. Nevertheless the method of the CCP–Nationalist alliance was different from what had been envisaged in Moscow in 1920. Sun Yixian, the Nationalists' leader, refused to sanction an inter-party alliance and insisted that CCP members join the Nationalist Party as individual members, a policy which came to be known as the 'bloc within'. Critics of the 'bloc within' approach argued that it would confuse the class composition of the parties, since they understood that a party could only represent one class. The CI counter-argument was that the Nationalist Party represented four classes, the national bourgeoisie, the petty bourgeoisie, the workers and the peasants, at least during the stage of the national revolution to expel imperialism from China.

Reorganisation of the Nationalist Party

Sun Yixian's acceptance of CCP members within the Nationalist Party and his successful negotiations with Soviet representatives opened the way to Soviet aid, which consisted of finance, military equipment and the sending of Soviet advisers. The exact

extent of the Soviet financial and military aid has never been
disclosed, but it is known that up to six ships plied regularly
between Vladivostok and Guangzhou after October 1924, bringing military equipment and oil. Some of this was a gift from
the USSR, but most of it required payment by the Chinese. To
assist in military preparations, Jiang Jieshi was sent to Moscow
in August 1923 for three months to observe Soviet methods.
Jiang had been militarily trained in Japan before 1911, had
joined the Tongmenghui, had fought in the 1911 revolution
and had worked in 1920 in the new Shanghai Stock and Commodity Exchange to raise money for Sun Yixian, but he was
not one of the inner circle of Nationalist leaders around Sun.
The major political organiser sent from Moscow was Borodin,
who arrived in Guangzhou in October 1923 and who immediately began to plan the reorganisation of the Nationalist Party
with Sun Yixian. Military advisers began to arrive in 1924, and
the most famous, General Bliukher (alias Galen), reached
Guangzhou in October 1924, to serve for almost three years in
China, although not all this time was spent in Guangzhou,
because the USSR was also providing military aid to warlord
Feng Yuxiang's Guominjun in the northwest of China from
April 1925.

The reorganisation of the Nationalist Party required a tightening of party discipline and the propagation of a new party
programme, with due attention paid to the military needs of
the party. Under Borodin's advice a provisional executive committee drew up a party constitution outlining a hierarchy of
branches according to geographic area, and providing for annual congresses, the first to be held in 1924. The congresses
would elect a central executive committee and a central super-
visory committee to run the daily business of the party, but it
was decided that Sun was to be designated leader, without the
necessity of election. The party rules, including the methods
for re-registering members, reflected the Leninist principles
of the Communist Party of the Soviet Union, thereby implying
the practice of 'democratic centralism', according to which each
level of the party is subordinate to its organisational superior
and each member is required to support publicly any resolution adopted after adequate discussion. The new constitution
and the alliance with the CCP drew criticism from some veteran

members of the Nationalist Party, even before the January 1924 Congress, criticisms which finally forced a split in the Nationalist Party in 1925, with the most vigorous anti-CCP members forming the Western Hills group, after a meeting in the Western Hills near Beijing.

1924 witnessed the consolidation of central Guangdong province as the base for the newly energised Nationalist Party, with the rudiments of a party army created. The First Nationalist Party Congress met in Guangzhou from 20 January, with 165 delegates present, for a party claiming some 28 000 members. Sun Yixian addressed the Congress on several occasions, stressing anti-imperialism, anti-militarism and the importance of the masses in the forthcoming national revolution, but he was non-committal over rural strategy. A Central Executive Committee was elected, with a quarter of its members also being in the CCP, and after the Congress the committee established the functional headquarters of the party in Guangzhou, with a secretariat, an organisation section and eight bureaux for party work.

The Nationalist Party sought to placate its military supporters by appointments in its upper levels and ordered the organisation of party cells in all army units in March, to begin the politicisation of the army towards party goals. In May 1924 the Huangpu Military Academy was opened near Guangzhou, with Jiang Jieshi as commandant and its students recruited from all over China through party organisers in the cities. The short three-month course was taught by the best officers available, including the Russian advisers and Chinese who had studied in Japan and at Chinese military schools. Huangpu graduates tasted military action in October 1924 when the government suppressed the Merchants' Volunteer Corps, which had been organised by businessmen opposed to Nationalist Party taxes and policies.

The Nationalist Movement after the Death of Sun Yixian

In early 1925 the Nationalist Party survived the death of its leader, Sun Yixian, without serious immediate disruption. Sun Yixian had gone north at the end of 1924 to meet military leaders there to discuss national reunification after the second

Zhili–Fengtian war. He visited Japan on the way, speaking there of the importance of Pan-Asianism, but he was too sick with cancer to negotiate on arrival in Beijing. He died on 12 March, after preparing a will advocating continued alliance with the Soviet Union and the prosecution of the revolution through to the end. After his death, Sun Yixian remained the most vital figure in Nationalist Party ideology, through his writings on the Three People's Principles, a body of doctrine that was powerful enough to be inspiring but vague enough to allow his successors enormous leeway in its interpretation. Even the CCP upheld Sun's role as a great revolutionary within the confines of his time and later the Party was grateful for the long-standing support of Madame Sun, Song Qingling, which provided a symbolic continuity with the pre-May Fourth revolutionaries, until her death at a post equivalent to vice-chairman of the People's Republic.

The Nationalist government in the south was not able to respond organisationally to Sun's death for almost four months for military reasons, but when it did, the new anti-imperialist atmosphere provoked by the incident of 30 May carried the party to new strengths. From February to April 1925 the Nationalist units, especially those from the Huangpu Academy, sought to drive Sun's one-time ally, Chen Jiongming, out of Eastern Guangdong province. This first Eastern Expedition witnessed the new party army style, the use of propaganda squads, the advice of Russian officers, stress on troop discipline in battle and towards civilians, and the principle of *lianzuofa*, collective responsibility for disobedience of orders, especially for unordered retreat.

In May 1925 CCP leaders, seeking to revive the organisation of the working class, organised a National General Labour Union after a conference in Guangzhou, and in Shanghai the Communists pushed for strikes against Japanese textile mills. Japanese guards at a Shanghai factory fired on Chinese workers on 15 May, killing one Communist. Protests mounted, culminating in an incident on 30 May outside a Shanghai police station, when the British inspector, fearing the crowd would invade the station, ordered his constables to fire into the crowd, resulting in twelve deaths. An immediate city-wide protest developed, with a general strike and further Chinese deaths in police repression of rioting. Demonstrations against the foreigner spread to other cities where more deaths occurred and foreign consulates were attacked. In Guangzhou, however, there was calm, because the garrison, consisting of nominally pro-Nationalist Yunnan and Guangxi units, had been courting foreign support in the absence of their more radical colleagues on the Eastern Expedition. The incident of 30 May clearly required a massive response from the centre of power of China's Nationalist Party, and therefore, without fully defeating Chen Jiongming, the Eastern Expedition troops returned to liberate Guangzhou from its inadequately nationalistic guest armies. This was achieved under Jiang Jieshi's direction by 12 June, opening the way to a general strike in Hong Kong on 21 June and to a massive anti-imperialist demonstration on 23 June in Guangzhou. The latter ended in tragedy with at least fifty Chinese deaths from British and French guns in the foreign concession on Shamen island, although the ultimate responsibility for starting the shooting is still in doubt.

The Nationalist Party announced the formation of a national government on 1 July 1925, with nine ministries and a National Revolutionary army (NRA), but with power controlled by the party's Political and Military Councils, both under the chairmanship of Wang Jingwei. The key figures in the Political Council were Wang, Hu Hanmin and Liao Zhongkai, but on 20 August 1925 Liao was assassinated. At Borodin's suggestion a committee of three, Wang, Jiang Jieshi and General Xu Chongzhi, investigated the crime, leading to the implication of a large number of conservative Nationalist Party figures: Hu Hanmin was sent off to the USSR, others were sent to northern China. Jiang then arranged for the expulsion of General Xu, thereby leaving only two major power-holders in Guangzhou, the civilian party veteran and Sun Yixian's close associate, Wang Jingwei, and the military commander, Jiang Jieshi. The physical security of the new government was enhanced by the decisive defeat of Chen Jiongming in the second Eastern Expedition of October 1925 under Jiang's command, and in the defeat of other enemies in northern Guangdong in October and southwest Guangdong in December. Nevertheless within Guangzhou itself the government was challenged by the increasing power of the Hong Kong–Guangzhou strike committee and its armed pickets under the control of the CCP. Although the committee was financed by the Nationalist government, it acted in many respects as a rival government.

Relations between the Nationalist Party and the CCP in Guangzhou were amicable in 1925, but soured in early 1926, only to be patched up under Soviet advice after Jiang Jieshi's coup on 20 March. Anti-Communist agitation within the Nationalist Party had been inspired by two books by party theorist Dai Jitao on the interpretation of Sun Yixian, published in mid-1925, and had been taken up by the Western Hills conference in November 1925. Dai and the Western Hills group were condemned by the Guangzhou Nationalist leadership and in particular by Jiang, who defended the alliance with the CCP in an open letter. The Nationalist Party's Second Congress met in January 1926 and elected a new central executive committee to include Jiang and exclude several northern conservative members; Communists gained a quarter of the membership. The Nationalist Party had now grown to somewhere short of 200 000 members, at least a sevenfold increase in two years, a growth rate more than matched by the CCP in the same period. Jiang, now clearly number two in the Nationalist Party, suspected that Wang Jingwei and the top Russian advisers under Kisanka wished to send him out of the way to the USSR, because of conflicts over allocation of Soviet arms and the forthcoming Northern Expedition and because of Wang's fears about Jiang's ambitions. Mysterious manoeuvrings by the gunboat, Zhongshan, near Jiang's headquarters led him to seize it on 20 March. He declared martial law and disarmed the guards of the Russian advisers and at the strike committee headquarters. All this was carried out without consultation with Wang or the Russians.

Solving the 20 March 1926 coup required all the authority of the CI in controlling the resentments of the CCP. Earlier in March the CI had resolved that a fighting alliance of the CCP and the Nationalist Party was essential. The continued growth of the national revolution in China was crucial to Soviet strategy and, in the CI analysis, also crucial to the best development of the CCP. The Hong Kong strike was viewed by Moscow as a vital part of anti-British activity and it was essential to keep anti-imperialist sentiments in China focused on Britain by

retaining the CCP role in propaganda work, because otherwise Chinese anger would naturally turn to the more immediate natural enemy, Japan, which the USSR wished to placate
for its own reasons in Manchuria. Therefore the CI urged compromise on the CCP, resulting in a package of concessions,
codified in the Nationalist Party Central Executive Committee
plenum of 15 to 25 May. The USSR promised to continue its
aid and to support a Northern Expedition, the Nationalist Party
expelled some more conservatives, Wang Jingwei retired to France
and the CCP was allowed a maximum one-third membership
in executive committees, with no CCP member as head of any
central bureau. The list of CCP members in the Nationalist
Party was revealed and all Nationalist Party members had to
re-register, pledging obedience to particular writings of Sun
and to the Congress resolutions of 1924 and 1926. CCP members were withdrawn from political work in the first army of
the NRA, the divisions drawing on the Huangpu graduates.
Nevertheless the CCP was allowed to continue its work with
labour and the peasantry, and the Hong Kong strike committee remained active, even refusing to control further strike actions
to coordinate with the Northern Expedition.

The Northern Expedition

With nominal unity restored between the Nationalists and the
CCP, the new aim of the Nationalist Party became to launch
the Northern Expedition against the warlords, whose lack of
nationalism had again been revealed in the gunning-down of
a demonstration in Beijing over unequal treaties on 18 March
1926, with forty-seven deaths. The NRA consisted initially of
five armies, but by the formal launching of the Expedition on
9 July 1926, there were eight armies, the two important new
units being the Seventh Army of Guangxi units under Li Zongren
and Bai Chongxi and the Eighth Army of Hunan units under
the ruler of southern Hunan, Tang Shengzhi. Tang had turned
to the Nationalists in the face of pressure from the north and
accepted his formal position over the Eighth Army in early
June. Troops from Guangdong and Guangxi went to his aid
during June, so that the capture of Hunan's capital, Changsha,

was effected on 11 July, two days after the nominal start of the Expedition. The Nationalists had to ensure that in their advance north they did not provoke either an alliance among the opposing warlords or an intervention by the foreign powers. Hence they negotiated with Sun Chuanfang in the lower Yangzi until they had isolated Wu Peifu in the middle Yangzi by besieging Wuchang in September 1926. The leadership also unilaterally called off the Hong Kong strike in October 1926 and kept issuing statements about the protection of the foreigner as an individual, while their subordinates attacked missionary properties.

By the end of 1926 the Northern Expedition had expanded Nationalist power enormously from the Guangdong and Guangxi base into Hunan, Hubei, Jiangxi and Fujian, the latter two taken after some stiff resistance from Sun Chuanfang's forces in November and December. The speed of the advance had been made possible by the quality of the NRA troops achieved through training and political indoctrination, by fiscal reforms which made the Nationalist currency acceptable to wider areas, by political work among the masses, who provided information, food and carrying power, and increasingly by defections from the opposing side. Since warlords retained power through the preservation of their troops, it made sense to avoid battle with the militarily keen southerners, and the Nationalists aided this process, by funds and by the promise of incorporation into a successful military machine. This dilution of the original military forces of the NRA with other troops still organised in their old units severely weakened the revolutionary thrust of the expedition, because many of the turncoat officers had previously used their military power to enrich themselves locally. Any attempt to apply social revolution in the rural areas would immediately impinge upon their privileges. Yet the organisation of the peasant masses into peasant unions, as in Hunan, although accepted by the Nationalists as necessary for helping the Northern Expedition, revealed a power potential which could not be constrained within the artificial boundaries of the policy of a national revolution before a social one. In theory the NRA should have moulded the ideology of the new officers and men to accept revolutionary goals through the appointment of political work officers in the new armies, but in practice Nationalist suspicions of the CCP strength in political work allowed new armies to avoid political retraining.

The very success of the Nationalist advance strained the relations between the elements within the Nationalist Party, as evidenced by the rivalry between Jiang Jieshi's military headquarters at Nanchang and the Provisional Joint Council set up in December in Wuhan. The Wuhan situation was heavily influenced by the CCP, which fomented a wide range of strikes against Chinese and foreign businesses. The CCP also urged strident anti-imperialism, which resulted in the takeover of the British concessions in Hankou and Jiujiang in early January 1927. These takeovers were tolerated by Britain in a new policy of acceptance of Nationalist power. The emerging military power-holder in Wuhan was Tang Shengzhi, the last general to join before the Northern Expedition began. In vain did Tang oppose Jiang's intention to march Jiang's troops into Nanjing and Shanghai, an area seen as providing too much wealth to Jiang. Jiang had prepared for the advance on Shanghai by raising money from sympathisers in the banking community there and by reassuring Japan that the position of powers in the city would not be challenged. The CCP too had prepared to win Shanghai for themselves, arranging three workers' uprisings against the warlord troops, the third of which on 21 March won the city just as NRA troops reached the city outskirts. Nanjing was taken by the NRA on 24 March, accompanied by looting of foreign consulates and the retaliatory use of shells by foreign gunboats killing up to thirty Chinese; responsibility for the looting has never been satisfactorily ascertained, but the powers came to accept publicly the Nationalist view that it was provoked by Communist agitators in the army.

Jiang Jieshi's Break with the Communists

Jiang's military advance was paralleled by the third plenum of the Nationalist Central Executive Committee, meeting in Wuhan in mid-March 1927. This resolved to restore power to the party, by restructuring all committees and returning the leadership to Wang Jingwei, who was due back from Paris via Moscow. The plenum also voted for greater Nationalist–CCP cooperation, but already in areas under Jiang Jieshi the suppression of labour unions and leftist branches of the Nationalist Party had begun, with deaths in the suppression of demonstrations in Hangzhou on 30 March. Executions of Communists also occurred in Chongqing on 31 March. Wang Jingwei reached Shanghai on 1 April and began a hectic round of discussions, promising Jiang another party plenum by mid-April to discuss policy on the CCP and issuing a statement on unity with the CCP secretary-general, Chen Duxiu. Wang left for Wuhan on 5 April, but the next day the foreign diplomatic corps allowed the Beijing police to enter certain buildings in the USSR embassy. The raid netted a vast body of documents detailing Soviet aid and plans in China and resulted in the arrest of over 50 Russians and Nationalist Party members. Twenty of the latter were executed, including CCP co-founder Li Dazhao. The information revealed in Beijing was the final straw for the already keenly anti-Communist Nationalists under Jiang and early on 12 April members of underworld gangs and disguised troops attacked all the centres of union activity in Shanghai. There was some brief resistance and then the slaughter of hundreds and possibly thousands of suspected leftists. An attempt at a general strike in protest failed and a new Nationalist-controlled trade union organisation was initiated, which effectively shut the CCP out of controlling or even influencing Shanghai labour until after 1949. A similar anti-Communist attack came in Guangzhou on 15 April, then in Changsha on 21 May and less bloodily in Jiangxi province at the end of May.

Jiang Jieshi's open break with the CCP posed enormous problems for the Wuhan government, for the CCP and more distantly for the USSR. The Nationalists in Wuhan expelled Jiang from the party and his NRA posts on 17 April, and Jiang's supporters in Nanjing replied by setting up a central government in Nanjing on 18 April. Wuhan now faced enemies on all sides except the northwest, where negotiations were being held with the Soviet-backed warlord, Feng Yuxiang, but when Wuhan's forces moved north into Henan in May against northern warlord troops, they sustained very heavy casualties in winning victory, with the result that Feng's forces reaped most of the territorial gains. The Wuhan government controlled three provinces, Hubei, Hunan and Jiangxi in April, but in May the local military in Hunan moved against the Communists, a move which top Hunan militarist and Wuhan supporter, Tang Shengzhi, failed to condemn when investigating for the government in June. The Wuhan government also faced grave economic problems, due to strikes and disruption in the business and banking sectors. Therefore Borodin offered to impose revolutionary discipline on the workers, i.e. to halt disruptions in order to consolidate the government, which gave some respite.

Soon after the Shanghai events, the CCP opened its Fifth Congress on 27 April, claiming to represent over 50 000 members, more than half of whom were workers. The Congress reaffirmed its commitment to alliance with the Nationalist Party's left-wing in Wuhan and confirmed the analysis that the events in Shanghai had revealed the counter-revolutionary nature of the national bourgeoisie. This left the Nationalist Party in Wuhan as a more revolutionary party representing only workers, peasants and petty bourgeoisie. Following the CI line of December 1926, the CCP now stressed the importance of the agrarian revolution to the current situation in China, but adopted a resolution of land confiscation which excluded small landlords and the land of the NRA officers. Chen Duxiu and others pointed out that stressing agrarian revolution would undoubtedly destroy the alliance with the Nationalists, who were very hesitant over land issues, but Roy, the leading CI speaker, dismissed such worries.

Behind the CCP's approach lay the directives of the CI, whose executive back in Moscow was divided over China policy in a debate that formed a major part of the Stalin–Trotsky divide with the Communist Party of the Soviet Union. Although the full details of Stalin's and Trotsky's differences on internal policy are beyond this book, a few salient points on external policy can clarify the China problem. Stalin had essentially come to accept the policy of 'socialism in one country' (USSR), implying that CI must serve the foreign policy needs of the USSR, whatever the short-term impact on local revolutionaries, whereas Trotsky argued that socialism in one country was a betrayal of internationalism and that revolution must be promoted wherever possible for the benefit of the oppressed. Stalin defined the Chinese revolution as a revolution in a semi-feudal, semi-colonial country in which the bourgeoisie could act progressively by destroying feudalism, whereas Trotsky perceived that feudalism had already given way to capitalism in China, with the implication that an anti-capitalist revolution could be organised effectively.

These two analyses provided the basis for two approaches, the Stalin–Bukharin line of alliance with the Nationalists at whatever cost in CCP concessions, and the Trotsky line of CCP independence, with the creation of soviets as the focus for mass loyalty. Stalin rejected soviets at this stage, arguing that the conflict between the left- and right-wing Nationalists was sufficiently clear-cut for mass understanding, without prematurely introducing a third centre of power in worker and peasant soviets. This line could readily be changed once the left and right Nationalists both turned on the CCP in July 1927. Stalin hoped that the CCP, through its mass organisations, could influence the Nationalist Party towards the left, but he also suggested in a telegram arriving 1 June in Wuhan that the CCP should create its own army, should support land seizures and should replace reluctant Nationalist Party leaders.

Stalin's telegram, which Roy naively showed to Wang Jingwei, and the subsequent decision by Feng Yuxiang to side with Jiang Jieshi spelt the end of the alliance between the Wuhan Nationalists and the CCP. Feng, after negotiating with both wings of the Nationalist Party, accepted the higher financial rewards offered by Jiang and sent an ultimatum to Wuhan on 21 June to expel Borodin and reunite the party. Workers' pickets in Wuhan were disarmed at the end of June and the CCP resolved to place their mass organisation under Nationalist orders, but it was too late. A further CCP resolution in line with new CI instructions proposed that Communists should leave the government, but remain in the Nationalist Party. On 16 July the Nationalists denounced dual party membership, published Stalin's telegram and began to hunt for Communists in Wuhan, although Borodin was allowed to leave peacefully, carrying a letter of gratitude from Wang Jingwei to the Soviet Politburo.

The collapse of the first united front between the CCP and the Nationalist Party paved the way for the eventual reunification of the Nationalist Party and began the CCP's career as the leader of anti-government insurgency. Three major CCP insurrections occurred in the latter part of 1927, the Nanchang Uprising of 1 August, the Autumn Harvest Uprising in Hunan in September and the Guangzhou Commune of 11–13 December, the last also providing the final link in the development towards Nationalist Party unity.

The CCP plotted the Nanchang Uprising on the basis of the extensive Communist influence among the troops there, with the expectation that the troops, preferably with their general Zhang Fakui, would march to Guangdong to continue the revolution. Despite a very cautionary telegram from Moscow, the local organisers felt that their planning was too far advanced to be stopped and therefore the military uprising began early on 1 August under Generals Ye Ting, He Long and Zhu De, all to become famous CCP military leaders; 1 August is now celebrated as Red Army day. This CCP revolt took place under the Nationalist banner, thus reflecting the CI line, but despite acquiring arms and money, the troops were forced out of the city, marching southwards. There were huge losses through disease, desertion and battle, and by the end of September the remaining troops had been scattered, some fleeing into the mountains under Zhu De.

The Autumn Harvest Uprising resulted from the line adopted by an emergency meeting of top CCP leaders on 7 August in Wuhan, advocating rural revolts in four provinces – Hunan, Hubei, Guangdong and Jiangxi. The meeting also elected Russian-speaking Qu Qiubai as head of the Politburo, laid the blame for the past errors on the opportunism of the previous CCP leadership and prescribed insurrection wherever possible, with the future aim of creating soviets. The intention of the party centre had been a simultaneous uprising in south Hubei and east Hunan, but activity in Hubei started prematurely and very quickly ran into insuperable difficulties, through betrayals by local self-defence forces. Mao Zedong, who had written so enthusiastically of the potential peasant rebellion, was placed in charge of Hunan preparations, but he quarrelled with the CCP centre over the use of the Nationalist Party banner, over the excessive geographic scope of the plans and over the CCP plans to use peasants alone, with no role for sympathetic military units. Mao in practice relied on two poor-quality army units, a local self-defence force and an armed group of unemployed miners from Anyuan. Although a few towns were briefly held, coordination between the sections was poor and the uprising was over by 15 September, with Mao retreating to the mountain bandit lair called Jinggangshan on the Hunan–Jiangxi border. Mao was subsequently dismissed from his alternate membership of the CCP Politburo for his errors. A CCP-led peasant uprising was more successful in eastern Guangdong, in the Haifeng and Lufeng area, where peasant unions created earlier by Peng Pai formed a government, later called a soviet, which lasted until February 1928.

As a movement claiming a working class base, the CCP was reluctant to see all urban control lost to the Nationalists, and this resulted in the CCP's last urban-based venture in more than 20 years, the Guangzhou Commune. The decision to move ahead in Guangzhou was inspired by a number of reasons, including a generally leftward shift in CCP policy in later 1927 and the analysis that urban revolution could be successful where the ruling class was in disarray. Such disarray had occurred in Wuhan in early November as Tang Shengzhi had been driven out by forces loyal to Nanjing, but the subsequent strike and attempted insurrection by the CCP had been very half-hearted; hence a coup among the military in Guangzhou on 17 November seemed an ideal opportunity on which to capitalise, only this time with a little more care. A revolutionary committee under Zhang Tailei sketched out the plans, with aid from CI agent Neumann. The uprising began on 11 December, with workers and some soldiers participating, but public response was limited. The rebels were crushed by returning Nationalist troops within two days, with a huge slaughter of suspected Communists thereafter. The attempted commune provoked the final diplomatic break between the Nationalists and the USSR. Although the internal logic of CCP policy can readily explain the Guangzhou commune, there has always been some suspicion that, as Trotsky insisted, the event was specifically timed to match a crucial meeting of the Soviet Communist Party, where it could act as proof for Stalin of the continued vitality of the Chinese revolution; the available evidence on this remains inconclusive.

While the CCP was attempting to regain governmental power through insurrection, the Nationalist Party finally thrashed out a compromise among its factions and its military supporters, which allowed the Northern Expedition to recommence in 1928 with the final goal as Beijing. The party was divided into three obvious factions, the Shanghai headquarters of party veterans who had opposed the pro-Soviet policy from the start, Jiang Jieshi and his colleagues in Nanjing and the Wuhan 'left-wing' under Wang Jingwei and General Tang Shengzhi. In July 1927 the Nanjing regime suffered battle reverses against the northern warlords, provoking criticism of Jiang, who in mid-August offered to resign. The offer, much to Jiang's annoyance, was accepted by his military council and Jiang went in September to Japan, where he improved his symbolic party credentials by winning the acceptance of the Song family for his proposed marriage to Song Meiling, Methodist-trained sister-in-law to Sun Yixian, on condition that he study Christianity. After his resignation Nanjing appeared in grave military danger, until internal military rivalries were put aside to allow an overwhelming Nationalist victory in the six-day Longtan battle against Sun Chuanfang at the end of August.

Negotiations between Nanjing and Wuhan in August and early September produced a formula for an extra-constitutional Special Central Committee, drawing on all factions, to discuss and settle party differences. Just as agreement seemed near, Wang Jingwei who had come to Shanghai for the talks, denounced the idea, retiring to Wuhan and then in late October to Guangzhou. Troops loyal to Nanjing marched on Wuhan at the end of October, taking it quickly, but Wang, in the south, insisted that a full Central Executive Committee meeting was the only constitutional solution to unity. Jiang Jieshi now returned to China, backing Wang's proposal and inviting Wang to Shanghai for preliminary discussions. On 17 November, the day after Wang left Hong Kong for Shanghai, a coup in Guangzhou under the leftist general, Zhang Fakui, drove out all troops opposed to Wang, an act of treachery which infuriated many Nationalist Party members in Shanghai and Nanjing and led to accusations of Communist influence in Guangzhou. When some three weeks later the Guangzhou Commune occurred, this proved devastating for Wang's reputation, forcing his retirement to France and leaving Jiang Jieshi free to hold the reuniting Central Executive Committee meeting in February 1928.

With Jiang Jieshi clearly in charge and the anti-Communist direction of the Nationalist Party spelt out, it was time to complete the Northern Expedition. The major enemy was the northeastern warlord, Zhang Zuolin, whose protector, Japan, had warned Jiang that the Japanese would tolerate Zhang's defeat south of the Great Wall, but would not let Nationalist troops enter Zhang's base in Manchuria. The forces available to the Nationalists were organised in four group armies, the first under Jiang, the second under Feng Yuxiang, the third under Shanxi warlord, Yan Xishan, and the fourth under Bai Chongxi of the Guangxi clique, which currently held the Wuhan area.

The advance proceeded smoothly, except for two issues, the presence of Japanese troops in the Shandong capital, Jinan and the question of who should take over Beijing from Zhang Zuolin. The Japanese government under Premier Tanaka Giichi, claiming the right to defend its nationals, sent troops to the Shandong coastal city of Qingdao. The general in command then decided on his own initiative to send troops inland to Jinan, just as NRA forces entered on 30 April, but he seemed ready to withdraw at Jiang's urging, when incidents between soldiers of the two armies occurred on 3 May. A truce was arranged, but Japan brought in reinforcements and the general in charge issued a humiliating ultimatum to China, resulting in full-scale fighting from 8 May until the Chinese were defeated. Japanese troops were to stay in Shandong for a year, despite Chinese appeals to the League of Nations and the USA. The Jinan incident turned China's anti-imperialist anger back against Japan, after the anti-British interlude under Soviet influence. It also revealed the weakness of international restraint against Japan and the dangers of independent action by the Japanese military, both phenomena which were indicative of events over the next ten years in China.

Despite the Jinan incident, the Northern Expedition achieved the capture of Beijing on 8 June 1928 after Zhang Zuolin had agreed to withdraw his troops. The Japanese had warned Zhang in mid-May that they would permit him to retire to the northeast with his army intact if he left Beijing quietly, but that should he stay and fight, his passage back to his north-east base would be blocked by Japanese troops. Zhang, feeling betrayed by Japan, agreed to leave, on condition that Beijing should not fall to Feng Yuxiang, Zhang's personal enemy after the Guo Songling mutiny of 1925. Thus it was that Beijing and Tianjin fell to soldiers under Yan Xishan, whom the Nanjing government appointed as garrison commander, while Feng, who had expected to take Beijing from the progress of the battles, was denied it, to his distress. Ironically, having sowed discord among his enemies over the Beijing issue, Zhang Zuolin was unable to capitalise on this, because his train was blown up on the morning of 4 June as it neared his north-east capital, Fengtian (Mukden). His death, plotted by middle-ranking officers of the Japanese army in Manchuria, was intended by them to spark such disorder in Manchuria that Japanese military intervention and conquest would result. In practice power passed relatively smoothly to Zhang's son, Zhang Xueliang, who declared the north-east as part of the Nationalist zone at the end of December 1928, despite Japanese threats and denials of involvement in his father's murder.

The completion of a Northern Expedition had been intended by its initial planner, Sun Yixian, as the fulfilment of national unity and the opportunity to lead the nation out of militarism towards a more effective republic. In the event the military compromises involved in a policy of victory by incorporating the enemy resulted in a country where armies were still not the servants of government and where unity, what there was of it, required constant manoeuvring among military factions. At least most military leaders in the eastern half of China now talked in terms of nationalism, of the quality of the Nanjing government leadership and of Sun's principles, but this new unity on the acceptable language for effective politics could not hide the fact that power, even after the end of the 'warlord period', depended overtly on military strength and not upon the merit of policies advocated and pursued for the reconstruction of China.

The existence of the Communist insurgency had also not been foreseen by Sun, who had anticipated a longer period of cooperation with the USSR and its Chinese disciples. Although the severely decimated CCP took time to recover from the events of 1927, there was never any tolerance within the Party towards the view that the whole united front approach in the 1920s had been wrong. The Party considered that the opportunities for growth, for training personnel, for experience in political work, for contact with the masses, and for learning about the class relations in China, all justified the policy adopted. The Party, always prepared to learn from short-term setbacks, could also point to a better understanding of the dangers of a 'bloc within' approach, and of the need to secure viable military force. At first publicly unexpressed but later admitted, there was also the lesson of the enormous problems which any revolutionary party faces, when it receives well-meaning but ill-informed advice from powerful sponsors, who are a long way away and who have experienced a quite different type of revolution. Although with hindsight we may bemoan the human cost of these negative lessons, there is little to suggest that the Party's analysis was at fault, as those early years did transform a small number of people from bitterly indignant but essentially intellectual radicals into the committed backbone of a mass-based party determined to build a new stronger China within their lifetime.

4 Reconstruction and its Problems

In 1928 after its victories in the Northern Expedition, the Nationalist government at Nanjing could fairly claim to be the strongest force within China, but the subsequent years of the so-called Nanjing Decade revealed that this strength was inadequate to overcome internal enemies and to defend against Japanese aggression at the same time. Problems unresolved by the Nanjing government were compounded by the deterioration of the Nationalist Party, which failed to provide the political leadership necessary for Sun Yixian's theory of political tutelage to work. Nevertheless, although it is easy to point to Nanjing's failures and possible to seek to excuse them because of the difficult circumstances, some attention must be paid to what was achieved, particularly in the economic and diplomatic sphere, otherwise the effectiveness of the government's call for resistance against Japan and the popularity of Jiang Jieshi in 1937 and 1938 become incomprehensible. The Nanjing Decade also provided a vital opportunity for the CCP to practise rural mobilisation in the restricted enclaves available to it, thus laying the basis for rural conquest of the cities in the 1940s.

The inheritance from the period 1916–28 was not entirely negative, but for the most part the positive aspects had not arisen from direct government activity, such as might be expected under a new government committed to national improvement. Such positive aspects included the growth of modern industry throughout the 1910s and 1920s, the development of modern higher education which could provide competently trained personnel for new tasks, the growth of urban nationalism with its matching dissatisfaction with the existing state of China and the increasing demand for political participation to give a real meaning to republicanism. Diplomatically the new government inherited foreign promises made at the Washington

84

Conference and since, which offered the possibility of major gains in Chinese sovereignty, if only China could persuade the Powers to deliver specific agreements. Nevertheless the negative inheritances of the warlord period presented an enormous burden for the new Nationalist government. These included the excessively large number of men under arms and still beholden to a variety of regional leaders, a national tax system that could not meet expenditure without extensive recourse to loans, and an agricultural economy which had suffered harshly from warlord depredations and from climatic conditions, which particularly in the north were less advantageous in the 1920s than in the 1910s.

Establishment of the Nationalist Government

Although the Nanjing government was officially established as the national government on 10 October 1928, the anniversary date of the 1911 revolution, the major Nationalist Party seat of power had been in Nanjing since April 1927 and the attempt to face the problems of governing central China had begun after this earlier date. To keep its now disparate army in the field the government could not rely on revolutionary promises alone but needed regular finance. Although the Shanghai business leaders were willing to advance funds to Jiang Jieshi before 12 April 1927 to gain the crushing of CCP organisations among the Shanghai workers, they were not willing to provide copious funds thereafter. This forced Jiang to use arrests, kidnappings and terror during the rest of April and May, to compel banks and businessmen to provide funds and to absorb government bonds. Such methods could not endear the new government to the capitalists of Shanghai and were only made possible by the close links between Jiang and the leaders of the Shanghai underworld, notably Du Yuesheng. When Jiang resigned in August, the Nanjing government found it impossible to sell its bonds and some units of the army refused to march as directed, because of pay arrears.

In early 1928, after his return to the leadership, Jiang appointed his brother-in-law, Harvard-trained Song Ziwen, as finance minister, and funds again began to flow through coercive techniques, although Song believed that in the long-term voluntary cooperation from banks would be more effective than coercion. With the completion of the Northern Expedition, Song called two conferences on the national economy and national finance in mid-1928, bringing together officials and businessmen, who discussed currency, budget and tax reform and threatened to withhold funds from the government unless it demobilised some of its soldiers. This threat was brushed aside by the Nationalist military leaders, but the Guomindang's Central Executive Committee plenum in August accepted Song's request for a proper budget and the unification of finances, even though implementation proved difficult in practice.

The establishment of the permanent government structure was intimately related to the interplay among the military leaders who supported the Nationalists, to the policy of victory by recruiting the enemy, and to the reunification of the Guomindang after the expulsion of the Communists. In order to reward the leading generals the authority of the centre was diluted by the creation of branch political councils, which operated as virtually separate governments during the second phase of the Northern Expedition. In order to gain expertise for the administration the central government recruited a large number of officials who had served the Beijing warlords, often inducting them as party members at the same time, in a move that critics entitled a 'southern expedition of bureaucrats'.

The new central government structure was outlined in the February 1928 Central Executive Committee plenum and then fully created by the August 1928 plenum and the subcommittees it formed. The government was to follow Sun Yixian's five-power structure, with five *Yuan* – executive, legislative, judicial, examination and control – under a State Council of seventeen, chaired by Jiang Jieshi and including the five *yuan* heads and the top military figures. The Nationalist Party, as the party training the people towards democracy, was to hold power through its Central Executive Committee and through the Central Political Council, a 46-member body large enough to allow representation for all groups within the party and military. The party resolved to close the branch political councils by the end of 1928, but effective achievement of centralised power would require much more than mere closure of regional offices.

Military Allies and Rivals of the Nanjing Government

The most pressing task for the government was military disbandment, since the number of men under arms was far in excess of any domestic need and their cost was overwhelming all other government expenditure. When the top generals met informally in Beijing in July 1928 after ceremonially reporting the end of the Northern Expedition to Sun Yixian's coffin, they estimated that the NRA contained 2.2 million men and Jiang suggested reducing this to 1.2 million, which would still consume 60 per cent of national revenues. The August plenum advocated a maximum 50 per cent military budget. The formal military disbandment conference met in January 1929 and adopted the quite illusory figure of 715 000 soldiers as the target, but when it came to deciding whose army should be reduced and at what rate there was no consensus. Jiang argued that his units needed to be preserved since they were already financed by the centre and would bear the brunt of any national defence against aggressors, but the others regarded reduction of their own forces as politically suicidal if Jiang's forces were not reduced at the same time. Although the conference ended without success, it did confirm one important principle which was to affect Nanjing thereafter, that all the land tax would be collected and retained by provincial governments. In practice this meant that each area militarist could obtain taxes for himself and that Nanjing could not draw tax from the most productive part of the economy, responsible for well over half the gross national product, therefore forcing it to tax trade and industry heavily, despite their role in modernising the economy.

The next forum for debate was the Third Nationalist Party Congress, meeting in mid-March 1929, but although it clarified the removal of Communist ideas from the party regulations, the Congress had to be abandoned when warfare broke out between Nationalist militarists. The major initial opponents were the Guangxi clique, whose area of authority included Guangdong, Guangxi, and the Wuhan area, with some influence in Beiping, the official name for Beijing from 1928 to 1949. The clique moved in March to remove Jiang's appointee from the Hunan governorship, which provoked an anti-Guangxi coup in Beiping and the arrest of the Guangdong governor at the party congress. War immediately followed, but the Guangxi forces failed to fight effectively in the Wuhan area, giving Jiang an easy victory by the end of April. During this war, the forces of Feng Yuxiang had begun to move in the north and war there seemed imminent, until Han Fuju, one of Feng's top generals, defected to the Nanjing side, thereby postponing Feng's war preparations until October. Battle was then joined in Henan after a telegram condemning Nanjing's policies, with both sides hoping to enlist the other powerholder in the north, Yan Xishan, in their support. In the event Yan did nothing and Feng's forces lost Henan by the end of November without being fully destroyed. Feng's manoeuvres in the north prevented the completion of any Nanjing campaign against the Guangxi remnants and Feng came to realise that he and Guangxi shared common enmity to Nanjing under Jiang Jieshi.

1930 witnessed the most intense of the intra-Nationalist wars, as all the major enemies of Jiang Jieshi allied together, linking their military effort with the political call of Wang Jingwei for a reorganisation of the party. The intention of the alliance was to strike southwards from north China using the forces of Feng Yuxiang and Yan Xishan and to strike northwards from Guangxi under Li Zongren, thereby forcing Jiang into a two-front war. After the offensive began in May, the Guangxi units advanced quickly after abandoning Guangxi province altogether, but problems of coordination led to logistical difficulties, culminating in a severe defeat near Hengyang in southern Hunan. The Guangxi remnants struggled back to their own province, thereafter concentrating more on provincial development than large-scale intervention in national politics, until the Anti-Japanese war in 1937. In the north the war of 1930 was much more evenly balanced, but both sides hoped that an added contribution by Zhang Xueliang and his north-eastern troops would decide the war in their favour. A full opposition government was inaugurated at Beiping on 1 September 1930, but after a defeat of Yan Xishan's forces in Shandong, the alliance collapsed in mid-September when the wavering Zhang Xueliang decided to intervene on Nanjing's side by moving troops into north China. Both Feng Yuxiang and Yan Xishan retired, Feng never again to be a major military figure with the independent troops, Yan for only a year before returning to his warlord domain of Shanxi province. Nevertheless although Nanjing could claim to have won the war, the spoils went to Zhang Xueliang, who could dictate the settlement in north China, preventing effective penetration of Nanjing power into the north.

Defeat in the north did not prevent the opponents of Nanjing from regrouping in the south and a new separatist government was established under Wang Jingwei and Sun Fo, Sun Yixian's son, in Guangzhou in May 1931. Their objections to Jiang Jieshi's rule in Nanjing resulted from their own ambitions and from the opinion that Jiang's 'dictatorship' was not preparing China for the fulfilment of Sun Yixian's democratic programme nor allowing the Nationalist Party to operate as an effective political party gaining popular support. Wang Jingwei was joined symbolically by the veteran politician of the Nationalist right, Hu Hanmin, who had been placed in custody in March 1931 over his opposition to Jiang's wish for a provisional constitution during the period of Nationalist Party tutelage. This was an idea nowhere mentioned by Sun Yixian. Before full-scale war between Nanjing and the south had developed, a national crisis intervened, when Japan attacked the Manchurian capital, Fengtian (Mukden), on 18 September 1931.

The Mukden incident and the subsequent Japanese conquest of Manchuria (to be discussed further in the next chapter) created a popular call for national unity, articulated by students, merchants and the press. Jiang Jieshi urged the Manchurian leader, Zhang Xueliang, not to fight the Japanese, but to allow international pressure through the League of Nations to redress Chinese grievances. This policy, although logically defensible given China's military weakness, could not endear Jiang to the public or to the Nationalist Party, as more and more of Manchuria was lost without resistance. Popular distress over Jiang's non-resistance policy and the insistence by the south that no reconciliation was possible while Jiang retained military control at Nanjing finally forced Jiang to resign in December 1931, after the Nationalist Party's Fourth Congress had called in November for a national emergency conference to unite all groups. The Guangzhou government was dissolved, and Wang Jingwei and Sun Fo came to Nanjing, with Sun Fo as the new premier, while troops of the Fujian 19th Route Army took over military duties in the Nanjing–Shanghai area. The new government proved unable to cope adequately with developments in Manchuria and within weeks Sun Fo had to beg Jiang to return to the government. A new compromise was achieved in January 1932 with the intention of sharing power among Jiang, Wang Jingwei and Hu Hanmin who had been released after Japan's attack. Hu, who had retired to Guangzhou, refused to serve and therefore power was shared between Jiang, who took military control and Wang, who headed the civilian government. With the Nationalist Party's crisis resolved, the national emergency conference proved an anticlimax, with limited attendance and largely controlled debate.

The new government under Jiang Jieshi and Wang Jingwei was still not the sole source of authority within China, for the north with Zhang Xueliang's Manchurian troops and the south under its branch political council at Guangzhou resisted central authority, as did Communist insurgents and those warlords of inland China untouched by the Northern Expedition. Two major confrontations occurred before 1937 between Nanjing and nominally Nationalist groups, one in Fujian in late 1933 and the other against the south in 1936. Military power in Fujian in 1933 belonged to the 19th Route Army, which had fought bravely against the Japanese in Shanghai from the end of January 1932. Upset by the continuing civil war against the Communists in neighbouring Jiangxi at a time when no resistance was being offered to Japan, the 19th Route Army leaders under Cai Tingkai established a People's Government in November 1933, proposing resistance to Japan and a liberal domestic programme. No support was received from other southern leaders, who saw their programme as too radical, nor from the Communists, who questioned the revolutionary advantage of having a third, middle-of-the-road government established in China. Hence the Fujian revolt in its isolation was readily put down by Jiang's soldiers in January 1934.

The revolt of the south (often termed the southwest revolt, from the official title of the Guangzhou branch political council) occurred after the death in May 1936 of Hu Hanmin, who despite a severe stroke was claimed to have dictated a will opposing dictatorial rule and urging resistance to Japan. The Nanjing government, whose troops had moved closer to Guangdong and Guangxi with the pursuit of the CCP's Long

March in 1934 and 1935, now demanded the submission of the two provinces to the centre. The south mobilised its troops on 1 June under the banner of resistance to the Japanese, but its advance north was quickly blocked by Nanjing units. Unwilling to engage in full civil war, Nanjing opted to buy over the Guangdong air force and its first army under Yu Hanmou, thereby leaving only Guangxi in revolt. The Guangxi leaders, badly defeated back in 1930, were in no mood to risk a fight to the finish, despite the mid-August appearance in Guangxi of keenly anti-Jiang veterans of the Fujian revolt. A negotiated settlement proved possible in mid-September, leaving Guangxi relatively autonomous, but confirming Nanjing's control over Guangdong.

Jiang Jieshi and Nationalist Party Factions

These repeated military crises and the ongoing military struggle against the Communists form the background for an understanding of the military bias of the Nationalist government during the Nanjing decade. The most important task for the government was to achieve national unity, but the only method consistently pursued was the military one. Jiang Jieshi, a military man by training, did not regard the Nationalist Party as a very effective tool for the reconstruction of China and, despite being party leader, did not pursue the rapid expansion of the party, whose regular civilian membership grew gradually from 266 000 in 1929 to 347 000 in 1935. Jiang preferred to build the party within the army, and military membership exceeded civilian membership throughout the decade, thereby giving a different emphasis from the one intended by Sun Yixian, who wished party tutelage to replace military rule. The stress on military issues also was reflected in the government's budget, in which about half of national expenditure went on the military from 1928 to 1934 and about a third from 1935 until the outbreak of the war with Japan in 1937.

Since Jiang Jieshi's greatest power base was the army and he readily expressed despair about the deterioration of the party, it is not surprising that Jiang's recipe for reconstruction stressed the role of the military over the party and the government.

Two obvious examples were the bandit suppression campaigns and the New Life Movement. Bandit suppression, the official title for the anti-Communist campaign, necessarily had military aspects, but Jiang used it as a means to detach provinces from the control of civilian central administrators by insisting that all administrative tasks needed to be carried out by the military. Anti-Communist campaigning also required the promotion of the *baojia* system, a traditional mutual responsibility scheme, with families grouped in hierarchical units of tens and hundreds of households, thereby in theory regimenting rural society for government purposes. The New Life Movement, launched in 1934, sought to inspire the population in Nationalist areas with a mixture of traditional Chinese moral ideas and respect for disciplined behaviour, which would allow the militarisation of society under the guidance of military officers and of the Blue Shirts. The latter were members of an organisation of personally loyal followers of Jiang Jieshi, created in 1932 to revitalise China through totalitarian methods under a supreme leader, and modelled in part on movements in fascist Europe.

The structure in Nanjing revolved around Jiang Jieshi, partly because of the continuing military tasks and partly because Jiang proved to be the only figure through whom the divisions within the government could be mediated. What Jiang lacked in revolutionary pedigree as compared with rivals such as Hu Hanmin or Wang Jingwei, he more than compensated for by his political ability and his range of personal connections. Jiang's original source of power had been the Huangpu military academy of the mid-1920s, where the young officers of the party army had been trained. The majority of these officers remained loyal to Jiang and confirmed his control over most of the centrally financed armies. From the activists among the Huangpu cadets emerged the Blue Shirts and their many front organisations, committed to militarising Chinese society under Jiang's leadership. Jiang's military influence was also increased by the work of Dai Li, creator of an effective military intelligence apparatus during the early 1930s, who also worked to bring the urban police fully under military control.

Jiang's major ally in the Nationalist Party was the CC clique, headed by the brothers Chen Guofu and Chen Lifu. These were nephews of Jiang's major early revolutionary model, Chen

Qimei, who had worked for revolution in Shanghai in 1911, 1913 and 1915. In 1924 Chen Guofu became Jiang's chief recruiter at Shanghai for the Huangpu academy and in 1926 became head of the Nationalist Party Organisation department, thus controlling appointments and developing the party's internal security work. The CC clique was apparently formalised in mid-1927, bringing together various anti-Communist groups based in the lower Yangzi area, and sought to promote Jiang, the pre-eminence of the Nationalist Party and traditional morality, the latter through extensive cultural and educational work.

Jiang's connections with older politicians came through his sworn brother and fellow-student in Japan, Zhang Qun, who introduced Jiang to the loosely organised Political Study Clique, created in the parliament in 1916. This clique included famous intellectuals, such as Wang Chonghui who helped to draft the organic laws for the 1928 government, several graduates of Japanese military schools, including the very able negotiator, Huang Fu, and capitalists of the Zhejiang financial circle, including Yu Xiaqing, chairman of the Shanghai Chinese Chamber of Commerce. Jiang's connections with the Zhejiang financiers were also strengthened by his Zhejiang birthplace and by his earlier work with Chen Qimei in Shanghai. Jiang's marriage to Song Meiling gave him ties with two top financial experts, Song Ziwen and Kong Xiangxi, and his conversion to Methodism won him the support of missionaries and of their converts, who were particularly well-placed in the higher education field.

Jiang's unusually wide range of relations with the various factions meant that no challenger within the Nationalist Party could hope to oust him successfully. The major attempt in 1931 proved a disaster, since the new leaders could not restrain inter-factional rivalries as Jiang did, and Jiang remained pre-eminent until his death in 1975, surviving war defeats against Japan and even the loss of nearly all of China to the Communists in 1949. Jiang's colleagues included those such as Song Ziwen, with modernising intentions and with programmes of interest to urban groups in China and those in the Huangpu and CC Cliques which were more organised and more traditionalistic. Jiang's preference went to the latter groups as far as ideology was concerned. Sun Yixian's Three People's Principles were interpreted with strong Confucian overtones and were supplemented by writings of nineteenth-century Confucian moderate reformers such as Zeng Guofan and Hu Linyi, who had helped in the suppression of the Taiping movement. Attempts by Song Ziwen to remove the anti-capitalist tendency from Sun's heritage were not successful as far as the party programme was concerned. Ironically Song Ziwen was one of those instrumental in restraining the activities of independent capital by what was in effect the nationalising of the major private banks in 1935 and by promoting the growth of bureaucratic capitalism. The latter implied the acquiring of business assets by officials of the government, who in no way tried to separate their private interests from their public duties.

The Nationalist Party had mounted its Northern Expedition to achieve national unity and to fulfil Sun Yixian's political programme as outlined in the Three People's Principles of Nationalism, Democracy and People's Livelihood. An examination of each of these themes will prepare the ground for a general assessment of the Nanjing decade, within the terms of its own programme.

Foreign Relations and Nationalism

Nationalism demanded the regaining of full sovereignty for China by ending the privileges granted to foreigners by unequal treaties, but the Nanjing government was unable to achieve this. The Nationalist government had come to power in a strongly anti-foreign atmosphere in late 1926 and early 1927, which did little to endear the new government to the foreign powers. Even after Jiang's break with the Communists, the powers still treated the new government distantly, rejecting out of hand the unilateral attempt to abrogate all unequal treaties in mid-1928. Nevertheless, once the Nanjing government was willing to accept responsibility for the existing state debts owed to the foreign powers, those powers were willing to discuss tariff autonomy, the USA leading the way with an agreement in July 1928. Japan, having roughly 25 per cent of its trade with China, proved the most obdurate, finally agreeing in 1930 to grant autonomy on most items in 1931 and on remaining sensitive items in

1933. With all the powers agreed, China set its own tariff rates in January 1931, for the first time in 90 years. Rates were generally raised to increase the revenue for the government, customs duties thereafter producing around 50 per cent of the national government's revenue, but tariff rates were not used to protect domestic industries or to promote exports. The only specific targeting of tariffs occurred from 1933, when categories of goods mostly imported from Japan gained punitively high tariffs, as part of anti-Japanese policy.

The restriction of more obvious privileges, such as concession areas and the right of extraterritoriality, proved much more difficult. Although Britain had abandoned two concessions under threat during the Northern Expedition, the next use of force, in Manchuria, proved a disaster for China. The Chinese government decided to seize the Soviet-owned Chinese Eastern Railway in northern Manchuria in July 1929, presuming that the USSR would be unwilling to attack a semi-colonial country and that the other powers would be delighted to see the USSR humiliated. In the event the foreign powers, recognising the dangers of tolerating the use of Chinese force to destroy treaty rights in China, backed the USSR, despite its diplomatic isolation, and the USSR advanced into the railway zone in November, defeating the Chinese troops there. The CCP was considerably embarrassed by the incident, because its commitment to the CI forced it to support the USSR in its propaganda, a view strongly opposed by former CCP secretary-general, Chen Duxiu, who was expelled from the CCP over this issue. Thereafter the Nanjing government pursued diplomatic means for the return of concessions, regaining twenty of the thirty-three. The foreign powers removed the arms embargo on China in April 1929 and accepted that extraterritoriality could be abandoned once the Chinese law code and courts were modified to match Western legal standards. After the Japanese attack on Manchuria in 1931, the Chinese government ceased to press for the end of extraterritoriality, recognising that in the event of full-scale war with Japan, the presence of legally immune foreigners would be beneficial to China's war effort. As a result the remaining foreign privileges were only relinquished in 1943, during the Second World War.

Despite the gains over tariff autonomy and foreign concessions, the Nanjing government record showed grave deficiencies over defence of national sovereignty in the face of Japanese aggression. Jiang Jieshi's policy was expressed through the slogan, 'internal pacification before external resistance', which resulted in appeasement of Japanese aggression in northern and north-eastern China. The students and parts of the media objected strongly to this appeasement, but from 1932 Jiang cleverly turned popular anger away from himself towards the civilian leader Wang Jingwei, who was severely wounded in an assassination attempt by a Chinese patriot at the Nationalist Party's Fifth Congress in late 1935. The logic of Jiang's policy was quite clear, that China needed time to build up its military resources before challenging Japan and that international reaction would restrain Japan. Jiang vigorously pursued the modernisation of his military forces, with the help of German army instructors and Italian aviators and although the League of Nations proved unable to restrain Japan directly, it did compensate for its diplomatic limitations by sending missions to China to advise on economic and educational development. Nevertheless the Nanjing government suffered badly in public esteem for claiming to defend the nation but seeming to stand aside while Japan dismembered it. Later the change to resistance against Japan in 1937 won the government widespread urban support and squared the propaganda line of the party with the reality of national defence.

Political Reform and Democracy

The second of Sun Yixian's principles, Democracy, took its inspiration from Sun's appreciation of the role of democracy in the strength of the Western Powers, but the implementation of democracy proved more difficult in China. Given the problems of the early republican period, Sun came to require a period of party tutelage before full democracy, during which time the party would develop democratic experience at the grass-roots level. Sun's timetable envisaged the development of self-governing counties, followed by self-governing provinces, with elected assemblies at each level, but the most notable feature of the Nanjing era was the reversal of this procedure. A great deal of energy was devoted, especially by Sun Fo, Sun Yixian's son, to the creation of a constitution and of legislative institutions at the centre, but almost nothing was done to develop local democracy. Even when tutelage finally ended officially in 1948, after a far longer delay than Sun Yixian had intended, the basis for popular participation had not developed and most observers described the change from party tutelage to constitutional rule as mere window-dressing. The reluctance to develop local democracy stemmed from the entrenched power of local officials and from the conservative inclinations of the lower-level Nationalist Party branches, but was enhanced by a more general intellectual tendency towards disillusion with democracy and appreciation of dictatorship as a way to strengthen China quickly. The Nationalist Party could have developed to represent wider interests and to keep a check on government, but its rejection of mass organisation work and its limited membership expansion meant that the party remained unrepresentative. In addition most senior and middle-ranking government officials were members of the party, so that the distinction between party and state became almost totally blurred.

Economic Policies and People's Livelihood

The third of Sun's principles, People's Livelihood, envisaged the promotion of popular wealth and welfare, through the control of capital and the equalisation of land rights, the latter open to many possible interpretations. The Nanjing government sought to develop people's livelihood by a range of economic and social policies, which achieved some successes, but which gained no relief for certain groups, especially in rural areas. Unfortunately for the Nanjing government its expenditures on the military and on debt-servicing consumed over 80 per cent of revenue between 1928 and 1934, and over 50 per cent thereafter, leaving very little for the implementation of any major programmes. The government became notorious for the number of programmes which it designed on paper, but proved unable to carry out. Nevertheless major advances were achieved in the provision of education and in the central control of educational standards, including the stricter regulation of the many foreign-financed and missionary schools. The railway network was restored to running order after warlord disruptions and new lines were completed between Guangzhou and Wuchang and from Hangzhou westwards across Jiangxi province. To complement the railways, road-building and the creation of civil aviation received government attention, although the total paved-road mileage available in 1937, 110 000 kilometres, was still woefully small for China's size.

Major success was achieved under the Nanjing government in the currency field. Merchant and business associations had been urging government action on the chaotic state of Chinese currency since the early Republican period, but action only became possible in the early 1930s with the increasing circulation of minted silver dollars and the greater stability of the government. In March 1933, the Nanjing government defined a standard silver dollar and organised one central mint in Shanghai, thereby replacing the variety of silver standards in different cities and gradually calling in uncoined silver. The new coinage was successfully launched during 1933, but grave problems arose in 1934 after the US Silver Purchase Act initiated huge exports of silver from China, at first legally and increasingly by smuggling, with Japanese connivance in the north. The depressive effects of the silver loss, added to the belated impact of the Great Depression upon China from 1932, forced the government to move, with British advice, to a managed paper currency in November 1935. The new currency was supported by Britain and the USA, which purchased large quantities of Chinese silver through official channels in 1936, and it gradually circulated throughout more and more of China, as the government called in silver coins, and as the use of the new currency became a test of loyalty to Nanjing. Although the paper currency allowed the possibility of unrestricted government issuance of notes, it is generally agreed that the new currency made financially possible the prolonged resistance to Japan from 1937. Up to 1937 the new currency held firm on the foreign exchange markets, even though the notes issue quadrupled between November 1935 and June 1937.

Paralleling the success in currency reform, the government also moved to develop the banking sector. In 1928 the Central Bank of China was created to handle government revenues, while the Bank of China was revamped to control foreign-exchange dealings, thereby challenging the near-monopoly previously enjoyed by foreign banks in China. Commercial banking flourished, with the number of firms nearly trebling from 1927 to 1934, while the uncontrolled activities of provincial government banks were severely reduced after the 1935 currency reform. The expansion of banking was vital to the budgeting of the Nanjing government, since over 20 per cent of revenue came from bonds, largely issued to the banking community at considerable discounts. These bonds served as the basis for speculative activity on the very volatile bond market and as security for bank note issue. The 12 to 20 per cent interest available on bonds at their discounted prices channelled over half of bank loans into government hands and raised the cost of investment capital for commerce and industry to prohibitively high levels.

Despite its achievements in the banking and currency field, the Nanjing government failed to register improvements in the agricultural sector, where the vast majority of the Chinese lived and worked. The Nationalist leaders rejected any redistribution of land holdings and held firm to the view that technological improvements would solve the agrarian problems created by small farms and subsistence incomes. Even the attempt to reduce tenant burdens by a proclaimed 25 per cent rent reduction received no effective backing from the lower levels of the party and the administration, in the face of landlord pressures. Where the central government had taxation powers, extraction from the rural sector continued to increase through the imposition of surtaxes, but no attempt was made to make the tax system more equitable by progressive taxation: rather, surveys indicate that the rural rich paid a lower proportion of their income in tax than did the middle peasants. The government did support credit cooperatives, claiming 1.5 million peasants enrolled by 1937, but these provided under 3 per cent of rural credit and mostly to the benefit of their richer members. The government also sponsored some ventures in agricultural extension, bringing new seeds and methods to selected areas, but the funding available was too small to be effective.

Meanwhile, as the government did little, the peasants suffered from the effects of an agricultural depression from 1931 to

1935, related to currency problems, to the collapse of silk markets and to poor weather, including rainfall in 1931 which produced a devastating flood along the Yangzi River, displacing over 25 million people. Agriculture produced less food during the early part of the 1930s, recovering only in the climatically bountiful 1936, the earlier period resulting in migrations from rural areas and widespread reports of poverty and desperation. Agricultural losses were compounded by sufferings related to the movement of armies and by the widespread use of forced labour for army transport and for rail and road construction.

The Nanjing Decade: An Assessment

This review of Nanjing's achievements and failures between 1928 and 1937 in terms of Sun Yixian's programme permits an evaluation of the government and an analysis of the basis for the Nationalist Party rule. Although the Comintern in 1927 defined Jiang's regime as representative of the national bourgeoisie, it should be quite clear from the above that the majority of the national bourgeoisie were not influential in the government and indeed suffered kidnappings, extra taxes and government control, culminating in government takeover of the strongest chamber of commerce, that of Shanghai, in 1930. The only group to win some benefits was the banking elite, at least until the government swallowed the banks in 1935. Nevertheless, there was some community of interest between the national bourgeoisie and the government over the reduction of foreign privileges and the control of labour, although the Nationalist-run trade unions did not halt all strikes, merely restricting their demands to economic, rather than political goals. The modern industrial sector of the economy did grow during the decade, at about 6 per cent per annum, a rate no faster than under the warlords and indicative of no outstanding support from the government. In the rural sector the Nationalists stood by the *status quo*, retaining existing tax methods and records and supporting the existing land-holding arrangements, even restoring landlords in areas where the Communists were cleared out, but the party at its higher levels showed little interest in agricultural questions.

The most important feature of the Nationalist government was its militaristic basis, created during the compromises of the Northern Expedition. Military organisation provided the strongest structures within the governing elite, since the party and mass organisations were both rejected as effective tools for long-term power at the centre or for penetration of regional strongholds. Some wished to spread militarisation further, on the fascist pattern, but the strength of the central government was inadequate for such totalitarian development, because it could only mobilise such a small percentage of the national wealth. Even with the stress on the military, the government was not able to unify the country over a ten-year period by conquest and although the provinces directly controlled by Jiang Jieshi did increase from two in 1928 to eight in 1936, this was still insufficient to provide Jiang with overwhelming force within the country. Despite its nationalistic propaganda, the military also failed in the most crucial role for an army, the defence of national sovereignty, thereby provoking widespread urban opposition to government policy.

Debate has raged since 1937 as to whether the Nanjing government could have achieved long-term viability and launched an effective modernisation programme, in the absence of the war with Japan from 1937. Early participants in this debate were arguing more in terms of their preconceived support for the Nationalists or the Communists than from any widespread appraisal of the events of the Nanjing decade, but the passage of time has allowed research to be done and passions to cool, especially when the Nationalists proved competent to rule Taiwan and the Communists ran into major difficulties in their rule of China after 1949. The Nanjing government represented the most effective of the central governments between 1911 and 1949, but its heavy dependence on military methods, the inefficiencies of its bureaucracy and its general neglect of the agrarian sector did not provide much hope for a modernisation programme. In particular the Nanjing government failed to apply its policies at a local level, through a failure to invigorate local officials with modernising energies. The central government seemed more like the thin icing on an unchanged regionalised cake than the penetrating yeast capable of creating a new national bread.

The Communist Party: Rural Soviets and the Sixth Congress

While the Nanjing government was seeking to win national unity and the many remaining regional warlords were continuing their own local exploitations, the ultimate victor of the Republican period, the CCP, was managing to survive through the creation of Communist-led enclaves in the border areas of several provinces. Although enormous claims were made for these Communist zones by the Comintern in terms of area and population controlled, Mao Zedong's peak estimate for 1932–4 was 9 million under CCP rule, and this seems to have been calculated by adding together the maximum populations attained by each zone, implying a lower figure at any one particular time. Although marginal in both geographic and numerical terms, the Communist zones were of vital importance for the development of the CCP and for the testing of policies for the rural sphere, whence the Party was to draw its greatest support. The interplay of personalities, the continuing problems with CI advice and the final humiliation of withdrawal from south China, producing the revolutionary epic of the Long March, formed the background for the emergence of Mao, the application of the mass line, the tempering of the Red Army and the growing independence of the CCP from outside authority. As with the united front period (1923–7), the lessons gained from 1927 to 1935 came as much from the negative examples of what not to do as from the positive achievements of the Party.

After the defeats of the latter half of 1927, the CCP, reduced in membership to about 10 000, consisted of two elements, the urban and the rural, which by force of circumstance operated with only limited communication. The urban Communists, who included the central leadership of the Party, were driven underground by the open Nationalist repression of 1927 and by the continued activities of the Nationalists' secret service agencies thereafter, preventing large-scale organisation of labour or propaganda work. Anti-Communist attacks made it impossible to hold the CCP's Sixth Congress in China, and as factionalism split the Party in the wake of defeats and problems, betrayals of factional rivals to the Nationalists produced further deaths and weakening of the urban Party base. The rural Communists, operating in unfamiliar territory geographically and ideologically, also faced attack and weakness, as military forces harassed their meagrely endowed bases, but they were able to operate openly as the local government within the enclaves which they held.

As Mao Zedong readily expounded, the strategic question was whether the revolution could best be served by efforts in the urban areas where the revolutionary forces of the proletariat were at their strongest or in remote border areas where the counter-revolutionary forces of the government and the warlords were weakest. If one assumed that class antagonisms throughout China offered scope for revolutionary mobilisation anywhere, it made sense to invest the energies of revolutionaries in areas where instant repression was unlikely and headway could be made, even if this contradicted the hitherto normal methods of a Communist-led revolution.

The Comintern too had to consider the best approach for the CCP. Having urged the crucial importance of the agrarian revolution in the early part of 1927, the CI could only applaud the rural successes of the CCP, but warned that care needed to be taken to ensure that the rural CCP did not lose its proletarian character or its obedience to the Party centre in the cities. Within the USSR the dismissal of Trotsky in December 1927 facilitated CI attacks on 'left extremists' in the CCP who had urged immediate national uprisings before the Nationalists could consolidate. Thereafter CI policy on China moved closer to Stalin's position that the CCP should seek to win local power in rural areas through land confiscation and the creation of soviets, while disturbing Nationalist counter-activities by urban subversion and propaganda. The Red Army should be developed by coordinating guerrilla activities but the CCP must recognise that victory in a national uprising would only come when peasant mobilisation was linked with a new revolutionary wave in the cities. The CCP Sixth Congress, held in Moscow from 18 June to 11 July 1928, adopted resolutions in this spirit, but under the influence of Bukharin, soon to be denounced as a rightist, the resolutions stressed the anti-imperialist tasks of CCP. The Congress, following CI February 1928 guidelines, also refined the theory that the Chinese revolution would occur in waves and that, given the unevenness of the revolutionary situation in regionalised China, it would be possible for a new revolutionary tide to succeed at first in one or more provinces, rather than nationally.

To set the Party in its new direction, the CCP Sixth Congress elected a new leadership, under the Shanghai proletarian figurehead, Xiang Zhongfa, but through selective transfer of leaders back to China from Moscow, the chief power within the Party centre in Shanghai fell to the Hunanese, Li Lisan. Li was under orders to develop the Party, the Red Army and the soviets, but at the same time to bolshevise the Party, implying stricter control over rural members by Shanghai. Among the Party members in rural areas Mao in particular resisted the organisational efforts of Li, who was known as a labour expert. This antagonism caused Li to oppose policies which he felt might benefit Mao, even if this contradicted CI directives, as it did over land policies in 1929. Within the urban Party Li was able to reorganise most of the provincial committees and to initiate purges of unsuitable members, but efforts to regenerate the mass movement within the working class proved very unfruitful and the CCP membership became less and less proletarian-based, only 8 per cent being of worker background in 1930.

While Li Lisan battled with urban problems, the rural groups of Communists gradually emerged in more stable formations by 1930, but conditions had remained very difficult for two years from late 1927 to late 1929. The most famous group, under Mao Zedong with Zhu De soon added, was established first in Jinggangshan on the Hunan/Jiangxi border, by combining military remnants from the 1927 uprisings with bandit groups traditionally operating in the area. Although religious and ideological challengers of the government in imperial times had usually diluted their fervour by recruiting militarily competent bandits as allies, the Communists were well aware of the dangers and through political work weaned the bandits away from their leaders towards service of the Party, a procedure aided by the considerable military experience available to the CCP and its earlier CI guides. Mao developed soldiers' committees within his army, in addition to the political commissars which the Central Committee required, and insisted that discipline and kindness must be shown in all dealings between soldiers and the people, an approach finally codified as the three disciplines and eight rules. Mobilisation of the local population was achieved with considerable difficulty and much propaganda work, by offering land redistribution and a reduction of taxes. At first Mao advocated total confiscation of land with redistribution to all except landlords, but in practice the limited politicisation of this remote border area meant that such a radical policy was unmanageable because of the opposition from rich peasants and general conservatism. Similar bases to Jinggangshan were created in 1928 in north-east Jiangxi, in northwest Hunan under He Long and in the Dabei mountains north-east of Wuhan.

The existence of the Communist border areas provoked military responses from the existing military authorities and in the process of conflict Communist methods of guerrilla warfare were developed. At first, attacks were mounted by local warlord units, which faced great problems of coordination because of rivalries and the existence of geographic frontiers through the Communist zones, but gradually the initiative passed to larger units under direct Nationalist control, culminating in five major encirclement campaigns from 1930 to 1934. Communist response relied heavily on the hilly terrain of the border areas, but also drew inspiration from earlier Chinese military traditions, particularly the writings of the pre-imperial Sun Zi on the art of war. Most crucial for the Communists was the avoidance of outright defeat, and therefore withdrawal and harassment played major roles, with battle sites and timings carefully chosen by the guerrillas to ensure maximum advantage. Although very effective militarily against an over-confident probing enemy, this was a much more debatable policy socially, because it allowed the counter-revolutionary forces to penetrate deeply into the Communist zone, destroying assets and threatening the security of residents of the zone for a period of time, even if the enemy was driven out eventually. Besides defeating enemy thrusts, the Communists also had to agree on a timetable for expansion of the base areas at moments of enemy passivity or inattention. This proved difficult as there was a constant struggle between the local wish to consolidate and the frequent desire at provincial and central level for an expansion of Red Army influence: Mao suffered temporary loss of power in 1928 after one such clash of opinion, but regained his control after military failures by his replacements.

In early 1929 Mao, Zhu De, and their new ally, Peng Dehuai, facing increasing supply difficulties in Jinggangshan under enemy blockade, moved their forces eastward, finally settling in south-east Jiangxi around the town of Ruijin, where Communist power was to grow more successfully. In the new area the land policy was changed to the confiscation of land only from the landlords, so as to disrupt the community less and in recognition of the important economic role of the rich peasants as efficient farmers and major suppliers for rural trade. The CCP moved ahead with its mass line work, whereby Party activists mobilised the mass of the population to join village militia, youth and women's organisations and to carry out land reform with the selective use of terror against class enemies. Recruitment for the Red Army expanded, leading to some concern at the growing power of Red Army commanders as viewed from the CCP centre in Shanghai, but Mao was determined to ensure the ideological discipline of these rural recruits, through the development of proletarian education, as he expounded at the Gutian conference in December 1929. As the CCP increased the percentage of rural members, it had to be argued that the CCP remained the party of the proletariat, not by its class membership but by its efforts towards 'proletarian goals', a line made easier for general understanding in China by translating proletariat as *wuchan jieji*, property-less class, a term devoid of any obvious industrial connotation.

Li Lisan and the Attempt to Retake Cities

The consolidation of the Jiangxi and other Communist border regions and the general developments in China and the world encouraged the CCP's urban leadership under Li Lisan to push in 1930 for the creation of an urban-based Communist regime. In late 1929, during the Chinese Eastern Railway crisis, the CI had ordered the CCP to increase preparations to take advantage of China's national crisis. The world economic crisis beginning in 1929 implied great hope for revolutionary achievement against faltering capitalism. On 26 February 1930 Li issued a circular calling for the coordination of increased urban strikes with guerrilla warfare, by pushing the Red Army towards major cities, especially in the Wuhan area, in order to win an initial victory in one or more provinces. Li's revolutionary optimism was not fully appreciated by Mao, who avoided sending delegates to conferences called by Li, or by the CI, which recalled Zhou Enlai to Moscow and began to send out to China the most staunchly pro-Stalin Chinese students from Sun Yixian University in Moscow. These latter had formed a group known as the 'Twenty-eight Bolsheviks' during the factional struggles at that university, and included four major figures of CCP history, Chen Shaoyu (alias Wang Ming), Qin Bangxian (alias Bo Gu), Zhang Wentian (alias Luo Fu) and Yang Shangkun.

On 11 June, after a conference without Mao's delegates, the Central Committee under Li adopted a resolution proclaiming a new revolutionary rising tide and ordering the combination of all revolutionary forces to achieve victory, by marching on the large cities of Changsha and Wuhan. On being informed, the CI expressed doubts, later turning to rejection of Li's policy, but Li suppressed the CI communications, isolated the CI representatives in China and placed members of the 'Twenty-eight Bolsheviks' group on probation. Whatever doubts they may have had, the rural-based Communists obeyed the centre's orders, with Peng Dehuai capturing Changsha for ten days from 27 July, but Mao and Zhu De failed to take Nanchang in the one 24-hour attack that they mounted there. At Changsha a provisional government had been established, but the mass support from within the city, which Li's line required, was nowhere in evidence, necessitating departure as the Nationalists counterattacked. Li had intended the upsurge to culminate in the capture of Wuhan, but the stronger defences there, the suppression of Communist suspects and the presence of foreign warships and troops discouraged full-scale attacks. Hence a second attack on Changsha was mounted in early September, ending in failure and the withdrawal of the Red Army back to the border regions.

The failure of Li Lisan's policy, even at a time of great disunity among the Nationalists, required the disciplining of Li without the attribution of any blame to the CI and forced the CCP to abandon any hopes of urban revolution in the short-term.

The problem for the CCP theoreticians was that Li's policy in many ways resembled the ambiguous statements from the CI and indeed Moscow had hailed the first capture of Changsha as a great step forward. Moscow sent Zhou Enlai and Qu Qiubai back to China in late August 1930 to terminate Li's line, but at the third plenum of the Sixth Central Committee in late September, they concluded that the CI and CCP lines had been identical, save for some tactical mistakes by the CCP leadership, especially over timing. Instead of criticising Li, the plenum criticised the moderate labour or 'Real Work' faction under He Mengxiong and Luo Zhanglong. In November CI letters arrived in China urging the whole Party to oppose Li and summoning Li for disciplining in Moscow, where he remained until returning to Manchuria with the USSR armies in 1945. Mif, the president of Sun Yixian University in Moscow, also arrived in late 1930 as the CI representative and organized a new leadership, confirmed at the fourth plenum in January 1931, consisting of members of the 'Twenty-eight Bolsheviks' and a repentant Zhou Enlai, and rejecting entirely members of the Real Work faction. The Real Work faction, objecting to this usurpation by inexperienced young Communists, then established a rival central committee under Luo Zhanglong, which struggled in the cities against the CI-recognised committee for two and a half years until Luo's arrest by the Nationalists in April 1933.

While the urban Communists were wracked with internal difficulties, the rural Communists continued to develop their soviets in 1930 and 1931 on the basis of Red Army strength and peasant organisation. The demise of the Li Lisan line had provided Mao with an opportunity to execute many local rivals in the Jiangxi Soviet after the Futian incident of December 1930, when some Communist units rebelled against Mao over his arrest of more than 4000 of their comrades as counter-revolutionaries or supporters of Li. The two largest soviets developed in southern Jiangxi under Mao and to the north-east of Wuhan, called the Eyuwan Soviet, where Zhang Guotao became senior leader in April 1931. Smaller soviets existed in the north in Shaanxi, under Gao Gang, and in several parts of Jiangxi, Hunan, Hubei and Guangxi. In addition there were Communist guerrillas in Hainan Island and, once Japan attacked in 1931, also in Manchuria, although the CCP-led operations in Manchuria never provided the main thrust of anti-Japanese resistance in the northeast. The first provincial soviet was established by the CCP in October 1930 for Jiangxi and in November 1931 the First National Congress of the Chinese Soviet Republic was convened at Ruijin, Jiangxi, with delegates from all major areas except the blockaded Eyuwan, which held its own simultaneous congress. The Congress created a provisional central soviet government, with Mao as executive chairman and Zhu De as chairman of the revolutionary military council.

Land Policy

The basis for revolutionary mobilisation of the peasantry was land redistribution, and therefore land policy was a vital issue in these early soviets. Originally it had been presumed that the peasantry could be divided into different categories for class struggle according to property qualifications, i.e. landlords, owner-farmers and tenants without personally owned land, but the complexities of village structure made such categories meaningless; there were some rich farmers who owned no land but were tenants on large efficient units worked with family and hired labour, and there were some poor farmers who still owned land but lacked the labour strength to work it effectively. Hence the criteria finally adopted looked more to yearly incomes and labour patterns of the peasants: a landlord was one who did not work his own land, but lived off rental income, a rich peasant had a regular surplus of income over expenditure and obtained part of his income (more than 15 per cent in the 1930s, more than 25 per cent on the later 1940s) from exploiting labour, a middle peasant had a balanced budget and only employed limited labour, if any, and the poor peasant could not survive on his income from land and had to hire himself out part or all of the time. Evaluation of peasant status proved incredibly time-consuming, given the difficulty of defining the category boundaries in many cases, and as the CCP became more experienced in land reform work, it was common to redefine category membership several times in each village before most villagers could be satisfied. Evaluation work was also complicated by the

existence of clan loyalty, by which those with the same surname tried to protect their relatives from definition in endan-
gered categories, such as landlord; such problems were particularly acute in south China where there were many villages
where all or nearly all families shared the same surname.

The process of land redistribution could be carried out once
the population of the village had been correctly categorised,
but there was a wide range of possible distributions. Some argued that the aim of a communist party must be the abandonment of private property and that therefore all land should be
nationalised and provided for the peasants either for collective use or on a contract basis. Others argued that this was too
radical for the peasants whose greatest goal was the personal
ownership of sufficient land, so the policy must allow real ownership titles to the redistributed land. Few would have denied
the correctness of confiscating the land of landlords and so-
called 'bad gentry', but what should be done with the rich
peasant land and land held by clans and temples? If only landlord or landlord and rich peasant land was redistributed, did
this mean adding scattered portions of their lands to the existing holdings of the poor and middle peasants or should the
whole village landholding pattern be resurveyed to create con-
solidated farms? If rich peasant lands were confiscated, should
the rich peasants receive some land in the redistribution? In
theory attacking the landlords and the rich peasants should
have won more support from the poorer peasants, because more
property became available for distribution, but in practice any
errors over the awkward boundary between rich and middle
peasants risked jeopardising the whole land reform effort by
alienating the middle peasants, so that tolerance of rich peasants often made tactical sense, even if it led to charges that
the CCP was no longer the party for the poor.

The actual land policy of the Jiangxi Soviet period tended
to become less and less sympathetic to the rich peasants, especially after the arrival of the CCP's young Russian-educated
leaders in the rural areas in late 1932. In 1929 Mao had advocated the confiscation of landlord land, but in early 1930, after
CI attacks on softness on the rich peasants, a new land law provided for the confiscation of landlord and rich peasant land, with
equal shares for rich, middle and poor peasants in the redis-

tribution. The 1931 National Congress proposed that the rich peasants should only receive shares of poor land and in 1933, after attacking Mao for his right opportunism, the Central Committee launched a land investigation movement to check on land reform results. This uncovered over 10 000 landlords and rich peasants who had slipped through because of earlier leniency.

Military Policy

The other major area for debate within the CCP was over military tactics and organisation, as military pressure from the Nationalists increased. The first three Nationalist encirclement campaigns from later 1930 to mid-1931 were defeated on the basis of Mao's guerrilla warfare tactics, which involved luring the enemy into the Communist zone and then destroying units which had advanced carelessly. In May 1932 the Nationalists began the fourth encirclement with half a million troops, with the main effort at first directed at the Eyuwan soviet north of the Yangzi and He Long's soviet in south-west Hubei. Both areas had to be evacuated under the intense military attack, with major columns of Communist troops evacuating westwards to form new soviets further from the reach of Nationalist forces. Meanwhile in the main Jiangxi soviet, the central Party leaders had from September 1931 proposed offensives to take advantage of the Japanese invasion of Manchuria and during 1932, under the advice of CI agent, Otto Braun, pushed for a 'forward and offensive line', in the belief that the growing Red Army could now tackle the enemy outside the Communist zone, thereby offering greater security to zone inhabitants. At the Ningdu conference in August 1932, Mao was criticised for his guerrillaism and his objections to regularising the Red Army structure, a process which involved separating state and military administration and which weakened Mao's position. The conference also supported the forward military line, which thereafter resulted in offensive actions by Jiangxi Red Army units to deflect some of the pressure from the other soviets being attacked in 1932 and to defeat the remaining impetus of the fourth encirclement when this turned on Jiangxi over the winter of 1932–3. These successes allowed the central leaders to mount a campaign from February 1933 against the 'Luo Ming line', in effect against Mao. Luo Ming was the Communist leader in Fujian, who had persisted in using guerrilla methods and who had resisted reorganisation of his local units under central authority. This purge, the greatest of the Jiangxi period, included accusations against Deng Xiaoping and other later CCP leaders.

The fifth encirclement campaign, begun in October 1933, concentrated all the available Nationalist pressure on the Jiangxi soviet in a carefully executed strangulation, which the Communists proved unable to counter with their available strength. The only possible escape mechanism was a massive withdrawal of Communist forces. The Nationalists employed up to 750 000 troops in the campaign, moved forward slowly with a system of military blockhouses and economic blockade, and engaged in propaganda and organisation of the local population through the *baojia* system. Under Jiang Jieshi's newly announced approach, Communist suppression required 30 per cent military and 70 per cent political efforts. Even the Fujian revolt of November 1933 to January 1934 failed to deter the Nationalist assault, which reaped major victories in April and July 1934 against the Communists who, by policy choice and by necessity, had to fight positional battles in which the advantage lay with the much-better-equipped Nationalists. As the Nationalists advanced, the CCP leadership, having rejected collaboration with Fujian, held the fifth plenum of the Sixth Central Committee in January 1934, attacking Mao and also the labour work of Liu Shaoqi. At the subsequent Second Congress of the Chinese Soviet Republic, Mao was re-elected as executive chairman of the republic and gave the main speech but lost his chairmanship of the Council of People's Commissars. Thereafter Mao's power declined until the Long March, with some reports of Mao having malaria and even of his being held under arrest. By May the CCP leaders were discussing contingency plans for abandonment of the soviet, but they still hoped that new recruits, mobilised by intensifying revolutionary terror, would step forward to defeat the enemy. By summer it was clear that the remaining few counties held by the Communists could not possibly survive and that increasing revolutionary terror was inducing desertions and purges, not extra strength.

The Long March

The Long March, by the First Front Army from the Jiangxi Soviet to north-west China, coupled with the equally long marches by remnants from other soviets, have become heroic symbols of the endurance and fortitude of the Chinese Communists, but at the time the Long March began much more as a disorganised retreat than as an ordered policy with new goals in view. Although Mao was later to blame the need to retreat upon the leftist leadership of the students returned from the USSR, the failure in Jiangxi related more to the outside pressures than to the internal policies. Nevertheless the methods of departure and of the early weeks of the Long March both evoked criticism, as the approximately 100 000 marchers were given little time to prepare, were ill-informed politically about the purpose of their journey and were expected to march in a straight line, thereby becoming easier prey for their pursuers. Within ten weeks, numbers were down by more than 60 per cent, as a result of battles and desertions, and increasingly heavy equipment had to be abandoned, including radio transmitters for contact with the USSR, although radio links were maintained within China on smaller equipment. These local contacts allowed Communists in the temporarily more stable areas to the north of the Long March route to provide vital military information on Nationalist movements, gained from monitoring Nationalist activity.

The original intention of the First Front Army had been to move westwards to join He Long's Communist units in western Hunan, but a minor meeting at Liping in December 1934 and a major conference at Zunyi in January 1935 altered this, while also reorganising the CCP leadership. At Liping the CCP leadership opted to move into poorly defended Guizhou province, rather than seeking immediately to join other Communist units, and to march in a zigzag fashion, requiring greater mobility, but also confusing the enemy more.

The Zunyi conference, one of the most important in CCP history, discussed the military problems of the Long March and of the Jiangxi soviet, with sharp attacks by Mao and Peng Dehuai on the military line of the students returned from the USSR and by Liu Shaoqi on activities in the Nationalist or 'white' areas. A resolution was adopted, reviewing the errors of Qin Bangxian, Zhou Enlai and CI adviser, Braun, and the conference agreed to drive north-westwards to meet with Zhang Guotao in Sichuan, under the new slogan of going north to fight the Japanese. The conference also reorganized the CCP leadership, granting Mao his first real position of Party power, on the Standing Committee of the Politburo, with Zhang Wentian, Qin Bangxian, Zhou Enlai and Chen Yun. Mao was not the Politburo chairman, but he did become director of the Central Committee's Military Affairs Committee, replacing Zhou Enlai. Zhang Wentian, one of the Russian-educated students, gained the Party's top post, general secretary, from his criticised colleague, Qin Bangxian. Thus Mao, the military and administrative architect of much of the Jiangxi period's successes, was finally granted high Party authority, not as absolute leader, but as relatively dominant within a collective leadership which had not yet criticized the political line of the recent years. Moscow thereafter spoke of Mao as the leading Communist in China, but not necessarily in the whole CCP, because of the ambiguous position of the leader of the 28 Bolsheviks, Chen Shaoyu, who had been recalled to Moscow in September 1931 to serve in the CI leadership.

With its leadership reorganized, the First Front Army spent several months in journeys around northern Guizhou, before finally crossing the Yangzi River in Yunnan in early May 1935 and pushing north. The pace of Communist manoeuvres was such that battle with pursuing units could often be avoided, but the Communists suffered from fatigue, illness and strained relations with the minority peoples who lived in these remote areas. A major disaster was avoided in late May at the Luding suspension bridge on the Dadu river in western Sichuan, where volunteers crawled across the chains in the face of enemy fire, to capture the last possible crossing-point unless one entered the Tibetan high country. Further marching led through mountain passes at over 4000 metres, until units of the First Front Army met up with troops of Zhang Guotao's Fourth Front Army in June 1935 in the north-west of Sichuan province.

The meeting of the two Communist armies, although a time for resting and recuperating for the rank and file, also provided the occasion for further leadership clashes, as Zhang

Guotao sought to turn his military strength into political power within the CCP. After the abandonment of the Eyuwan Soviet in 1932, Zhang Guotao had led the Fourth Front Army westwards into Sichuan, rebuilding numbers and creating Communist zones without applying all the leftist policies of the late Jiangxi period. As the First Front Army entered Sichuan, Zhang's forces had moved further west to link with the Jiangxi remnants and, despite losses in this move, they still totalled about 40 000 men, four times the size of Mao's army. In the CCP leadership, however, the Fourth Front Army was severely under-represented, with only Zhang Guotao in the Politburo.

In late June at the Lianghekou conference, Zhang challenged the leadership arrangements of the January 1935 Zunyi conference, which had lacked the full Central Committee membership. The Jiangxi Communists rejected Zhang's formal bid to become CCP general secretary although they did coopt some of the Fourth Front Army commanders into the Party leadership. Zhang also proposed that the Communist armies should consolidate in Sichuan with the possibility of retreat into the Chinese northwest, while the First Front Army leaders urged moving north to the small soviet in Shaanxi, so as to appear to be preparing to fight Japan, and possibly to gain USSR aid. No decision could be reached, but Zhang did gain acceptance of the use of revolutionary committees and people's governments instead of soviets.

A further conference therefore proved necessary in August at Maoergai, as Nationalist pressure increased. A compromise decision was reached to split the Communist forces into two, with the eastern column including Mao, Zhang Wentian and Zhou Enlai, and the western under Zhang Guotao and Zhu De, both expecting to move a little to the north. In the event, parts of Mao's column moved quite rapidly north, reaching the Shaanxi Communists near Baoan in October 1935, while the remainder of the eastern column of Zhang's western column remained in Sichuan until driven out towards Tibet in March 1936. In mid-1936, these units began to move northwards towards Shaanxi, because of bitter conditions and of CI offers to mediate the Mao-Zhang dispute. Their progress proved disastrous as Zhang continued to strive for new Communist zones in the north-west against local Muslim and Nationalist opposition.

By the end of 1936, the remnants of Zhang's forces and units of He Long's Second Front Army had all reached the Baoan area in northern Shaanxi, where the balance of strength now favoured the leaders around Mao. These men had rebuilt their armed forces and successfully mediated the disputes which had riven the Shaanxi base prior to Mao's arrival.

One other major issue divided Mao and Zhang Guotao in 1935, the choice of the best policy towards a united front against Japan. Although the Jiangxi Soviet had symbolically declared war on Japan in 1932, the CCP had been reluctant to work with any established authorities to promote the anti-Japanese struggle. Zhang Guotao argued that this policy was too extreme and that the greater success against Japan could be obtained by wider collaboration with others in China. Although an appeal was launched in August 1935 from Maoergai for resistance against Japan, Mao did not envisage much collaboration with others nor a dilution of the soviet-building work of the Party. If through his restricted access to radio Mao did know anything of the simultaneous moves in the CI Seventh Congress towards broader united fronts worldwide, he did not disclose it, in the context of his battle with Zhang. It was only in December 1935 at the Politburo meeting at Wayaobao that the Party declared formal support for the united front and openly attacked the political line of Russian-educated students in the Jiangxi period as leftist and arising from inability to apply Marxism–Leninism effectively to the concrete conditions of China. It is perhaps ironic that the last important ingredient of Mao's ultimately victorious strategy, the use of the united front, should have been prompted by the Comintern, at the very moment when Mao was establishing his political supremacy against the CI and its Chinese trainees. The success of the united front, in saving the CCP from possible destruction and then opening the door to great expansion, forms the subject of the next chapter, in which Japanese aggression forms the essential background.

5 The Second Collapse

To a country grown accustomed to the depredations imposed and the privileges demanded by the Western powers, the Japanese onslaught from 1931 to 1945 represented a heightened danger from the maritime side of China. Here was a conquering force which had definite ambitions for a monopoly of control in China, either to be exercised directly or through collaborationist governments which would serve Japan's whim. The result was almost a return to the earlier experience of overall conquest of China by outsiders, but this time it was carried out by a country which, although once in awe of China, had now progressed to account China as backward and in need of guidance. Although the Japanese had reached their position of military strength with the help of Western-style industry and training, they regarded many aspects of the West as unacceptable. In particular in the 1930s they attacked liberalism and communism as threats to the Eastern way of life. They anticipated the stemming of Western influence in China by the promotion of the older ideologies of China and by restricting China's role to that of provider of raw materials for Japan's industry. What the Japanese could not understand was that, after nearly a century of humiliation by the Westerners, Chinese leaders could not openly cooperate with the Japanese aggressors without risking severe attacks from within the urban literate community. Replacing Western domination with a racially closer Eastern domination was no substitute for the full independence which the Chinese sought. Moreover the Chinese were not sufficiently swayed by Japanese talk of Pan-Asianism to refrain from using Western power to thwart the Japanese, realising that eventually Japanese ambitions would provoke a Western reaction.

Besides its direct impact upon the areas invaded, the Japanese military advance also played a major role in long-term battle between the Nationalist government and the Communist Party, resulting in a quite different internal balance in China in 1945

117

from that in 1931. This change in the relative strengths and in the apparent administrative competence of the two Chinese rivals set the stage for the full-scale civil war which engulfed China in 1946, culminating in the overwhelming victory of the Chinese Communists.

Much argument has raged over whether the Nationalists could have created a stable united China in the absence of the Japanese invasion and whether the Communists were 'saved' by the out-break of war in north China in 1937. In both cases the conclusions reached tend to reflect the individual's general evaluation of the Nationalists and Communists. It seems more helpful to realise that the Japanese invasion was a continuation of that foreign aggression which had allowed the growth of both parties in the 1920s, and as such was part of the problem to be solved by the two party leaderships in their search for a stronger China, rather than something to be ignored or used as an excuse for failure. Both parties can be said to have neglected up to 1935 the positive role that promoting active resistance to Japan could play in national political life; the Nationalists preferred to stress internal pacification before external resistance, while the CCP, taking its lead from the Comintern, argued that class struggle within China was much more important than national defence for achieving the revolution desired by the Party. Both parties however kept open the possibility of a different orientation – the Nationalists through the anti-Japanese stance of the Blue Shirts, the Communists by nominally declaring war on Japan in 1932.

It was the renewed Japanese threat south of the Great Wall from the end of 1935, coupled with the Comintern shift towards popular-front governments, which permitted both parties to re-consider their positions, culminating in the second united front in mid-1937. Although the loss of the north-east to Japan in 1931 had provoked outraged demonstrations and boycotts in China, the government's policy of appealing to the foreign powers to turn back the Japanese army could be justified, because the northeast, since its administrative and demographic incor-poration into China at the end of the Qing dynasty, had never been fully under central government control, because of foreign machinations. The threat to Beiping (as Beijing was then called) and even to five northern provinces as implied in Japanese actions in late 1935 was symbolically more important. Beiping was still recognised as the cultural centre of China, despite the removal of the political capital to Nanjing. It was also dangerously prophetic of the growing range of Japanese ambitions, which threatened the gradual submission of China to Japan, in the absence of any military response from China and of any meaningful diplomatic pressure from the foreign powers.

Japan's Military Advance 1931-6

The Japanese conquest of the north-east began on the evening of 18 September 1931, when a Japanese-arranged bombing incident on a railway near Fengtian (Mukden) provided the pretext for a general Japanese advance. Unlike the 1928 plot to assassinate the Manchurian warlord, Zhang Zuolin, which had been conceived by middle-ranking Japanese officers without consultation with their superiors, some indication of Ishihara and Itagaki's 1931 plan had been revealed to higher levels and it was clear that the senior leadership of the Japanese Army would welcome an opportunity to act vigorously, whatever the views of the foreign ministry under the pro-Western Shidehara. Jiang Jieshi and the GMD leadership responded to the Mukden incident in two ways, by urging the north-eastern commander, Zhang Xueliang, to withdraw without resistance and by seeking to enlist foreign support to condemn and roll back Japan. Thus while the diplomatic process through the League of Nations gradually moved to censure Japan in a limited way, the Japanese were able to consolidate their position in the whole of Manchuria, despite the initial overwhelming predominance in numbers of the Chinese over the Japanese forces in the area. Most of Zhang's troops were withdrawn from Manchuria, although some, notably under Ma Zhanshan, undertook some resistance in the north for a few months until defeated in the absence of military support from the rest of China.

The Japanese declared the establishment of a new, separate state of Manzhouguo (Manchukuo) in February 1932 with the last Qing Emperor, Henry Puyi, as chief of state, but the new state was not recognised by the Western powers nor by Nanjing. Puyi's status was raised to Emperor in 1934, but this did not alter the fact of Japanese military control of most aspects of the new state. Manzhouguo was intended to be a major economic asset for the Japanese Empire, with its iron, coal and soya bean production, and considerable Japanese investments were channelled to the area for a decade, reinforcing the differences between a rapidly modernising Manchuria and a much-less-developed rest of China. Japan's capture of the whole of Manchuria, when her previous treaty-interests had been only in the south, required careful handling of USSR interests in the north. Although the USSR responded to the Japanese aggression in Manchuria by reopening diplomatic relations with Nanjing in 1932, the USSR was not willing to risk a major conflict with Japan in the area. This meant that the Manchurian committee of the CCP was instructed not to make anti-Japanese resistance its main task in the early 1930s. Later the USSR sold the Russian-built north Manchurian railway network to Manzhouguo in 1935, to reduce the possibility of disputes with Japan.

Although the main focus of Japanese army action was in Manchuria in 1931 an important separate battle developed in Shanghai in late January 1932. The Japanese attack in Manchuria had provoked a very extensive anti-Japanese movement in the cities of the remainder of China, with particular activism among the students who repeatedly petitioned for direct resistance to Japan. A major focus of the anti-Japanese movement was the boycott of Japanese goods and this boycott readily spread to attacks upon shops stocking such goods. Anti-Japanese activity was particularly severe in Shanghai, where the Japanese naval commander repeatedly called on the local authorities to restrain it and finally sent his marines ashore. Fighting soon erupted between the local Chinese forces, principally the Nineteenth Route Army, and the marines, with severe losses for the Japanese. The Japanese navy, which had intended to gain its share of glory and extra funding through the Shanghai venture, was thus compelled to call in the Japanese army to rescue it. The battle lasted some six weeks, ending with a limited Japanese victory and an internationally negotiated settlement demilitarising the Shanghai area. Although public acclaim for the defence went to the ex-warlord Nineteenth Route Army, Jiang Jieshi committed units of the centrally organised army and those units suffered higher casualties than the Nineteenth Route Army.

Nevertheless Jiang did not seek to publicise his action, fearing that it could provoke even harsher Japanese reprisals.

In North China Japanese military pressure continued after the formal establishment of Manzhouguo in March 1932, with the main focus on Rehe (Jehol) province, but with some Japanese forces taking Shanhaiguan, at the coastal end of the Great Wall on 1 January 1933. The takeover of Rehe was essentially completed easily in ten days in February 1933, despite much spirited talk by the Chinese side, and Rehe was included in Manzhouguo. The only serious resistance was offered by the Twenty-ninth Army under Song Zheyuan, making him into a national figure. Nevertheless the Chinese and Japanese reached a local agreement, the Tanggu truce of 31 May 1933, whereby areas to the north and east of Beiping were demilitarised. The Japanese had also taken over parts of Chahar province in May 1933 but were temporarily pushed back by an army specially organised by the warlord Feng Yuxiang on a patriotic basis. His actions only proved an embarrassment for the Chinese central government and he was persuaded to dissolve his army, whilst the Japanese returned to their earlier gains. Thereafter the Japanese sought to increase their influence in western Inner Mongolia, where tensions between Mongol leaders and the Chinese gave fertile ground for intrigue.

In 1935 relations between Japan and China began to improve on the national diplomatic level, but deteriorated at the local level in the north. Nanjing moved to curb anti-Japanese materials in the press, sacking the anti-Japanese Minister of Propaganda, and in May Tokyo and Nanjing announced the exchange of ambassadors, thus raising representation above the ministerial level, which China experienced with all the other powers. The Chinese ambassador on arriving in Tokyo offered a settlement of outstanding issues on the basis of friendship and some compromise on the Manchuria question, but Hirota, Japan's foreign minister, after consultation within Japan's foreign policy drafting bureaucracy (which included the military), replied with his three principles:

- Chinese cessation of anti-Japanese activities;
- China's *de facto* recognition of Manzhoukuo;
- Sino-Japanese cooperation in suppressing Communist activities.

Such terms were unacceptable to Nanjing, the third because it implied sanction for Japanese military presence in China, even though anti-communism was the Nanjing policy.

In the north Japanese plans gradually coalesced around the idea of a pro-Japanese government independent of Nanjing based on the five provinces of Hebei, Shanxi, Shandong, Suiyuan and Chahar – the brainchild in particular of Special Affairs officer Doihara Kenji. Initial pressures in Hebei and Chahar had resulted in two local agreements in June 1935, the He-Umezu and Qin-Doihara agreements, which sanctioned further Japanese advances and local withdrawal of Chinese forces. The wider plan for the five provinces was discussed with the local north-China leaders in the latter part of 1935, but its implementation proved politically impossible after nationalistic demonstrations in Beiping on 9 December 1935 led to widespread opposition to pro-Japanese institutions in the north. The Japanese were only able to establish a fully pro-Japanese regime in East Hebei under one of China's most notorious collaborators, Yin Rugeng. The great advantage of Yin's regime was that it bestraddled the railway from Manzhouguo into north China and the Japanese were able to give a false legality to their already extensive smuggling programme, by claiming that customs duties on goods, at very low rates, had been paid to Yin's government and that thereafter the Chinese customs could not challenge the goods. The economic losses by smuggling in the north were very large and of great importance to the Nanjing government which relied on customs revenue for much of its income.

During 1936 Japanese advances in China were limited, with slight gains in military presence south-east of Beiping. This slowdown was the result of two factors: turmoil within Japan after the Mutiny in Tokyo on 26 February 1936 and the growing unity in China around resistance to Japanese aggression. Within Japan the failure of the Mutiny placed the army under the Control faction, which argued for long-term mobilisation of Japan to create a total war economy, but which was divided over the value of military involvements in China south of the Great Wall, which might weaken the army for its major potential fight against the USSR. Within China the drive for unity drew mainly on the urban intellectuals and students, but it received support from the change of line advocated by the CCP.

Although the Comintern in Moscow had adopted its policy of anti-fascist popular fronts in August 1935, it seems that the CCP only adopted the united-front approach as its policy at the end of 1935 and even then the Party was unwilling to include the Guomindang in the front at first. The united front for resistance was the last major policy change by the CCP that was directly ordered by the Comintern, but the CCP leadership under Mao was not willing to accept the complete Comintern approach, nor to tolerate for long the return to power of Wang Ming. He had been representing China in Moscow in August 1935 and was to return to China in 1937 to carry through Moscow's programme based on full cooperation with the Guomindang and the hope of urban revolutionary activity to supplement the countryside. By May 1936 the intellectuals and students had coordinated their activity into a National Salvation Association, which sought to pressure the government for resistance. The revolt by the southern provinces in mid-1936 chose anti-Japanese resistance as a major slogan, although the sincerity of the revolt was questioned by many, especially because it was known that Japanese help had been offered to the rebels.

The Xi'an Incident

Despite the calls for a united front, the Communist–Nationalist civil war within China continued until the Xi'an incident in December 1936. Although minor anti-Communist activities continued throughout China, the major campaign, under the command of Zhang Xueliang, warlord of the lost northeast, was in the north-west against the remnants of the Long March. The Communist armies had advanced briefly into Shanxi province across the frozen Yellow River in February 1936, but retired by May, despite some success with land reform propaganda, in the face of military opposition from the local warlord, Yan Xishan. Thereafter the main front between the Communists and Zhang's troops was quiet, as a result of a tacit ceasefire at the front line which gradually developed into more formal cooperation as the Communists argued the futility of Chinese fighting Chinese while Japan held the north-east and threatened further advances. Such a halt in the anti-Communist campaign was unacceptable to Jiang Jieshi and he urged Zhang to continue the attack, first at a conference in Luoyang in October 1936 and then by flying to Zhang's headquarters at Xi'an in December.

Zhang refused to follow Jiang's orders and, under threat of dismissal, Zhang, with the cooperation of north-western warlord, Yang Huzheng, arrested Jiang on 12 December. They issued a list of eight demands, including an end to civil war. The central government reacted cautiously, although some leaders advocated an immediate bombing of Xi'an, and troops were prepared for possible action. The Chinese Communist reaction seems at first to have been delight at the capture and possible execution of their enemy Jiang, but reconsideration of the national situation and the horrified reaction of the USSR quickly prompted a change towards the need to preserve Jiang as a national leader and the despatch of Zhou Enlai to negotiate at Xi'an. Full details of the Xi'an negotiations are unknown, but it is clear that some sort of agreement was reached on the ending of the civil war, although Jiang denied that he had promised anything to gain his release. Jiang returned to Nanjing on 25 December together with Zhang Xueliang, who was stripped of his posts and held under house arrest thereafter, even in Taiwan after 1949.

The aftermath of the Xi'an incident was the continuation of the ceasefire between the Communists and their attackers, and the beginnings of political manoeuvring towards a viable co-operation between the two sides. In February 1937 the Communists called on the Nationalists to end the civil war and to work for a more democratic government, offering in return to end their insurrection, to stop land confiscation, to rename the soviet area and to redesignate the Red Army as part of the national revolutionary army. The Nationalists replied with four conditions, the abolition of the Red Army and the soviet government, the acceptance of the Three People's Principles and the halting of class struggle and of propaganda for sovietisation. The Communists were determined not to lose their independence by sacrificing their army or by forcing members to join the Guomindang as in the 1920s' strategy of the bloc within, but there were sufficient parallels between the two programmes to imply that a compromise solution could be attained once the situation became critical after a Japanese attack. The likelihood of a united resistance in China was threatening to Japanese ambitions, but the accumulated evidence now available implies that the Japanese did not intend to begin a full-scale war in mid-1937, although the opposite interpretation was adopted at the time in ignorance of the internal politics in Japan.

The Anti-Japanese War

Japanese Campaigns

Open hostilities between Japan and China recommenced after a trivial incident in the late evening of 7 July 1937 near Lugouqiao, or Marco Polo bridge, south-west of Beiping. The Japanese North China army, legally stationed in China since the 1901 Boxer Protocol and greatly increased in numbers in the 1930s, was engaged in night exercises of questionable legality in an area technically beyond the privileges gained in 1901. An unexplained shot was heard and on taking the roll call the Japanese discovered a man to be missing, although the man returned later in the night. The Japanese assumed that the shot had come from the nearby Chinese town and demanded the right to enter the town to search for their lost man. When the demand was rejected the Japanese attacked the town on 8 July, whilst local Chinese forces of the Twenty-ninth Army under Song Zheyuan prepared for further conflicts. Nevertheless the battlefield situation remained relatively calm for three weeks, as the local commanders sought to establish a local agreement, such as had been possible in 1933, 1935 and 1936.

The reactions of the two central governments stymied any local settlement. Jiang Jieshi realised that all previous local settlements had resulted in losses for China and therefore insisted that this time there should be no sacrifices to Japan and that the central government must be involved in the negotiations, reinforcing this position by sending central forces northwards towards the Beiping area. The Japanese, under a new premier, Konoe, also interpreted local settlements as unsatisfactory in that they gave excessive diplomatic power to local military commanders and therefore demanded direct communications between Tokyo and Nanjing. Japan also strengthened its position by the despatch of reinforcements to north China, after considerable debate within Japan's military hierarchy. Thus a small local incident was turned by intervention of the two central governments into a major conflict of wills, in which the Japanese were finally required to remove their military opponents in the north, which they did by the capture of Beiping and Tianjin by early August.

The Nanjing government realised that a war in the north was both unwinnable and insufficiently provocative of the other powers involved in China, and therefore desired to expand the war to the Yangzi area, where the Western powers could be expected to intervene as they had in 1932. A number of minor incidents had occurred in Shanghai involving Japanese military men and on 13 August the Chinese began to move against the Japanese area of Shanghai known as Hongkou, with an attempted major air attack on Japanese shipping in the harbour on 14 August which culminated in disaster when several bombs landed short in the streets of Shanghai. Jiang committed his strongest troops to the attack on the Japanese positions, held by marines, and the Japanese were obliged to call in army units, which fought for three months in the Shanghai area before breaking out, with the help of a flanking action to the south-west near Hangzhou in November. The Chinese losses were very heavy, but the powers on whom Jiang had called for intervention refused to make any vigorous response after a conference in Brussels in November.

The Japanese advanced rapidly after the end of Chinese resistance near Shanghai, taking Nanjing on 13 December. They nearly risked serious international complications by bombing attacks on the USS *Panay* and the British HMS *Ladybird*, attacks prompted by officers seeking to widen the war to attain Japanese ambitions in East Asia but quickly disavowed by the central authorities in Japan with adequate apologies. Meanwhile in the north the Japanese had continued to advance against the wide variety of local military forces, winning all the major battles, but being delayed by some strong resistance including the ambush of part of a Japanese division at Pingxingguan by Communist troops, which was later extolled as a major Chinese victory. By December the Shanxi capital, Taiyuan, and northern Shandong province were under Japanese occupation.

The Chinese government was offered terms by the Japanese through German mediators in early October, but by the time it had agreed to these terms as the basis for negotiation in early December, the Japanese had stiffened their position as a result of military success. The capture of Nanjing prompted the Japanese army in north China to establish a full-scale puppet government in Beiping in the hopes of forestalling any attempt to base a Japanese-controlled China in Nanjing. This government, named as the Provisional Government, drew its personnel from politicians of the warlord era who had been kept out of politics during the Nanjing decade. After capturing Nanjing the Japanese allowed their army to range through the city at will, creating over a period of six weeks the Rape of Nanjing, which resulted in the death and humiliation of tens of thousands of non-combatant Chinese, witnessed and reported by the handful of foreigners in the city who had tried to establish zones of safety. Exact responsibility for the Rape has never been satisfactorily established, although the post-war trial of war criminals blamed the local Japanese commander, Matsui. The prolonged nature of the outrage implied that it was a major policy decision, not a mere temporary failure of discipline, and it seems to have been intended to shock the Chinese government into an awareness of Japan's seriousness of purpose in bringing China to its knees. In practice it forced Jiang to reject any compromise solution with Japan, and the Japanese replied in January 1938 with an announcement that they would have no more to do with Jiang, whom they now saw as no more than a regional warlord.

The Japanese spent the next fifteen months expanding the area under their control, but without achieving their goal of pacifying China or of gaining acceptance of their ambitions by any major military leader in China. After the loss of Nanjing the Chinese government had moved its long-term capital to Chongqing in Sichuan, well-protected by the Yangzi gorges from land and river attack and by very frequent mist and cloud from air attack, while the temporary forward capital was at Wuhan. The Japanese therefore strove to take Wuhan and to control the railway line from Tianjin to Nanjing, allowing communication between north and central China. Although suffering a severe defeat at Taierzhuang in southern Shandong in April 1938 and being hindered by the deliberate breaching of the Yellow River dikes in June 1938, the Japanese pushed forward relentlessly with both tasks and in October 1938 took Wuhan. In the same month they dared to occupy Guangzhou close to Hong Kong in south China, after witnessing British appeasement policy in Europe at the Munich conference. Further advances resulted in the capture of Nanchang, the capital of Jiangxi province in March 1939, and the occupation of Hainan island off the southern coast in February 1939. During this period of advance the Japanese had established a puppet government, the Reformed government, at Nanjing in March 1938 and had also attempted to court disgruntled Nationalist politicians. This policy resulted in the unexpected defection of the major GMD leader, Wang Jingwei, from Chongqing in December 1938, to discuss plans for a national government for the Japanese-occupied areas of China.

After March 1939 the front-line between the Japanese and the Chongqing-led forces of Free China was largely stabilised until 1944, although the Chinese attempted an offensive in late 1939 and the Japanese moved to occupy a few extra towns, especially along the coast. Free China was essentially isolated from coastal trade and after Japanese pressure on French IndoChina in 1940, the only routes open to the outside were from the USSR and from Burma, both long and tortuous, although Shanghai as an international concession remained open to Free Chinese influence. Foreign aid in the early part of the war came to China principally from the USSR which signed a non-aggression pact with Nanjing in August 1937 and provided aircraft and pilots for use against Japan. The other powers were more tardy, with Britain aiding in maintaining the value of Chinese currency and France offering railway loans. With both belligerents using American equipment, neither side wished to initiate the operation of the US neutrality laws by declaring formal war, this being in particular China's view since China realised that in its financial and economic weakness it could not replace American supplies elsewhere, whereas the richer Japan would not suffer so severely. The USA issued a warning to Japan in 1939 over renewal of navigation treaties after the

Japanese moved into islands in the South China Sea, but only began serious aid in 1941. From March of that year China was allowed access to equipment under lend-lease. In July the USA froze Japanese assets and imposed an oil embargo after Japan moved into southern IndoChina.

The outbreak of the Pacific War after the attack on Pearl Harbor by Japan in December 1941 allowed Free China to declare war on Japan openly and to solicit large-scale help from the USA and Britain. With the loss of Burma to Japan, all aid had to be flown over the Hump route, over the mountains from India into Yunnan, a route which at its maximum could only bring in 20 000 tons of supplies a month. US aid included the operations of aircraft under the command of Chennault, who had previously served unofficially as the leader of the volunteer Flying Tigers, the support of ground forces under Stilwell and the provision of large loans, for government operation and currency maintenance.

Although the involvement of the USA in the war presaged the ultimate defeat of Japan outside China, which allowed the Chinese to be less urgent in the prosecution of their own war against Japan, its direct impact was very negative because of the issue of US planes operating from China. The Japanese were very worried about the bombing of the Japanese mainland and after American carrier-based planes launched the Doolittle raid on Tokyo in April 1942 and flew on towards China, the Japanese launched a land campaign in China to destroy all airfields south of the Yangzi within range of the coast. In 1944 with the advent of longer-range planes, a further and deeper campaign was necessary, resulting in the Ichigo campaign in which Japanese forces sought to take control of the complete north–south railway in China and to destroy all the air bases used by the Americans in south-west China. The campaign, at a time when Japan was losing the island war in the Pacific, was remarkably successful and revealed the weakness of the Free Chinese forces after seven years of war. At the time of the Japanese surrender in August 1945, the Japanese army was still in control of most of the areas in China which it had ever occupied, except in the north-east where the entry of crack USSR armoured forces pushed back the Japanese Guandong army, poorly equipped in comparison.

The Impact of the Anti-Japanese War on the CCP

The eight years of war in China south of the Great Wall had a profound effect on the competing Chinese forces which had begun the war under a united front, allowing the Communists to spread geographically and to gain in administrative experience while the Nationalists faced mounting problems. Under the united-front arrangements the Communists were allowed to run the ShaanGanNing border area government based at Yan'an, and the Communist military forces were reorganised as the Eighth Route Army with three divisions to operate in north China. In October 1937 permission was granted for a further unit, the New Fourth Army, to operate south of the lower Yangzi River. With their scanty equipment the Eighth Route Army soldiers were not prepared for positional warfare with the Japanese and their main task was to spread behind the Japanese front line in north China. Although many Eighth Route Army commanders argued that their soldiers should be kept together in units large enough for mobile warfare, the CCP leadership under Mao finally persuaded them that in most areas it was necessary to break the army down into smaller units suitable only for guerrilla warfare, until sufficient penetration and recruitment had been achieved.

Although the GMD had publicised the CCP's July offer of collaboration on 22 September 1937 and the CCP formally accepted the programme for resistance and reconstruction drawn up at the GMD Extraordinary National Congress (27 March–2 April 1938), there was nevertheless considerable uncertainty over the exact methods of implementing the united front. Within the CCP the differences were most clearly articulated between Mao, as the resident leader, and Wang Ming, China's leading figure in the Comintern, who returned to Yan'an from the USSR in late 1937 to assist the war effort. Although Mao had gradually endorsed the widening scope of the united front before July 1937, he did not intend that the CCP should lose any independence of action or that the CCP should tone down its programme too severely just for the sake of cooperation with the GMD. Mao suspected that the GMD resistance effort would only be partial and insisted the resistance war must provide an opportunity for political reforms in China. Wang Ming on his return to China had confirmed Mao's leadership while urging the need for a more collective leadership and for the strengthening of Mao's ideological understanding. In December 1937 Wang insisted that the resistance war was crucial to China's survival and that therefore the CCP must cooperate wholeheartedly with the existing, unreformed GMD. Wang's policy, which drew on Stalin's instructions, was accepted by the Party for most of 1938 and assumed a long-lasting collaboration between the CCP and GMD, whose clearest manifestation was to be the joint prolonged defence of Wuhan, a defence which the GMD refused to sanction after the defeats along the Yangzi valley. With Wang temporarily dominant, Mao turned to writing on military issues, until the loss of Wuhan in October 1938 spelt the end of Wang's policy at the forty-day-long Sixth Plenum of the Sixth Central Committee.

The advances of the Chinese Communists in the first three years of the war were spectacular, with Party membership ballooning from 20 000 in 1936 to 800 000 in 1940, whilst the Red Army reached 500 000 by 1940. Such expansion was achieved almost entirely in the liberated areas – that is, areas behind the most advanced position of the Japanese army – but it would be wrong to assume that this growth was entirely the result of Japanese atrocities forcing Chinese peasants to seek the protection of the Red Army. The only concern of the Japanese army up to the end of 1938 and the principal one thereafter until later 1940 was the defeat of the Nationalist government and the control of the main cities and communication routes in China. Hence in their advance they bypassed most of the areas in which the Chinese Communists were to become established – that is, the hilly areas of north-west and south-east Shanxi and the border straddling north-east Shanxi and north-west Hebei, where the central government agreed to the formal creation of a second border government called JinChaJi in January 1938.

Major debates among historians have raged over the causes of the CCP's advance since the publication of Chalmers Johnson's book, *Peasant Nationalism and Communist Power*, in 1962. Johnson argued, on the basis of mainly Japanese military sources, that the Chinese peasants were inspired to join the Chinese Communists because of the Communists' harnessing of nationalism in the war situation and their abandonment of class struggle and radical social policies. In Johnson's view the Chinese peasants could not be mobilised effectively by revolutionary propaganda, as proved by the Communist failure in south China by 1935, but Japanese aggression forced the peasants into unaccustomed military and political activity to seek to defend their territory. This defence against a non-Chinese enemy rapidly led to the emergence of nationalism among the mass of the rural population, who had previously been unaffected by the urban and intellectual nationalism of movements such as the May Fourth. This thesis clearly seeks to argue the vital importance of the anti-Japanese war in the rise of the CCP, but has been attacked both for its sources of evidence and for the limitations of its interpretation, which allows no serious role to the social policies of the CCP during the anti-Japanese war. It is also open to question on geographic grounds for the early period of the war in that the main Communist expansion occurred in many counties with limited, if any, contact with Japanese troops. Unless one is prepared to argue that the reputation of atrocities committed elsewhere caused the peasants to seek to organise for their defence, which would imply a higher level of political consciousness than Johnson accepts for peasants, it becomes necessary to modify Johnson's view considerably.

The Japanese invasion of north China swept away the established higher levels of authority in north China – that is, the provincial governments in Hebei and Shandong – and reduced the hold of Shanxi governor, Yan Xishan, to the south-west of that province. At the lower administrative levels, some magistrates fled at the news of the Japanese attack, while others remained in place but without clear direction from above. The invasion thus caused a breakdown in authority patterns, but did not necessarily result in a complete political vacuum. Some formal local authority figures remained, while the local rural society was able to turn to existing unofficial structures to retain some cohesion. The Communists were now able to penetrate the local society for one of two reasons. First, in those areas which had experienced Japanese military activity there was a strong desire for effective military means to protect villages and the Communists came armed with suitable military techniques practised over a decade of fighting against better-equipped enemies. Second, in those areas where the Japanese had not been militarily active, the Communists arrived as military representatives of the national government, with a commitment to organise village life for the development of national resistance. Since the military aspects were less urgent in these areas, the Communists relied more heavily on the involvement of the peasant population in reordering the social and political patterns of village life. The disappearance of open Guomindang repression of the Communists and the Communists' commitment to the united front allowed the Communists to create new patterns of village leadership, although this intrusion by outsiders was resented and often resisted by the existing village elites.

In order to reorganise village life the Communists had to discover ways to enhance the power of the poorer peasants without so antagonising the rural elite that it would prevent change. Since the Party had made a public commitment in its united-front agreements not to pursue open class warfare, this meant that landlords and rich peasants could not be openly attacked for their status, but had to be persuaded to surrender some of their previous power to the larger numbers of poorer peasants favoured by the Party. The only exception against open attack occurred in the case of traitors and collaborators, whose land was usually confiscated and redistributed to other villagers; there was a tendency for such collaboration with the Japanese to be carried out by the richer elements of the rural society who had property in, or connections with, the towns which the Japanese held. The major tools for reordering the villages were the tax system, the application of rent and interest reductions and the organisation of village governments through mass participation and in some cases elections.

The Chinese rural tax system had become notorious for its many anomalies and abuses, which made it highly regressive – that is, those with highest rural incomes paid the lowest rates of tax, while those with low incomes paid high rates of tax. The Communists moved rapidly to equalise the tax burden, with slogans such as 'those with money contribute money, those with strength contribute strength' and with the abolition of the many surtaxes which had accumulated since 1911. The Communists gradually moved to the reasonable-burden tax system implemented in firmly controlled areas in 1938–9, which tended to tax the rural rich very heavily, in the name of the resistance effort, and some authors have seen the tax policy as a slow method to confiscate land from the rich who were in many cases unable to meet the taxes over seven years of war without selling off their land to meet their tax payments. Such a view probably overestimates the ability of the Communists to extract so much without provoking resistance and the Party was forced to compromise and reformulate tax policy several times by 1945.

Rent and interest reduction was an obvious target for a party seeking to reduce the burden on the poorer sections of the rural community and it had the great advantage of being totally acceptable under united-front policy, since rent reduction had been sanctioned by the Guomindang's own land law of 1930. Exact details of the reduction varied locally, but the general principle was to set rents at 37.5 per cent of the main harvest, a supposed reduction of 25 per cent, and to fix interest at 10 per cent per annum. Since high rates of tenancy were unusual in north China, it was the interest reduction which had the larger effect, since interest rates had ranged up to 10 per cent per month. Although these policies can be viewed as harming the interests of the rural elite, there was also an advantage for the elite. The new village governments guaranteed that in the interest of national unity the new lower rent and interest payments would be handed over on time by the poorer villagers, if the level of charges had been approved by the governments. Such public scrutiny of financial deals between rich and poor was also intended to end the wide range of other burdens imposed on the poor, often described as 'feudal dues', such as gifts to the landlord at new year, or unpaid labour for the landlord at his family festivities.

Nevertheless the economic changes resulting from tax and rent reforms were not enough to reconstruct rural social relations. The villagers had to become involved in the running of their villages and not merely to accept the authority either of the older village elites or of the new military and political arrivals. The Communist Party began to recruit extensively among those who were seen as active in the development of mass organisations, the self-defence and militia groups, the women's associations, the youth corps and various peasant associations, that were the means to incorporate the peasants into the public life of the villages. In order to create an effective resistance, the pre-war society with its unequal sharing of power and burdens could not be recreated, since the peasant majority had then been given almost no incentive to become active in causes proposed by outside authorities. Therefore there had to be rewards for the peasants to ensure their commitment, including a chance to exercise more control over village life within the limits of wider government policy. This political role for the peasant masses, culminating in secure areas in village assemblies and direct elections, also served the Party's long-term goal of weakening the rural elite, which had previously been and would again later be defined as the class enemy. To ensure widespread participation in government, the Communists evolved by 1940 the 'Three Thirds' systems, whereby CCP members occupied a maximum of one third of places in assemblies, with one third for other progressives and one third for enlightened members of the rural elite, including Guomindang members.

The expansion of the Communist influence up to 1940, although it was achieved with the help of an unsystematic mixture of social and military policies applied according to local conditions, relied above all upon the absence of a clear rival for power. The Guomindang was neutralised by the united front and had never been politically well-established in north China anyway, while the Japanese had other priorities. This is not to say that the Communist policies for mobilisation had no importance in building Communist power. They clearly did, but in the period, 1937–40, they were given an unusual opportunity which the Communists employed to the maximum extent. This expansion allowed the Party to build a strength that could meet the enormous military challenge which arose from 1940 and to emerge invigorated and ready for new expansion when the military challenge reduced from 1943. This military challenge arose from two sources, the major one being the new focus of Japanese military efforts upon rural pacification and the minor one being the decay of the united front in military and higher political fields which culminated in the New Fourth Army incident of January 1941.

The change in Japanese military action in 1940 was provoked by the massive scale and unexpected nature of the Communist-led Hundred Regiments campaign from August 1940. During

1939 the Japanese Army had mounted a couple of unsuccessful single route attacks upon the core areas of Communist bases
in north China, but had then turned to a so-called 'cage policy',
whereby they divided up the more low-lying areas with thousands
of fortification points, ditches and walls, which cut mobility
between liberated areas and hurt their supply lines. The
Communists therefore had to devise a strategy to reduce the
effectiveness of this Japanese activity and one solution was an
all-out attack upon the whole range of Japanese positions in
north China, to allow the destruction of the fortified points
and of the Japanese-held roads and railways. Another reason
for such a large gesture was to convince the Jiang Jieshi
government in Chongqing that resistance was viable and
continuing, since there were fears that Jiang might seek an
agreement with the newly established puppet government of
Wang Jingwei in Nanjing, whereby Guomindang forces and the
Japanese would unite in anti-Communist suppression. Debate
continues among historians over the responsibility for the
Hundred Regiments initiative, arising from suggestions in the
1960s that General Peng Dehuai had acted without approval
from the Central Committee and Mao. This seems unlikely,
but the campaign was far removed from Mao's cautious military
style and his view, stated in 1938, that a Chinese counter-offensive
was a long way into the future.

The campaign involved some 400 000 troops of the Eighth
Route Army attacking Japanese positions in five provinces of
north China in August 1940, but by October the Japanese were
beginning to counterattack and the campaign petered out by
December. The Communists claimed a victory in terms of 3000
fortifications destroyed, but the longer-term results were desperately harsh for the Communists. The Japanese now turned
their full attention upon the Communist areas, reintroduced
the fortification policy and supplemented it with an attempt
to destroy anything which could assist the anti-Japanese resistance.

The method was the 'Three-all' campaign, interpreted by the
Chinese as 'Burn all, kill all, loot all'. Under this assault the
Communist areas shrank, with liberated area populations being
nearly halved and the Eighth Route Army being cut by a quarter. To defend communities the Communists devised new
methods such as extensive tunnels below villages and were forced

to increase the cooperation between the regular forces of the Eighth Route Army and the local guerrillas and militias. Given the Japanese attacks on agricultural production, it became essential for the Communist forces to become as self-reliant in food as possible, so as to minimise the burden upon the Chinese peasants, and production campaigns, by both the peasants and the military, were an essential new part of the resistance effort.

The intense Japanese pressure also required the Communist Party to ensure that its members were ideologically prepared to meet such a challenge, especially where Japanese activity left local Party organisations out of contact with their superiors for long periods of time. The 1937–40 expansion of the Party had been achieved without great concern about the quality of the new members, beyond their activism. Thus the Party had to launch a 'Rectification Movement' to discipline and direct the new members by raising their understanding of political theory and its application in the context of the resistance war. The main rectification campaign lasted from 1942 to 1944 with detailed study of writings by Communist leaders, including many by Mao Zedong. In the more politically aware rear area around the Communist capital Yan'an, the campaign met considerable opposition from those such as Wang Shiwei who feared the Party's drift towards bureaucratic methods, but in other areas the campaign served its purpose in providing a wider awareness of what being a Communist Party member entailed.

From the Party leadership's viewpoint, there was a second advantage in the Rectification campaign, because by careful selection of the study texts it was possible to eliminate views associated with Wang Ming and other Moscow-trained Party members. These had tended to interpret Marxism–Leninism in ways which were seen by Mao and his supporters as less appropriate for Chinese conditions. The approach preferred by Mao has often been called the sinification of Marxism, that is the application of the general theories and insights of Marxism–Leninism to the concrete realities of the Chinese revolutionary situation. This blend of revolutionary theory and practice in China is often called Maoism by foreign observers, although the Chinese then and now only acknowledge the role of Mao Zedong Thought, a political tool of lower intrinsic value than the supposedly universal tools of Marxism and Leninism.

Among other important ingredients it included ideas on the role of people's war, the importance of the rural areas in the revolutionary process, the need for the 'mass line' and the call from 1940 for 'New Democracy'. The mass line implied methods to ensure that the Party did not lose touch with the masses, by requiring Party policy to be derived in part from the wishes of the masses as refined by the Party's leadership in view of the total picture facing the revolution. New Democracy argued that China could move forward politically under the CCP's leadership without the destruction of the bourgeois class, since China needed its skills in modernising the nation.

Although the major pressure on the Party in 1940 to 1943 came from the Japanese, the deterioration of relations between the CCP and the Guomindang must also be mentioned. The Communists had begun the resistance war with legal acceptance from the Guomindang and received a central government subsidy for their effort to place the Eighth Route Army into battle on the basis of the very limited resources of the ShaanGanNing area. Nevertheless tensions arose between the two parties, both in Chongqing where the Communists were allowed to operate a liaison office and in the liberated areas, where military conflicts over control of territory began to occur from as early as 1939. The Communists and the Nationalists were both seeking to gain influence behind the Japanese lines, with the Communists clearly most successful in the early war years in the north.

In the area south of the Yellow River – that is much of Shandong, Jiangsu and Anhui – the situation was more confused. These were areas which had been closer to the centre of pre-war Nationalist power and the Nationalists were gravely concerned about any large-scale Communist activity there. Although the Communists' New Fourth Army had been permitted in this area, its expansion proved unacceptable to the Nationalists, who during 1940 negotiated with the Communists on the basis that Communist troops be withdrawn eventually to the north of the Yellow River. Presumably the Nationalists would not challenge them there for the length of the resistance war. As a result of these talks the New Fourth Army began to move its main operations north of the Yangzi River, possibly in preparation for a later move further north. That Army's Headquarters was however slow to move from south of the Yangzi. In January

1941 after appearing to march away from the Yangzi southwards, it was attacked and decimated by Nationalist forces. Public argument raged for several weeks over the responsibility for the incident, the Communists blaming anti-Communist feelings among the Nationalists, the Nationalists claiming insubordination. The war of words was largely won by the Communists, who highlighted the patriotic issue of the destruction of an actively anti-Japanese military force by its own side. The incident ended any remaining military cooperation between the two parties, saw the Yan'an area blockaded thereafter by some of Jiang Jieshi's best troops and left the rest of the New Fourth Army to become active in competition with the Nationalists south of the Yellow River.

At the end of 1943 the resistance war entered its third phase for the Communists, the chance to expand as Japanese forces were diverted to other war activities in the wider Pacific War. The results were impressive, with the Party at its Seventh Congress in April 1945 claiming control of nineteen liberated areas with a population of over 90 million people. This expansion drew on the skills gained by CCP members during the previous three years of difficulties which meant that this enlarged population base was firmly and actively committed to the support of the Communists when the Japanese surrendered in August 1945.

The Impact of the Anti-Japanese War on the GMD

While the Communists were expanding their popular support and gaining administrative experience in the Resistance War, the Nationalists, in contrast, faced increasing difficulties in achieving their goal of organising an efficient modern government for China. Part of the blame for these difficulties lies with the Nationalists' situation, for they were driven from their major base of activity in east China, they had to maintain a huge army in the field and they had to meet responsibilities as the internationally recognised government of China. Nevertheless it must be admitted that the major part of the problem arose from the behaviours of the civil and military officials of the government. Acts of corruption and cases of military inefficiency, although common enough before 1937, took on a new character when the economy faced extreme shortages and rising inflation and when the military were urgently required to defend the nation. The Nationalist government failed to find fully acceptable ways to share the burdens of the war and as a result, despite its apparent power on paper, it emerged in 1945 as an organisation with very weak links with the general population.

The Nationalists at Chongqing, like the Communists, regarded the war with Japan as involving a period of extensive Japanese advance, followed by a long period of stalemate, when the Japanese could not expand their territorial control. If the Japanese did attempt a local offensive, then their success at that location would be matched by small Chinese advances elsewhere. Once the stalemate was reached in early 1939, the Chongqing government only attempted one major offensive effort against the Japanese, in the early part of the 1939–40 winter. Although the Chinese won some minor victories, the conclusion reached by Jiang Jieshi and other Chinese military leaders was that the campaign was too costly for the Chinese side. Hence no further Chinese offensives were carried out.

Nevertheless, the Nationalists did continue to offer some support to the efforts of anti-Communist guerrilla forces behind the Japanese lines, especially in Shandong province, but, unlike the Communists, the Nationalists were never able to spread sufficient Party discipline to allow unified control of these guerrillas. The result was that these nominally Nationalist guerrillas, who had developed from former warlord armies or local militias, were not fully trusted by the central government which feared to strengthen local military power, and hence, with only limited material support, they were gradually eliminated in three-corner fights with the Japanese and the Communist guerrillas. To avoid destruction many of these guerrilla units defected to join the puppet armies of the Japanese, claiming later at the end of the war that they had been ordered by Chongqing to become puppets to maintain their anti-Communist activities. It is still unclear how far such defections were approved by Chongqing, but we do know that some puppet leaders remained in radio communication with Free China and that in August 1945 much of Japanese-occupied China passed into temporary puppet control which preserved these areas for the Nationalist government until the movement of formal Nationalist army units back to the eastern half of China.

The most immediate problems facing the Nationalist government after it was forced westwards in 1937 and 1938 were economic. Although the government organised the transfer of some 120 000 tons of factory equipment out of the coastal cities, the inland parts of China were unable to produce sufficient goods to satisfy the war effort and to provide adequate rewards for the government and Party elite. Thus prices of goods began to rise as demand outstripped supply.

This inflationary pressure was greatly increased by the total inability of the government to achieve a balanced budget. With the loss of the coastal cities and severe cuts in Free China's international trade, the main revenue sources of the Nanjing Decade had disappeared and hence the government was obliged to print money to overcome the fiscal deficit. It was only in 1940 that the central government was able to begin to lay claim again to the land tax as a national revenue, but by then expenditure had risen so far that the extra revenue could not cover it. Nevertheless the collection of land tax in kind and the system of compulsory purchase of grain in Free China imposed heavy burdens on the peasants, especially as the government failed to impose that burden evenly across the social spectrum, and peasants' revolts followed, as in Sichuan, the heart of Free China, in 1942 and 1943. As the inflation rate rose to 10 per cent a month by 1940, it became more profitable to hoard goods than to market them. Producers of goods found it increasingly difficult to acquire the necessary raw materials, especially cash crops from peasants, because the paper money in circulation was not respected.

The inflationary process struck hardest at the urban dwellers on low or fixed incomes, such as teachers, students, low-ranking officials and small shopkeepers, elements in society who could be expected to be more sympathetic to the long-term goals of the Nationalists, rather than of the Communists. Nevertheless their sufferings were compounded when it became clear that some other members of society were making fortunes out of profiteering in one of two ways. The first way was through insider information, which enabled senior government and Party officials or their families to manipulate access to raw materials, or to take advantage of changes in foreign exchange rates, especially against the US dollar from 1942. They acquired the assets of failing businesses at low cost and were able to arrange the letting of government contracts at a fee. The second way was through the existence of a huge trade across the front-line between Free China and the Japanese-occupied areas. Although defended by some as the rightful sharing of goods between all Chinese, in practice this trade provided war materials, such as tungsten and antimony, for the Japanese and destroyed the myth of all-out resistance to Japan. At its worst, it could even lead to Free Chinese deaths, as in the case of a famine in Guangdong, when hoarders were sending rice stocks into Japanese-held Guangzhou even while Chinese starved in Free China.

Inflation was less of a problem of survival for the peasants in Free China as compared with urban dwellers, because peasants could hope to consume their own food production within the limits of tax demands, but they faced an equal danger, conscription. In order to maintain its armies in the field, the Nationalist government had to replenish its forces with new recruits. According to official records 14 million people were conscripted, although the actual figure was almost certainly higher, given the recruiting activities of local armies beyond central control. Government regulations stated that under-age children and only sons could not be conscripted, but they often were. In the absence of a clear census or any centralised record of population information, the conscription process was carried out by quota, with the provinces allocating quotas to the counties and the counties to the villages. Local officials responsible for meeting the quotas tended to recruit from the poorer parts of the village community, who could not bribe their way out. Often the village sick were offered to meet the quota. In such circumstances the numbers conscripted bore little relation to the number of men arriving at divisional headquarters sometimes hundreds of kilometres distant: many died en route and even more tried to desert. Given that China's battlefield casualties were up to 3 million dead and that there was no official permission to leave the army after conscription, desertion and death under harsh conditions in the army must account for most of the gap between conscript numbers and the increase of at most 3 million men in the size of Chinese armies between 1937 and 1945.

Although China began the resistance war against Japan with no allies, that situation had entirely changed by 1945, with China recognised as one of the Big Four powers and in receipt of considerable overseas aid, but this diplomatic change was not without its problems for the Chongqing government. In the early years of the war military aid had come from the USSR, but had not involved any formal structures linking Soviet personnel with Chinese officials, in the absence of war between the USSR and Japan. Hence this aid did not result in any foreign interference with China's military or general policies. China's situation after Pearl Harbor in December 1941 was entirely different. China was now incorporated as part of a regional war zone, covering China, Burma and India, and was expected to cooperate with its Allies in forwarding the war against Japan. American military arrived in China, to help with training and with aerial warfare and to oversee the distribution of military aid. General Joe Stilwell was appointed as chief of staff for the war zone under Jiang Jieshi and tried to persuade Jiang to prosecute the war in ways to benefit the Allies' global ends, rather than to satisfy Jiang's own domestic ambitions of keeping Communists and regional militarists at bay until the Japanese defeat. The USA also extended US$500 million in credits in 1942, but then insisted on interfering in the use of these credits, especially when China sought to use $200 million of the credits to buy gold to sell in China.

Hence the end of diplomatic isolation brought new tensions, for China's allies expected an all-out effort against Japan, without providing sufficient compensation. Thus at the December 1943 Cairo Conference Jiang Jieshi was promised the return of all Japanese-conquered territory, including Taiwan, lost in 1895, but in immediate terms few resources were provided to China and expeditions to reconquer Burma were repeatedly postponed. This Allied approach derived from a firm US decision to devote its major effort to the defeat of Germany in Europe first, with only secondary priority to the Asian situation, but from Jiang's viewpoint it was hypocritical of Stilwell and other American officials to demand more Chinese war effort against Japan, when the USA had only a limited commitment. During 1944 the situation worsened, as Nationalist forces buckled under the Japanese Ichigo campaign. Stilwell complained of the misuse of American military aid which was provided only to units regarded as loyal to Jiang and finally sought to take personal command of the fighting including the possibility of sending US aid to Communist units. At this point Jiang demanded and received the dismissal of Stilwell by US President Roosevelt, but the opinions which Stilwell held were shared by most of the US diplomatic staff in China, whose appreciation of the Communists' fighting potential had increased after the despatch of a US observers' mission to Yan'an in mid-1944. From Jiang's viewpoint the only bright hope in 1944 was the success of US-trained Chinese troops in the reconquest of northern Burma, but even this Jiang could turn against Stilwell by claiming that these successes were at the expense of Chinese defeats in China itself.

During the last ten months of the Pacific War, Jiang Jieshi's freedom of action was restricted by two aspects of US foreign policy. One was the desire to ensure long-term peace in China and the other was the need to involve the USSR in the Pacific War to limit US casualties. The USA was aware of the con-tinuing enmity between the Nationalists and Communists in China and President Roosevelt had sent Patrick Hurley to Chongqing in September 1944 to act as a mediator. With the departure of Stilwell in October 1944 and the subsequent res-ignation of US ambassador Gauss, Hurley became ambassador and began to plan for a coalition government in China. Visit-ing Yan'an he obtained Mao's agreement for a sharing of power, but then when Jiang opposed it, Hurley was persuaded to re-pudiate the agreement, thereby earning suspicion from Yan'an and opposition from his own diplomatic staff. Nevertheless it became clear that the USA would be directly interested in the promotion of negotiations between Communists and National-ists, rather than allowing Jiang to pursue anti-Communism with-out restriction.

The USSR had not been at war with Japan up to this point, but at the Yalta Conference in February 1945, at which China was not represented, Stalin and Roosevelt discussed the condi-tions for a Soviet entry into the Pacific War. Stalin's conditions were quite clear, although historians have argued that the USSR would have joined the anti-Japanese war even if the USA had not accepted such wide-ranging terms. The USSR would enter the Pacific war three months after the defeat of Germany, as long as all the gains made by Japan at Russia's expense since 1875 were cancelled. This meant not only the return of the Kurile Islands and south Sakhalin, but also the recovery of rights in Manchuria.

Fearing leaks of information about the Yalta decisions, the American leadership – first Roosevelt and then after his death, Truman – delayed telling China of the conference details until June 1945, when Jiang was urged to seek a USSR–China treaty to embody the Manchurian arrangements. Although angered by the US diplomacy which had brazenly bargained with sovereign rights of China, Jiang was unwilling to irritate the Americans by rejecting the bargain or to risk open support by the USSR for the Chinese Communists. Hence after weeks of difficult negotiations a Sino-Soviet treaty was signed on 14 August 1945, less than a week after Soviet troops entered Manchuria against the Japanese. The treaty promised Soviet support for the National government and respect for Chinese sovereignty in Manchuria, while providing for joint exploitation of Manchurian railways for the creation of a joint Sino-Soviet base at Port Arthur and a free port at Dairen, and for a plebiscite in Outer Mongolia to allow the population to choose its future. When the plebiscite was held later, the vote was almost unanimous for the creation of an independent nation separate from China, although in practice the new state of Outer Mongolia was part of the Soviet sphere.

The End of the Second World War in China

The end of the Second World War came suddenly for China in August 1945 and was essentially unrelated to events in China. During 1945 the Japanese Army had still been able to mount offensives in China, although these were less devastating than the Ichigo campaign of 1944, and the success of the US island-hopping campaign across the Pacific meant that no landing on the China coast was necessary, despite diversionary rumours about one. The Japanese surrender came after the dropping of atomic bombs on Hiroshima and Nagasaki and news of Russian entry into the Pacific War. The surrender of the Japanese in

China was confirmed by the despatch of Prince Asaka of the Imperial family to the Japanese headquarters in China.

The surrender implied the disarming and ultimate repatriation of more than one and a quarter million Japanese troops then in China excluding Manchuria. Immediately this issue came to divide the Nationalists and Communists, for whoever took the surrender of a particular unit could anticipate gaining the weapons and territory that this unit had controlled. Hence the two sides sought to compete in accepting these surrenders. Once unofficial news of Japanese acceptance of the surrender terms reached Chongqing on 10 August, Jiang issued orders for Japanese units to remain in place and to surrender only to officials authorised by the National government, while Zhu De, the Communist commander, ordered his troops to accept Japanese surrenders without delay. Within two days, Zhu was ordering Communist units to proceed to Manchuria, while Jiang was telling Zhu to refrain from independent action. Thus the scene was set for immediate conflict between the Nationalists and Communists. The Japanese leadership in China decided to surrender only to the representatives of the national government and on 20 August sent a directive to their troops to assist the Chongqing government and to take retaliatory action if the Communists attacked. Some 1500 Japanese died in battles with the Communists over the next couple of months, as this policy was applied, although this did not prevent the Communists from taking some major towns, such as Zhangjiakou (Kalgan) in Inner Mongolia and Yantai on the Shandong coast.

The war had ended with the Communists in the rural areas of north and east China, the Japanese in the main cities of the east and the Nationalist forces mainly in the south-west, but Jiang Jieshi regarded the return of Japanese-occupied cities to Nationalist control as vital and ordered his units to proceed to them as rapidly as possible. This proved easy along the Yangzi river, where Hankou, Nanjing and Shanghai were reoccupied by mid-September, but the cities of the north were more remote from Free China. Hence it proved necessary for Jiang to seek US help on 20 September, whereupon US marines, ultimately totalling 53 000, landed at Tianjin, Qingdao and other ports, and US and British warships entered Shanghai. Further US help came in the form of an airlift of over 100 000 of China's best troops from south China to the Beiping area in October in preparation for the reoccupation of Manchuria.

US ships sought in late October to deliver Nationalist units to the Manchurian coast, but this proved impossible. The Soviet army, which had occupied Manchuria in the last days of the war, refused permission to land at Dairen or Port Arthur, claiming these were not open to non-Chinese ships, while other ports had fallen into CCP hands, as the USSR began its withdrawal from southern Manchuria. The Nationalist units finally landed south of the Great Wall at Qinkuangdao and began to fight their way north towards the Manchurian border. Nationalist victories were achieved by late November, but the rate of advance was so slow that Jiang was forced to ask the Russians to delay their required withdrawal from Manchuria, which was due to happen by early December. The Russians agreed to delay and to allow China use of major airfields close to the cities of Manchuria, thereby allowing Nationalist power to be projected into the region, without the loss of the Russian-occupied zone to the Chinese Communists. In practice the delay allowed the Russians to complete the dismantling of most of the heavy industrial plants in the area, as so-called war reparations, an estimated loss to China of US$2 billion.

While the scramble for territorial control was occurring, the Nationalists and Communists were actively discussing a political solution to their differences. To achieve this, Mao, now the undisputed head of the CCP since the Seventh Party Congress, travelled to Chongqing under the protection of US Ambassador Hurley, for a six-week stay, to meet with Jiang Jieshi. Mao did not take part in any detailed negotiating, leaving that role to Zhou Enlai, but gave an impression to the media that he was ready to collaborate wholeheartedly with the Guomindang. In the formal talks involving Zhou the two sides agreed to establish a Political Consultative Conference to discuss the general principles for achieving a 'peaceful, democratic, united and unified China' under Jiang's leadership, but it was impossible to reach specific agreements on military force reductions and on methods of appointment of officials in Communist zones. After Mao returned to Yan'an in mid-October 1945, he announced the withdrawal of Communist forces from south of the Yangzi River and the Communists began to destroy railway

lines in north China, to hinder a Nationalist return to the north.
Seeking to prevent an all-out war, the Nationalists proposed to
call the Consultative Conference immediately and urged the
Communists to cease military advances, but Mao rejected this.
On 25 November Zhou left Chongqing, signalling the end of
top-level contacts between the two sides and the following day
Ambassador Hurley resigned at the failure of his peace-mak-
ing efforts, which he blamed largely upon the allegedly pro-
Communist sympathies of his embassy staff.

Realising the serious threat of civil war in its war-time ally,
the US government decided to send one of its most illustrious
citizens, General George Marshall, to China as personal ambassador from the President. Marshall, the former chief of staff,
was instructed to make peace between the Nationalists and Communists, but his mission faced enormous difficulties, because,
despite Marshall's avowed personal neutrality as a mediator,
the US government was clearly favouring the Nationalists, in
such ways as sales of excess military equipment and the provision of military advisers. Nevertheless the early months of the
mission from late December 1945 looked very promising for a
long-term peace. Within three weeks of his arrival a truce had
been concluded, the Communists had agreed to the reoccupation
of Manchuria by Nationalist troops and the Consultative Conference opened, with a Nationalist commitment to end party
tutelage and call a National Assembly for May 1946. By the
end of February a scheme for military cutbacks had been agreed,
envisaging a Chinese Army of sixty divisions by July 1947, fifty
Nationalist and ten Communist.

Despite these hopeful signs, the situation on the ground remained tense, especially in Manchuria. There Jiang Jieshi was
now ready to request a rapid Russian departure, while Communist forces under Lin Biao were well-established in rural areas.
When the Russians withdrew from Fengtian (Mukden) on 12
March, the Communists immediately entered the city but were
driven out at once by advancing Nationalist forces. At Changchun
further north, the reverse occurred, as on 14 April the Russians handed the city over to 4000 Nationalist soldiers previously airlifted in, but these were overwhelmed by Communist
attackers in four days. The Nationalists were now obliged to
fight their way north from Mukden, finally capturing Changchun

on 23 May after a major victory over the Communists at Sipingkai.
Meanwhile, however, the Communists had taken over all the
Russian-evacuated cities in the northern half of Manchuria, such
as Harbin and Qiqihar. As the Communists were losing ground
in central Manchuria, other Communist units took the opportunity to expand in north China, threatening in particular Jinan,
the capital of Shandong province.

Marshall had been out of China when the Changchun battle
began, but on his return strove to re-establish the momentum
towards peace. Jiang Jieshi was not prepared to discuss a truce
until the capture of Changchun, but then one was agreed for
15 days starting on 7 June, later extended for another eight
days. During the truce period, negotiations continued fruit-
lessly on the issue of troop reductions and the Nationalists
demanded Communist evacuations from Manchurian cities and
other territory in inner Mongolia, Shandong and Jiangsu. Full,
open civil war dates from 30 June 1946, when the truce ended,
but in fact hostilities had never fully ceased since the Japanese
surrender. To Jiang the successes of May 1946 proved the
certainty of victory through the use of force, while to the
Communists their achievements in the resistance war and their
expansion thereafter convinced them that if handled correctly
as a mixture of political and military offensives, a civil war must
weaken and eventually destroy the Guomindang.

The Civil War

The first nine months of the civil war from July 1946 to March
1947 appear on the surface to confirm Jiang Jieshi's view, for
this was a period of Nationalist expansion. The Nationalists
managed to clear almost all Communist units from central and
south China. They also set a number of specific targets further
north for capture, including most notably the Communists'
resistance war capital, Yan'an, taken in March 1947, but success
in these ventures did not mean increased power for the
Nationalist armies for three reasons. First, the Communists
avoided large-scale battles, hence the Nationalist advance did
not imply the destruction of Communist military forces. Second,
the Nationalists were not able to consolidate their hold on lines

of communication such as roads and railways and hence the wider dispersion of Nationalist units entailed increasing problems of supply, with the risk of units becoming cut off from all supply, except expensively by air. Third, the Communists continued to expand the size of their forces, by promoting voluntary enlistment from villages engaged in land reform and by careful handling of Nationalist deserters and prisoners, who were encouraged to fight on the Communist side after a short period of political education. This last point contrasts heavily with the Nationalists' approach to Communists taken prisoner, who were regarded as security risks and hence herded away into special prison camps.

The tide of the civil war began to turn militarily from about April 1947 and during 1948 the Communist advances were spectacular, culminating in the complete capture of Manchuria in November 1948. Meanwhile Communist units had pushed south of the Yellow River into the northern side of the Yangzi valley. Moreover, as the Communists captured increasing quantities of war equipment from defeated or deserting Nationalist units, it became possible for the Communists to move in mid-1948 to large-scale positional warfare rather than depending upon guerrilla methods. The most crucial battle of the civil war was fought in late 1948 at Xuzhou, the main defence point for denying the Communists access to the lower Yangzi region from the north. The battle lasted two months, with over half a million men committed on each side, and culminated in a total Communist victory by 10 January 1949, with over 300 000 Nationalist troops taken prisoner. Thereafter the Communists were able to negotiate the peaceful surrender of Beiping and later to push across the Yangzi on 20 April 1949. Shanghai and Nanjing fell rapidly, followed later by Guangzhou in October and Chongqing in the west at the end of November. During December the remaining areas of the mainland turned to the Communists, leaving only islands, such as Taiwan and Hainan, in Nationalist hands, and areas in the far west, such as Tibet and parts of Xinjiang, to be incorporated during 1950.

The scale and speed of the Communists' military victory were impressive, but it remains to explore why the victory occurred. Any explanation of these events must draw upon at least five strands of argument, relating to the military strengths and sociopolitical programmes of the Communists, to the military weaknesses and other failures of the Nationalists and to the international context of the civil war. Neglect of the necessary complexity of the explanation will distort our understanding and lead to simplistic viewpoints, such as that, espoused by the opposition Republican Party in the USA, that US actions had 'lost China' or by Jiang Jieshi in his 1950s writings that Soviet aid had been the main ingredient in the Communist victory. Several books have stressed the collapse of the Nationalists, without admitting that what resulted was not a political vacuum which the Communists just happened to fill, but rather that the Communists planned a comprehensive programme for the replacement of Nationalist power. Some authors, dazzled by the Communist victory, have failed to note that it was not inevitable in 1949, that the Communists made mistakes and suffered some defeats and that Nationalist ineptitude was very helpful to the Communists. A heavy focus on the military aspect of the war is favoured by some, but cannot fully explain the demoralisation of the Nationalist forces and the commitment of the Communists, which relate in part to the socio-economic events in the two rival areas of China.

The military outline of the civil war has been covered above, but some comments on military strengths and weaknesses are necessary. The Nationalists began the civil war with at least a three-to-one superiority in military manpower, with a huge advantage in weaponry and with total air superiority. Nevertheless, they were unable to convert these into military victory, for two main reasons, the type of leadership in the Nationalist military and the condition of the rank-and-file soldiers. In many ways the Nationalist armies retained aspects of warlordism as generals refused to cooperate and would prefer to conserve their own units rather than help a beleaguered colleague.

These habits were reinforced by Jiang Jieshi's own leadership, which tended to reward loyalty over military effectiveness and which interfered, often disastrously, in battlefield affairs, by insisting on the defence of untenable positions at the risk of his personal displeasure. Many would regard the decision to reoccupy Manchuria in 1945 as a major error by Jiang. Jiang's desire to hold territory also led to a defensive mentality among his generals, who would not fight to break out of impending

Communist sieges, but preferred to remain safe in the short term behind city walls. This preference for garrison activity also affected the lower ranks who, while fearing to be out in the countryside, failed to maintain adequate military preparedness or discipline towards civilians in the boredom of waiting for war to reach them. The availability of a wide range of modern weaponry tended to make Nationalist officers less concerned with the morale of their men, in the confidence that firepower alone would win battles, yet it was the failure of the men to use and conserve their weapons which destroyed the Nationalists. Conditions for the peasant conscripts remained extremely poor, with officers ready to beat their men and swindle them of their pay and food, with no adequate medical back-up for battle injuries and with no organised programme to explain to the men why they were fighting. Hence desertions were rampant, especially as there was no support scheme for the soldiers' families, who had lost their labour and yet faced harsh economic circumstances.

In contrast the Communist armies had major strengths, which compensated for their early limitations in manpower and equipment. Their generals were prepared to cooperate in regional strategies, without continually looking to petty personal advantage. The central political leadership trusted that the generals understood the Party line and left the details of military affairs to the generals. The rank and file were given regular political training to create an understanding of the purpose of the civil war and received regular confirmation of the intentions of the Party in the support for their own families and in the promotion of land reform in areas conquered. Within the economic limits of the rural area, the army was supplied with arms and medical services, and food was provided for all, without undue privileges being enjoyed by the officers. Relations with the civilian population were controlled by very strict rules of conduct, with severe punishments meted out to those who did disobey. Care was taken to ensure, as far as possible, that units only fought in battles where there was a good chance of victory, although this proved impossible on occasions in 1946 in Manchuria. The Communist strategy did not require the holding of specific points, but rather the continuous reduction of Nationalist numerical strength by the elimination of weaker or isolated units. All in all the Communists had a united, able leadership commanding a motivated soldiery with flexible tactics against on enemy which lacked these qualities.

Nevertheless military factors alone could not decide the war and therefore attention must turn to other factors, both domestic and international. In my view the international factors are less important than the domestic, but by no means negligible. The civil war in China was fought in the context of the emergence of the so-called 'cold war' between the two major military victors of the Second World War, the USA and the USSR. Each side in the civil war received some support from its ultimate ally in the cold war, but the scale was limited. The most clear Soviet support was the delaying of the arrival of Nationalist troops in Manchuria in 1945, but the delay was only about six weeks. In addition the Soviet armies handed over a proportion of the Japanese arms captured in Manchuria, which allowed some upgrading of CCP weaponry, but such a windfall was more than matched by the transfer of Japanese arms in the rest of China into Nationalist hands. Formal Soviet aid was extremely limited until the dispatch of an official military mission in July 1949, but useful trade occurred between Communist-held areas of Manchuria and the USSR. Throughout the civil war the USSR maintained very correct relations with the Nationalist government and in one instance actually damaged the CCP's prospects. The CCP felt itself unable to protest the USSR's extensive looting of Manchuria, resulting in widespread criticism of the CCP as unpatriotic.

The USA was a much more active player in China, but its ability to control events was limited. With the rapid demobilisation of US forces from late 1945 and the growing financial commitment to the economic reconstruction of Western Europe, the USA lacked the resources, military or financial, to change the situation. US marines had been sent to China in September 1945 but were gradually withdrawn by February 1949, and there were no other American forces available to replace them in any possible combat role in China. US military advisers remained in China, but found their advice often disregarded by Jiang Jieshi. The US role in transporting Nationalist troops has been noted, but in the end this contributed to Jiang's defeat, for it allowed him to extend into the north and north–east beyond his capacity to supply the troops adequately or cheaply. Financial support for the Nationalists was extensive, both by the USA directly and through the largely US-financed United Nations Relief and Rehabilitation Agency (UNRRA), but the amounts never satisfied the Nationalist leadership. The Americans were aware that the aid was being squandered corruptly and, given the needs of Europe, would not offer more. The April 1948 China Aid Act authorised another US$ 460 million aid for the fiscal year, 1948–9, but was interpreted by the Nationalists as virtually a betrayal, since they had requested far more. It can well be argued that US aid to the Nationalists damaged their prospects, for it made them less willing to seek domestic ways to control their finances and it seemed to prove Communist allegations that the Nationalists were American lackeys, especially when the new China–USA treaty of November 1946 was so commercially favourable to the USA.

It remains to sketch the non-military factors which played a role in the civil war and this will also provide an opportunity to detail some of the non-military events between 1945 and 1949. On the Communist side, the most important change was the turn away from the rent and interest reduction campaigns of the resistance war years, towards full land reform – that is, the abolition of tenancy by the destruction of the landlords and the redistribution of land to the poorer peasants. Although the rent and interest reduction campaigns with their associated tax changes had caused some redistribution of village lands, this had rarely occurred with open attacks against landlords, except for traitors.

The new direction was heralded by a Central Committee directive of 4 May 1946, to transfer land ownership to the existing cultivators of the land, but the methods available were many. They included movements to struggle against landlords and settle accounts with them, direct confiscations of land, the sale of landlord holdings to tenants, the voluntary donation of land by landlords and the equal redivision of village land. Direct confiscations played a major role in Manchuria, where large tracts of land had been held by the Japanese or by their Chinese collaborators, but such confiscation did not mobilise the peasants as effectively as the movement to 'settle accounts'. In this the peasants were required in public meetings to recall the exploitation they had suffered at the hands of landlords and of the vaguer category of 'local tyrants' and to calculate what should be repaid. These repayments almost always exceeded the immediate cash resources of the landlord, and could result in the loss of some or all of his land. Theoretically the Party attempted to separate the capitalistic activities of the landlords, such as investments in local industries, from their other exploitation, but in practice such distinctions were difficult to maintain, once peasants were aroused to demand compensation.

The reasons for this shift to a more radical land policy arose from the context of impending civil war. When the enemy had been an invading foreigner, it had been possible to talk of a united front of all classes in resistance to this aggression and to demand sacrifices from all. Now that the enemy was within the nation and would seek allies within the Communist areas who could not be branded as traitors, it was necessary for the Communists to eliminate the potential power of those allies. In so doing, the Party was confirming more openly its commitment to the poorer sections of the rural community and offering them further rewards, in terms of land and goods, for their loyalty to the Party. The Party's aim was not so much the elimination of landlord economic power, which was limited in north China, but rather the overthrow of the local elite in ways which would teach the peasants that they could exercise local power.

The policy, however, was fraught with practical problems, which taxed Party leaders for two years, culminating in the Outline Agrarian Law of October 1947 and the Directive on Land Reform and Party Rectification Work of February 1948. The practical issues included the methods for distributing confiscated property, the timing and necessity of land reform in relation to the military security of an area, the problems of assigning appropriate class labels to the peasants and the task of recruiting peasants for the army without making peasants interpret land reform as merely a prelude to conscription. The Outline Law had stated that all property in the village must be equally divided, but this was seen as too much of an attack upon the middle peasants and was stopped in the February directive. Land reform had been urged even in areas where the military situation did not ensure likely protection of the confiscating peasants, such as close to or even behind Nationalist lines, but by 1948 much more caution was suggested, with newly liberated areas told to wait to implement full land reform, until the overall military situation had improved. The question of class label was of vital importance to the peasantry, since it defined who would benefit and who would lose from the redistribution process. Nevertheless the assigning of labels was incredibly difficult and was often carried out more than once in the same village with the help of visiting work teams. The most crucial boundary was between middle and rich peasant, since the middle peasants were not be forced to lose property, while the rich peasants were. To reduce the likelihood of serious mistakes, the Central Committee in 1948 finally decreed a very lenient definition, that those earning up to 25 per cent of their income by exploitation could still be classified as middle peasants.

The Party implemented the land reform through the local Communists and the despatch of work teams from higher levels, but the complexities and temptations of the process required a further round of Party rectification beginning in 1947. It was essential for the local reform cadres to understand, rather than mechanically apply, the land reform directives as these were altered in response to the analysis of the general situation. It was also necessary to maintain Party morality at a time when class enemies in the rural areas would engage in bribery and other means to gain a satisfactory outcome to the redistribution process. One common area for corruption was in the resurveying of village land, an immensely time-consuming process, given the division of village land into tiny plots. Party rectification was in part by study of relevant documents, but more importantly was by public announcement of Party memberships and subsequent public assessment of members by non-Party villagers.

As the Party gained sufficient support through its land reform programme to maintain and expand its army in the field, so that army began the gradual conquest of the cities of China, which presented new problems for the Party. Although the Party had been a co-partner in city activities before 1927, it had not run a major city alone until the capture of Zhangjiakou (Kalgan) in the north in late August 1945. To that city were gradually added the cities of Manchuria and then from late 1948 the cities of the rest of China. Some of the early takeovers in Manchuria were marked by excessive destruction and confiscation of property, but these mistakes were quickly rectified and did not occur for the later cities. On a superficial level, the Communists strove to tidy up the appearance of the cities by suppressing drug abuse and redirecting beggars, thieves and prostitutes into more productive activity, which won the praise of all outside visitors, but more fundamentally the Communists searched for means to make the cities into productive entities. This required the stimulation of industry and the control of excessive labour agitation, within an essentially capitalist structure. Gradually the Communists devised effective labour policies through trade unions to reward workers for their productivity without jeopardising the profitability of their firms. Efforts were also made to control inflation through the issue of currency not tied to the Nationalists, but results were mixed, given the Party's heavy military costs and continued inflation in Nationalist areas. Nevertheless it can safely be asserted that the Communists achieved a stability and limited prosperity in the cities, which contrasted very favourably with life in the Nationalist zones.

The Nationalist Government had ended the Second World War as the recognised government of a Great Power, with diplomatic support from the USA and the USSR and with a large army, which included thirty-nine divisions trained and, by December 1945, equipped by the USA, yet these advantages were squandered over the following four years leading to the ignominious route to Taiwan. This loss of power, although ultimately experienced on the battlefield, was also linked to the failings of the Nationalist leadership in other areas, political, economic and social. Some of the blame can be personally ascribed to Jiang Jieshi, but he only represented the most visible part of an organisation which had lost touch with the immediate needs of the general Chinese population. The Nationalist Party, which had in the mid-1920s appeared dynamic and able to generate unselfish sacrifice for China's betterment, had turned through the 1930s into a self-serving, largely military-dominated group which failed to inspire the general population or even its own members with any vision of the future. By 1945 its cynical manipulation of government and ruthless suppression of opposition had begun to lose it the support of those urban groups who might in theory have been expected to prefer its economic policies as against the potential socialism of the CCP. Nevertheless the Nationalists still retained the support of most of the rural elite, who recognised that the Nationalists would preserve traditional rural power structures, whatever nominal lip-service they paid to Sun Yixian's Principle of People's Livelihood.

The Nationalists' first commitment in August 1945 was to retake authority from the Japanese and their puppets and this task was handled badly. The inhabitants of the occupied areas were not treated as if they had suffered under the Japanese, but were regarded with disdain by the returning Nationalists. The Nationalists took several months to decide on the fate of the puppet leaders, many of whom stayed in their posts or were incorporated into the national army rather than facing trial as traitors. Property which had been taken over by the Japanese was not returned to its original owners, but became government property or was sold off to those close to the government. What is worse, in many cases where factories were taken over, they were not maintained as going concerns but their machinery was broken down and sold in pieces or as scrap. On Hainan island for example, where Japan had invested heavily, a Nationalist government survey in the late 1940s found not a single piece of machinery still complete and operable. Puppet currency which had suffered a similar inflation to that of Chongqing was redeemed at a rate of 200 to one, virtually wiping out any remaining cash assets of the citizens of the occupied area.

Despite the return to its coastal base, the Nationalist government was still unable to balance its budget and continued to depend upon the printing of banknotes to pay its way. The inflation rate began to climb, from its 10 per cent per month rate, towards 30 per cent a month and then higher. This compounded the earlier impact upon groups with relatively fixed salaries such as teachers and increased the opportunities for hoarders and speculators. Surprisingly it did not spark major unrest in industry, because the government had insisted upon indexing wages there to the cost-of-living, in the belief that no Communist insurrection could succeed if the workers were contented. In 1948 inflation reached such levels that the government decided to issue a new currency, the gold Yuan, backed by gold, silver and foreign currency which citizens were to hand in. The government guaranteed to restrict the total volume of banknote issue and to freeze prices, with Jiang Jingguo, Jiang

Jieshi's son, overseeing the programme in Shanghai. Prices held in Shanghai for a few weeks and then the currency collapsed totally, dropping almost a millionfold against the US dollar over a nine-month period.

Politically from 1945 the Nationalists claimed to be further-ing democracy and achieving the constitutional phase of Sun Yixian's vision, but this claim was severely challenged, both by the Chinese Communists and by many Western observers. In line with the Mao-Jiang talks of mid-1945, a Political Consulta-tive Conference was held in Chongqing in January 1946, attended by delegates from the Nationalist, Communist and other smaller parties. The conference reached major agreement on most matters, including the reorganisation of the government and the military and the move towards constitutional rule, but this agreement was subject to confirmation by the formal leadership of each party. When the Nationalist Central Executive Com-mittee met in March 1946 and under pressure from right-wing members revised the party's acceptance on certain issues, such as provincial autonomy, the conference unanimity began to collapse, with charges by the Communists and the smaller Democ-ratic League that the Nationalists had violated the earlier agreement.

In response the Nationalists decided to push ahead with the constitutional revision process without the participation of the Com-munists. In addition pressure was brought to bear on the smaller parties to restrict their criticism of the Nationalists, culminat-ing in the assassination of two leading Democratic League members in July 1946, one being Wen Yiduo, a leading poet. The constitutional assembly of November 1946, new constitu-tion of January 1947, elections of November 1947 and National Assembly meeting of April 1948 were thus seen as imposed by the Nationalists, without any acceptance by most of the politi-cal opposition, which boycotted these events. Although inca-pable of winning sustained support for the Nationalists, these constitutional manoeuvres did have one very long-term effect, in that the members elected to the 1948 Assembly were still sitting in the formal legislative body in Taiwan in the early 1990s, further elections having been prevented by the loss of the Chinese mainland to the Communists.

In sum, then, the Nationalists failed to expand their politi-cal legitimacy through their constitutional programme. They also failed to achieve adequate economic stability, to eradicate their image as dependent upon foreign aid or to eliminate corrupt practices from within government. With these failures, they gradually lost the support of the population of urban China, who had hoped for a period of effective reconstruction after the years of foreign aggression. The Communists, meanwhile, had increased their ability to mobilise the rural areas through the radical, but technically non-socialist policy of land reform, while achieving some success in returning cities to productive activity. The final test of strength came on the battlefield, but the result had been strongly influenced in advance by the relative qualities not just of the armies, but also of the two party organisations, of their leaderships and of their ideologies. In almost all senses, the Communists won and the Nationalists lost. Moreover this result did not depend upon late 1940s actions of those foreign powers with interests in China.

6 The Early People's Republic

The establishment of the People's Republic of China in 1949 represented the greatest opportunity for China during the twentieth century. The country was essentially geographically united, although there was some mopping up still to be done, especially in Tibet and Taiwan. The military forces which had conquered the country in the final year of the civil war remained firmly tied to the authority of the central government and its political leadership. Foreign special privileges had been eradicated, save for those of the USSR in the north-east, and foreign countries either had recognised or seemed likely to be about to recognise the new administration as the legitimate government for all China. The government had a detailed programme for development and had the aid of a large corps of dedicated and experienced administrators who could be expected to give the lead in the implementation of this programme. The rural political mobilisation by the CCP and the urban problems of the GMD in the civil war years enabled the government to hope that it was firmly supported by the majority of the peasantry and viewed with sufficient goodwill by the urban population, especially as the harshest anti-Communist critics had had time to move away to Hong Kong or Taiwan.

Although the potential for successful advance was high, a number of negative factors must be noted, some of which impinged on the immediate situation, others on the longer term. The incredible inflation in the cities was difficult to cure, given the total suspicion towards any kind of printed money, yet the Communist administration could not function without money, even if the role of barter was extended. The experience of most of the Communist cadres had been with rural and less-developed parts of China, but the government's economic development programme focused on the cities and industry, whose non-Communist experts the CCP would be forced to consult, whatever their political leanings. Moreover the economic programme with its industrial emphasis threatened to provide no adequate recompense for the peasants, the most ardent supporters of the CCP before 1949, whilst the alternative of emphasis on the peasant economy which could produce limited growth would condemn China to comparative weakness. The decision to 'lean to one side', thereby joining China with the socialist bloc, allowed access only to the technology which the USSR was willing and able to provide It also implied that China would follow Soviet advice and the Soviet model for its own development, however inappropriate that might prove to be over time.

Consolidation

The first task of the Communist government was consolidation:

- to destroy the remaining enemy troops;
- to restore the economy to its previous peaks of production;
- to reopen the networks of public transport and governmental communication;
- to spread to the whole of China the social reforms which had proved the basis of Communist strength in the Communist-held rural areas during the civil war.

The consolidation phase was estimated by Mao in June 1950 to require three years and this timetable was achieved for the most part, despite the additional strains from the Chinese involvement in the Korean War from October 1950. Success in this phase owed much to the organisational skills of the CCP and to the desire of the population for law and order and for a sense of direction after years of conflict and uncertainty. In this regard the sheer length of the previous period of national distress helped the creation of a strong thrust for an effective government. Unlike many colonial countries where an efficient if ruthless power had maintained the colonial cities and their economies until the decolonisation, China experienced the collapse of urban power in the absence of an adequate foreign protector for the cities and this allowed the rural-based revolutionaries to impose their will more easily.

The termination of the civil war and the occupation of the Qing geographic heritage was essentially achieved by the end of 1950, except for the major offshore island of Taiwan and a few small islands such as the Pescadores (Penghu), Quemoy (Jinmen) and Mazu. These remained independent of the mainland, much as Taiwan had between 1644 and 1683 at the Qing conquest. Along the coast the second largest island, Hainan, was conquered in April 1950, after Jiang Jieshi, preferring a controllable single-island haven in Taiwan, refused further help to Hainan's defenders. The Zhousan Islands off the Yangzi River mouth fell in May 1950, thereby reducing the Nationalists to aerial attacks on Shanghai as the only means of damaging central China's trade development. Gradually these attacks petered out as Soviet military aid stiffened China's air defences. Preparations were in hand in Fujian in May and June 1950 for an invasion of Taiwan, which foreign observers rated as highly likely to succeed, when the outbreak of the Korean War on 25 June resulted in American policing of the Taiwan Straits to prevent further Communist advances in East Asia.

On the Inner Asian frontier, China put an end to the various independent regimes in Xinjiang and in October 1950 troops under Liu Bocheng advanced into Tibet, fulfilling Beijing's October 1949 promise to 'liberate' Tibet. A Tibetan appeal to the United Nations won no support from the Security Council Permanent Powers, who accepted, largely at the urging of the Chinese Nationalist delegate (The People's Republic only gained its place in the UN in 1971), that China had undisputed sovereignty over Tibet. Tibetan resistance in East Tibet was crushed by the advancing Chinese army and negotiations were held in Beijing, resulting in an agreement in May 1951, whereby Tibet was granted regional autonomy within the Chinese state. In practice this meant Chinese control over the armed forces and foreign affairs, but it allowed Tibet to retain its existing social structure, including the authority of the Dalai Lama, who returned to Lhasa from India.

Restoration of the Chinese economy required a new level of expertise from the Communist leaders in the management of large economic units, and several leaders emerged to guide the economy, including Bo Yibo, Chen Yun and Li Xiannian. The main economic policy in the cities was dictated by the political line that China was in the new democratic stage of the revolution in which the national bourgeoisie was included among the progressive forces, assuming that as individuals they had not compromised too heavily with the Nationalists. Fortunately for the Communists the Nationalists had already nearly completed the expropriation of the bourgeoisie through their practice of bureaucratic capitalism, whereby state officials came to control most of China's private assets, and by the state's confiscation of all Japanese-held property in China at the end of the Second World War. As a result, after the flight of leading Nationalist officials there were few large holders of capital left and the major areas of the modern economy fell directly into the new government's hands. The government used its control over resources and power supplies to restrict the activities of the bourgeoisie within the channels acceptable to the Communists. Further pressure was placed on the national bourgeoisie by the autumn 1951 'three-antis' (*sanfan*) campaign against waste, corruption and bureaucracy, which broadened in early 1952 into the 'five-antis' campaign against bribery, tax evasion, fraud, theft of state property and theft of state economic secrets. Although these economic crimes might attract severe fines, much more damaging was the risk of being transferred across into the simultaneous, more punitive campaign against counter-revolutionaries.

The conquest of inflation was achieved through a policy of restricting government expenditure to move towards a balanced budget and the use of commodity vouchers to stabilise the market. Under this system people could surrender existing paper currency for vouchers which guaranteed the purchase of a specific quantity of vital necessities such as food and fuel, supplied from the government stores, whatever the market price. Balancing the budget proved easier for the Communists than for the Nationalists because they could draw upon the rural surplus and their officials were accustomed to lower wages often paid in kind. In addition Communist control and rapid rehabilitation of the transport system allowed more efficient distribution of the taxes collected in kind. Prices stabilised during 1950 and the *Renminbi* or people's currency, first issued locally in late 1948, was circulating nationally by early 1951, administered by the People's Bank of China. Prices expressed in the new currency rose very gradually during the 1950s (about 10 per cent rise in retail prices for 1952 to 1959) but after rising sharply between 1960 and 1962 (about 25 per cent rise in retail prices) settled into great stability, until inflation began again in the late 1970s.

Land Reform

In the countryside restoration of economic activity was directly tied to the revolutionary programme of land reform, which was extended to the centre and south of China during 1950. It was assumed that peasants who gained land from redistribution would be keen to raise production and thereby provide sufficient food for the urban areas while enriching themselves. It was also assumed that removal of the landlord class across the whole of China would reduce fears of restoration of Nationalist rule and would create a secure atmosphere conducive to the achievement of production. Although this latter assumption proved correct, especially where involvement in the accusation and death of landlords tied the peasants to the new regime, the first was less clearly correct in practice. Peasants often found they could raise their own standards of living while producing less output, as they no longer lost a considerable proportion of output as rent and high interest on loans to the landlord or moneylender. The process of land reform in the PRC was to be carried out in accordance with the Land Reform Law of 30 June 1950, which provided for the classification of peasants into five categories (landlord, rich, middle, and poor peasant and rural worker) and the redistribution of land from the landlord and rich peasants to the others. Classification work was aided by work teams of outsiders, 270 000 in the case of the East China region, who entered the villages to meet with peasants, discuss grievances and establish peasant associations, relying on the tenants and small farmers. General rules for peasant associations were issued in July 1950 and guidelines for rural class determination in August 1950, drawing on CCP documents from 1933. The Land Reform Law prohibited the use of force, but in many cases this proved impossible, especially where peasants became incensed in bitter accusation meetings against landlords, as the land reform campaign merged into a movement for 'settling accounts'.

The land reform in the whole of China from 1947 to 1952 resulted in the confiscation of 46.6 million hectares of land, about 40 per cent of China's arable area, from about 4 per cent of the population and its redistribution to some 300 million peasants, 60 per cent of the rural population. In addition, rents totalling up to 35 million tonnes of grain per annum were cancelled and draft animals, tools, hoarded foodstuffs and much landlord housing were redistributed. The process was officially ended at the issuance of new land certificates in each village, although in practice land reform often led directly into the development of mutual aid teams and more advanced forms of collective farming. The exact level of violence in land reform has been difficult to verify, the government later admitting 800 000 executions in the land reform and suppression of counter-revolutionaries campaigns, and careful analysis of local figures issued at the same time implying anything up to three or four times this amount. These deaths were seen as justifiable by the new government in terms of eradicating the power and prestige of the landlord system and in ensuring peasant commitment to the new society.

Land reform also played a role in the emancipation of women, a task which the CCP saw as vital to improve basic social conditions and which was more directly tackled by the Marriage Law of 1 May 1950. This law prohibited arranged marriages, provided for the dissolution of forced marriages through easier divorce proceedings and ordered secondary wives or concubines to leave their husband's homes. Later regulations of September provided people's courts for cases of tyrannical husbands. Divorces numbered 186 000 in 1950, 409 000 in 1951 and 396 000 in the first half of 1952, as many unsatisfactory arranged marriages were dissolved, but divorces also proved necessary where the now very socially acceptable Party activists, who might be already married, acquired new, more desirable brides, who also might be married. Tensions in the divorce situation and the plight of secondary wives induced many suicides by women, well over 10 000 in 1950 alone. Land reform seemed to offer greater opportunities for women's status and independence, since women received land in the redistribution, but by 1953 the central government recognised that marriage reform had been only hesitantly accepted, as old practices of arranged marriages, use of marriage go-betweens and bride-price continued. Despite this realisation the government insisted that divorce should be granted as sparingly as possible, after the initial rectification of pre-1949 anomalies, and encouraged mediation and community pressure to keep marriages intact, except in cases where one partner had been accused of severe political crimes.

The Political Structure

The political structure established in 1949 was a mixture of Communist practice in the pre-1949 liberated areas and of additions necessary for ruling the whole nation. Control at the day-to-day level rested with Communist cadres and with the military commanders who had completed the civil war victories, but long-term arrangements had to be codified by new institutions. The Party had decreed that a people's democratic dictatorship would serve as the basis for rule, following the analyses developed by Mao since his essay, 'On New Democracy', of 1940. Under this scheme, the CCP, as the party of the proletariat, was the leader of the working class in alliance with the peasantry, while a broad united front including the petty and national bourgeoisie would be given a role in government, under the guidance of the CCP. Elements from the bourgeois classes could be represented by the eight 'democratic parties' allowed to operate under the new regime, including the Democratic League and the Guomindang Revolutionary Committee, formed from disaffected Nationalist Party members. These parties were only granted very limited rights for new recruitment and propaganda, and in practice only 9 per cent of the population could enlist in them.

The first national political institution established by the CCP was the Chinese People's Political Consultative Conference (CPPCC), which met in Beijing from 21 September 1949 after a preparatory session in June. The delegates, presided over by Mao, were drawn from the political parties, mass organisations, the army, and the provisional regional governments, and adopted two vital documents, the Organic Law of 27 September and the Common Programme of 29 September, which provided, in effect, a provisional constitution for China. The Organic Law established the Central People's Government Council which in turn was to set up the State Administration Council, the Revolutionary Military Council, the Supreme People's Court and the People's Procurator-General's Office. The Government Council was chaired by Mao, with six deputy chairmen, Zhu De, Liu Shaoqi, and Gao Gang, from the CCP, Madame Sun Yixian, as a symbol of continuity with Sun's revolution, Li Jishen from the Revolutionary GMD and Zhang Lan of the Democratic League. Total membership was sixty-three, with thirty-two Communists. The State Administration Council, later known as the State Council, under premier Zhou Enlai, had ten CCP and eleven non-CCP members in its consultative and decision-making bodies and oversaw thirty-one ministries, shared among fifteen CCP and sixteen non-CCP ministers. The Military Council was dominated by the CCP, with twenty-one out of twenty-eight members. The power-sharing in the government organs was symbolic of the approach adopted in the Common Programme, that China was a state under People's Democratic Dictatorship with state power exercised by a people's democratic united front.

The CPPCC was to exercise the functions of an all-China People's Congress, until the latter could be convened with the development of representative structures. Local representative conferences to replace military rule at the township and county level were convened in a third of China's counties in 1950 and in almost all in 1951, with the members nominated, but in 1952 moves were made towards open elections. Elections for a 1953 National People's Congress were announced in December 1952, with the electoral law promulgated in March 1953. By this law township elections were direct, by show of hands or secret ballot of all over 18 years old, except those deprived of voting rights. The township congress elected delegates to the County Congress, which in turn elected delegates to the Provincial Congress, which then chose delegates for the National level. Such a hierarchy of indirect elections could not be completed quickly. The National People's Congress – delayed a year – first met in September 1954, and passed the Constitution on 20 September.

Major administrative power in the first years of the PRC lay in the regional structure, which developed from 1948 to 1950 with the advance of military operations and in recognition of the disparities within China. Six regions were created under an Organic Law of December 1949, two under civilian regional government in north China and north-east China, and four under military administrative committees in the north-west, centre–south, the east and the south-west. Each regional government had a majority of CCP members in controlling positions, with the military officers of the four Field Armies dominant in the four military committees. Although the central government claimed all taxes for the Centre in 1950, from 1951 some taxes were allotted to the regions.

The north-east area, under Gao Gang, was regarded by observers at the time as being much more closely tied to the USSR than were the other areas of China. It had its own 1949 agreement for exchange of Chinese agricultural products for Russian industrial equipment, to replace what the Russians had stripped out of the north-east in 1945 and 1946. It also received the help of Russian advisers. Some leaders in the north-east suggested that the policy of new democracy was unnecessary there as full socialism could be attained in this area, because of the background of Japanese rule and capitalist development from 1931 to 1945. The six-region structure was abolished in June 1954. Gao Gang and the leader of east China, Rao Shushi, were both expelled from the CCP in early 1955, because their previous handling of their regions was seen by the central government as too independent. This expulsion marked the first internally disciplined dismissal of top leadership of the CCP since its consolidation under Mao in the early 1940s, but unlike subsequent dismissals this one has not been the subject of re-evaluation and argument in later CCP struggles.

Early Foreign Relations

The initial consolidation of the PRC required the formulation of a comprehensive foreign policy, both to deal with the remnants of foreign activity in China and to chart a new role for China in the world. This policy was a continuation of the CCP's anti-imperialist policy and a confirmation of China's adherence to the socialist bloc. Although the unequal treaty rights had been abolished in 1943, there did remain the presence of foreign businesses, consular establishments and missionaries, which could be viewed as still harming Chinese sovereignty. The new government set out to destroy those remnants belonging to all countries save the USSR, by a policy of harassment, taxation and control, with the result that nearly all non-Soviet foreigners were either withdrawn or ejected by 1952, with the foreign-held property being taken over by the Chinese. This process of virtual confiscation soured relations between the PRC and the Western nations, which were to be further embittered by the Korean War. Financial problems relating to confiscated assets were only finally resolved in the case of the USA in 1979.

Relations with the USSR provided a direct contrast, with the visit of Chairman Mao to Moscow for almost three months from December 1949 to discuss at the highest level the amicable ending of Soviet special rights in China and the extension of Soviet aid to China. The length of Mao's stay was exceptional and has been taken to imply that the negotiations were by no means easy. Although Mao and the CCP had been careful, especially in CCP materials put out in the Russian language, to give due deference to the Soviet leader Stalin, the CCP was not prepared to be totally subservient to the USSR and Mao saw himself as an important theoretician. The addition of China to the socialist bloc was a propaganda victory of enormous worth, but the request to supply China with large-scale aid cannot have been too welcome, given the demands within the USSR itself from losses in the Second World War and continuing tensions in Europe.

The negotiations with the USSR produced agreements in February and March 1950, which were formally ratified on 30 September 1950, relating to Soviet rights and to an alliance between the USSR and the PRC, in theory directed against the resurgence of Japanese militarism. The USSR agreed to return the Manchurian railways to China without compensation by the end of 1952 and to abandon its position in Port Arthur and Dairen at the signature of a peace treaty with Japan or by the end of 1952, whichever was earlier: the Korean War caused the extension of this time limit, but the two towns were relinquished in

1955. Three joint-stock Sino-Soviet companies were established, one to operate airlines between China and the USSR, and two to develop Xinjiang's oil and non-ferrous mineral resources. Direct aid was a loan of US$ 300 million, to be used over five years to buy Soviet equipment, with repayment between 1954 and 1963 at 1 per cent interest payable in raw materials, gold and US dollars. Agreement was reached on 141 projects to be built with Soviet aid, and Soviet advisers and technical data were made available to China. The alliance was for a thirty-year term, renewable thereafter. Despite the deterioration of Sino-Soviet relations from 1960, the treaty was not abrogated, until Chinese notification in 1979 that an extension would not be sought.

The international situation of the PRC changed with the outbreak of the Korean War on 25 June 1950, which rapidly reversed the withdrawal of US interest in the Chinese civil war. The US Seventh Fleet was ordered into the Taiwan Strait, preventing the Communist takeover of Taiwan, and some analysts have suggested that although China would have welcomed a North Korean advance into the South in or after August 1950 the June timing could not have been worse for China, when the Chinese civil war seemed so close to completion. In Korea the North Korean advance was met by military intervention under United Nations auspices and with US forces as the main units. The Chinese response was to suspend talk of demobilising the army and to proclaim support for the North Koreans. After the UN landing at Inchon on 15 September Chinese denunciations of the USA increased and after South Korean forces crossed into North Korea on 1 October, Premier Zhou informed the Indian ambassador on 3 October that China would intervene if UN forces crossed the 38th parallel into the North. After US forces under General MacArthur had crossed the parallel without due attention to the Chinese warnings, Chinese troops, officially known as volunteers, moved quietly into Korea. Initial clashes with UN forces on 25 October were followed by a three-week lull, during which the UN forces did not withdraw despite proof of Chinese commitment. Renewed fighting in November pushed the UN forces back with heavy losses and the war reached a stalemate near the 38th parallel, until an armistice was finally signed in July 1953.

The Korean War played a crucial role in establishing the pattern of China's foreign relations for more than twenty years. First, the intervention of the USA in the Taiwan Strait prevented the conquest of Taiwan, and the USA undertook to develop Taiwan economically and militarily under Jiang Jieshi as a bastion of anti-Communism in East Asia. Second, the enmity of the USA and its allies was directed very vigorously against the PRC, both in trade terms, whereby the restrictions on trade with the PRC were among the most stringent restrictions imposed against the Communist block countries, and in political terms. Third, the USA, using Japan as a base for UN operations in Korea, pushed for a Japan peace treaty, which was signed in San Francisco in September 1951, by all the opponents of Japan in the Second World War, except China and the USSR. Furthermore Japan, although now nominally independent and no longer occupied by its conquerors' forces, still played host to American forces and followed American foreign policies, especially over close relations with Taiwan and a closed door against the PRC. Fourth, there was no longer any possibility of the PRC taking over the China seat at the UN from Jiang Jieshi's representatives, since the PRC was branded as the aggressor in Korea and votes at the general assembly by countries friendly to the USA would keep the PRC out until 1971. Fears of Chinese expansionism in Asia led to a US–South Korea mutual security pact in October 1953 and to US support for the French in Indo-China up to 1954 and to the South Vietnamese government thereafter. Lastly the Korean War pushed the PRC more firmly into the socialist bloc, but at the same time the PRC was to receive its first demonstration of the limited largesse of the USSR, which failed to provide its best equipment to the Chinese forces and expected China to pay for its provisions, despite the role of the war as a defence of the socialist bloc. Internally the Korean War served to develop national pride by showing that China had now regained sufficient strength to challenge American might successfully and the demands of the war were an effective patriotic means of tightening controls on the economy and of pursuing counter-revolutionaries more relentlessly.

Economic Growth and Socialist Transformation

With its economy basically rehabilitated to pre-war peak levels by 1952 and with the political structure determined as a CCP-dominated people's democratic dictatorship, the PRC was ready in 1953 for attempts to accelerate economic growth and to carry further the socialist programme of the CCP. The major model available for the CCP planners was that of the USSR, with its reliance on heavy industry and on the role of the central bureaucracy in determining targets. Care however would be needed to avoid heavy losses in the socialisation of agriculture, losses which might have been politically acceptable in the early USSR with its historic surplus of exportable grain, but which were economically impossible in the subsistence-level small-farm Chinese countryside. Complications arose for the Chinese leadership from two sources as the Soviet model was applied in the period, 1953–7, most importantly because the model proved unsuitable in certain respects given China's economic conditions and also because the USSR entered into a period of change after Stalin's death in 1953, culminating in the de-Stalinisation moves under Khrushchev in 1956, which called into question parts of the Soviet methodology.

Officially the General Line of Socialist Transformation was announced by Mao on 1 October 1953, after two major work conferences on economic and organisational questions between June and September, but in practice changes in agrarian organisation had begun before this date. Although land reform had solved the immediate problems of inequality in the countryside it alone did not seem to offer great opportunities for raising production further, since each private land-holding was so small and there was a lack of capital to invest in better tools or land improvement. The only major resource available in rural areas was manpower, which was generally under-employed, except at certain peak moments of the agricultural cycle, when there was a temporary shortage of labour. The obvious course, which was also positively encouraged by socialist theory, was to organise labour collectively in such a way as to raise the number of days worked in the fields, thereby allowing the development of new land and the more intensive cultivation of the old, by double-cropping, by improving water

control or by increased application of fertilisers. Some traditional Chinese villages had had labour-sharing schemes, especially
on a seasonal basis, and the CCP encouraged the creation of
Mutual Aid Teams of five households on average on this pattern, whereby team members cultivated fields jointly and sometimes acquired tools in common. By December 1951 43 per
cent of rural households were in mutual aid teams, 58 per cent
by March 1953. Although the teams could operate successfully
to overcome labour shortages at peak times, there were difficulties over the timetabling of group labour and over the allocation of labour to improvement work, because the private nature
of land ownership repeatedly brought selfish wishes to the fore
in the decision-making process.

To overcome these problems it was necessary to pool land
in the gradual development of collective farming in which individual claims to land would disappear, thereby allowing the
collective unit to benefit from land and productivity improvements. The timetable for the collectivisation process was a subject
of considerable debate among the higher leaders of the CCP.
Some argued that it was not possible to achieve full collectivisation before mechanisation was widely available in agriculture
and that too rapid a development would exceed the political
consciousness of the peasants. Others such as Mao placed trust
in the revolutionary potential of the rural areas and in the
ability of collectives to finance future improvements such as
mechanisation. Experimental regulations for Agricultural Producer Cooperatives (APC) were issued in December 1951 and
further revised in February 1953 with 14 000 cooperatives in
existence by March 1953.

These APCs were nearly all lower-level cooperatives – that is,
agricultural land remained under private ownership with members receiving payment according to their property input and
their work. These differed from fully socialist or higher APCs
in which payment was only for work done, with private ownership restricted to houses and vegetable gardens. In the lower
APCs, which up to 1954 averaged from ten to twenty households, two share funds were created, a production expenditure fund into which cash was paid on joining to meet crop
expenses under ordinary circumstances and a common property share fund. This latter fund represented the sum required

to buy the members' large tools, and in many cases all the animals from the members: each member was credited for the items supplied to the cooperative on joining it and any deviations from the average ownership of tools and animals were to be rectified, either by paying the cooperative in cash if he owned less than the average or by the cooperative paying out cash if he had contributed more than the average. In both cases cash payments could be delayed for up to three years and state loans were made to poor peasants with few assets seeking to join cooperatives: these loans were often written off later, resulting in state subsidy for the cooperative process. Distribution of lower APC output to the members was on the basis of land shares and labour input. Where land had been evenly distributed the initial ratio for output distribution could be 40:60 or even 20:80 for the land:labour input, but where it was necessary to get middle peasants to join, ratios of 60:40 were common. Although land shares were recognised the actual boundary markers in the fields were removed and the land cultivated in larger units.

Development of the lower APCs became accepted general policy in late 1953, when it became clear that land reform was not guaranteeing adequate food supplies to the cities nor providing sufficient capital for industrial development. The cooperative would be a much simpler unit to deal with administratively than would individual farmers, especially when the state in November 1953 imposed the planned purchase and supply of grain, whereby the state monopolised the bulk grain market with prices set on the basis of the 1953 free market prices. This soon developed into a quota system whereby the peasants were to produce certain quantities of crops with 80 to 90 per cent of the surplus production having to be sold to the state. The state monopoly on grain was paralleled by the creation of a national grain rationing system and of a system of residency permits.

The Chinese were divided into rural growers of grain and essentially urban ration-card-holders, with residency permits granting urban or rural residence in a fixed place. People were not allowed to move without the permission of their local leadership and of the leadership where they wished to go, which in the case of a city, would have to guarantee a job and sponsor an urban ration book. Although this package of measures was designed to ensure equitable distribution of grain and to prevent speculative profiteering by the peasants, its long-term effect was enormous and not all to the good. The urban–rural divide became increasingly marked, with the urban population secure in food and privileged in income, medical care, education and recreation and with the peasantry less well provided for, except possibly in housing. Movement between the two became very difficult and acquiring an urban permit or transferring permits between cities became a frustrating task for the individual and a source of immense power to the lower bureaucracy.

The numbers of lower APCs grew rapidly to 114 165 by the autumn of 1954, after Mao in December 1953 had threatened purges of officials dissolving APCs. Local officials and cadres were sent down to the peasants to explain the advantages of the cooperative system and in some cases offered material inducements to peasants to join, but problems arose from the poor quality of local leadership and from attempts at coercion. Because of these problems the drive towards APCs was twice halted or even in some places reversed, but it began again in 1955. When the First Five Year Plan (1953–7) was finally officially published on 5 July 1955, it estimated that 33 per cent of rural households would be in APCs by 1957, but Mao, following two months of high level argument on the pace of cooperativisation, addressed a meeting of provincial CCP secretaries on 31 July 1955 with a demand for 80 per cent of peasant households to be in lower APCs by spring 1957. This acceleration of the APC programme was accompanied by a growing push towards the fully socialist higher APCs in which work alone determined income and the dividends on land were ended, with the land no longer withdrawable from the common pool. The acceleration was aided by the good harvest in 1955 and by the renewed search for village activists, but in 1956 signs of resistance to collectivisation appeared with some slaughter of livestock and hoarding of grain. Nevertheless the programme was essentially completed by spring 1957, with 670 000 higher APCs providing for 114 million peasant households, an average of about 700 people per collective.

Although agriculture was called upon to grow at least as fast as population growth of about 2 per cent per year, the major aim of the CCP was to boost the growth of the rest of the economy, in particular industry. Such growth would reduce the impact of the weather on the economy, by reducing the relative importance of agriculture, and would allow the development of the industrialised society which the CCP regarded as modern and as the only viable basis for socialism. The First Five Year Plan allocated 46.5 per cent of investment to capital goods industry in an attempt to create a heavy industrial base in China. Most of the investment was internally generated in China, with domestic saving vastly increased over the levels of the 1930s. Calculations imply that by the end of land reform in 1952 about half of this increased domestic saving was generated by agricultural taxes and by raising prices of items sold to peasants and it seems likely that further savings were squeezed out of the peasantry from 1953 on. This was in strong contrast with the 1930s situation where the central government was unable to mobilise agricultural resources for its own needs and had to resort to taxing the modern sector of the economy.

Although internal savings were dominant, the role of Soviet aid was crucial for more complex projects. Soviet aid credits by agreements in 1950 and 1954 totalled US$425 million towards 156 major projects and in 1956 the USSR agreed to supply 55 new projects for US$625 million to be paid for out of current trade. Not all these projects were completed but 166 were, in iron and steel, power generation, machine tools, chemicals and other industries. Further projects were sketched out in 1958 and 1959, only to be halted by the withdrawal of Soviet advisers in 1960. Some 10 000 Chinese went to the USSR for technical training in the 1950s and over 10 000 Soviet technicians went to China to provide support for the projects and to explain technical data, including the blueprints for over 1400 other factories.

Growth was not the only commitment in the industrial and commercial sectors, because the socialist transformation which was occurring in agriculture was also extended into these areas. Private ownership was already limited in the industrial sector by 1952 when consolidation was completed, and the move to end private ownership in late 1955 met with little difficulty, the remaining entrepreneurs being awarded dividends on their capital investment at 5 per cent per year. In many cases they were kept on as managers in the nationalised firms, since other expertise was lacking, but they were joined by CCP cadres to ensure the political rectitude of their management decisions. More problems of organisation faced the ending of private ownership in the commercial and service sector, much of which had been carried out by individuals or very small concerns. Here the main thrust was towards the creation of state-controlled cooperatives, a process completed by 1957.

The Intellectuals

Besides reorganising agriculture and industry, the CCP had to devise policies for the mobilisation of intellectuals throughout the community. For the CCP, 'intellectuals' implied all those who had completed higher middle school education, although the Party also talked of 'higher intellectuals', defined as professionals, scholars and creative artists, numbering about 100 000 in the early 1950s. Two conflicting forces were at work in mobilisation policies for intellectuals – the desire to take advantage of the intellectuals' skills, which might need a relatively free and open atmosphere to flourish, and the fear that the intellectuals might not uncritically support the general line of the CCP, therefore requiring care and control from the Party. Given the Party's commitment to industrialisation, it was essential in economic terms to employ the highly educated minority in China for the most rapid development possible, especially those with technical and scientific knowledge. The Party believed that it had gained general support from the intellectuals in 1949 as an organisation deemed capable of restoring order and re-establishing China's national prestige, but this did not mean blanket approval of all Party policies nor did it necessarily guarantee intellectual commitment to Marxist–Leninist ideology.

The Party's approach relied upon a mixture of coercion towards and support for intellectuals and was promoted through a series of campaigns usually termed 'thought reform'. To support the intellectuals, the state arranged for the provision of salaries and other facilities for them and organised them into Party-controlled associations for each intellectual area, such as the Chinese Writers Union. Our knowledge of the thought-reform campaigns in the 1950s draws heavily upon the criticisms of literary figures, since the available written evidence is greatest in this field, but it is assumed that those in the creative arts and humanities were more severely involved and affected by the campaigns than were those in scientific pursuits. In 1951 a campaign was launched to persuade intellectuals to turn from Western theories and to adopt theories from the Soviet Union, while a rectification in literary fields was promoted by the novelist Ding Ling, herself a target of Party criticism in the early 1940s. A more relaxed atmosphere followed in 1953 and early 1954 with the ending of the Korean War, as intellectuals were permitted to criticise Party cadres and many appealed for higher professional standards with less involvement of Marxist–Leninist theory.

In the latter part of 1954 with the anticipated announcement of the First Five Year Plan the Party began a vigorous effort to control the intellectuals, culminating in the 1955 campaign against Hu Feng, which was extended beyond the intellectual community to enter the general populace. The 1954 campaign began with attacks on Yu Pingbo, a literary scholar who had failed to remould his interpretations of an eighteenth-century novel to conform with Marxism–Leninism, but soon spread to include attacks on the May Fourth leader, Hu Shi, then in Taiwan, for his pragmatic methods of gaining knowledge without preconceptions, and the writer, Feng Xuefeng, for his denunciations of the falsifying of reality in Chinese literature since 1949. The target changed to Hu Feng in 1955, first because he had called for more personal autonomy at a time when the state required dedication to Party-determined goals and second because he had been at odds with leaders of the Party's Propaganda Department, especially Zhou Yang, since the 1940s. The anti-Hu Feng campaign developed into a general attack on all those holding views differing from the current orthodoxy, with many labelled as counter-revolutionary, not only among the intellectuals, and with Hu and those close to him purged from their positions, imprisoned and denounced by their colleagues.

The intensity of the attack against intellectuals in 1955 meant that when the Party sought to mobilise support for economic programmes to increase production at the end of 1955, the intellectuals were unwilling to contribute effectively, for fear of possible future persecution. In response the premier, Zhou

Enlai, in January 1956, proposed reforms to improve the working conditions and the independence of intellectuals. In May, in a speech, the full text of which was not published, Mao offered the slogan, 'Let a hundred flowers bloom, let a hundred schools contend', the flowers referring to creative work in arts and literature, the schools to theories in the scientific arena. Mao's speech drew not only on the Party's desire to encourage intellectuals, but also on the realisation that the new Soviet leader, Khrushchev, had denounced the former leader, Stalin, in February 1956 and that Stalinist abuses must be prevented in China, by allowing some criticisms to be voiced. Nevertheless the readiness of the intellectuals to speak up was limited, with some short stories appearing in 1956 depicting problems of bureaucratic heavy-handedness and urging a more independent press. These stories, although portraying idealistic youth struggling for a more socialist future, were regarded with distaste by Party cadres who saw the relaxation of controls as a threat, and articles began to appear in early 1957 against the Hundred Flowers approach.

Into a situation where the Party was uncertain of the value of relaxing controls on intellectuals and where the intellectuals were reluctant to speak out, Mao introduced his speech, 'On the correct handling of contradictions among the people' on 27 February 1957. This speech spelt out his theory that contradictions and class struggle remained within a developing socialist society and that many of these contradictions could be resolved non-antagonistically – that is, through democratic methods of discussion and criticism. The speech was not presented at a Party meeting, but at a state conference, where many Party members reportedly walked out, and the contents of the speech were not reported in the official press immediately. The intellectuals' response was still muted, but finally after more urging by Mao, the Party accepted by May 1957 that a rectification movement could occur, with non-Party members offering criticism of the Party members. What followed was a growing rush of criticisms by intellectuals and students, not merely of individual Party members but of the system, with calls for a more open society and even for the disbanding of the Party. Opinions vary as to whether Mao provoked this whirlwind of criticism in order to deceive and later remove all the major non-Party critics or whether Mao hoped that the intellectuals after more than seven years of CCP rule would be favourably disposed towards the Party and its achievements in the economic and social spheres. The latter opinion has more to commend it, since Mao would hardly have struggled so hard to activate the intellectuals in the face of strong Party opposition, if his purpose was to prove his Party opponents correct in their dim assessment of intellectuals.

The Hundred Flowers movement was transformed in June 1957 into a vigorous anti-rightist campaign, particularly after the publication on 18 June of an amended version of Mao's February speech, with precise limits on the scope of criticism spelt out, limits which had clearly been exceeded in May. Those who had spoken out in May and June were subjected to condemnation, but more importantly the anti-rightist campaign was spread to include others such as the writers Ding Ling and Feng Xuefeng who had been criticised in previous campaigns but had remained quiet in 1957. Quotas of 5 per cent of rightists in a unit were set and had to be fulfilled, even in units with few educated personnel. The punishments applied to rightists included loss of position and political rights, being sent to the countryside for labour reform and, for many Party members, loss of that membership. It is estimated that somewhere around half a million intellectuals were branded as rightists, and these labels, along with the stigma they imposed, stayed with many of these individuals until the late 1970s, when a major effort to reverse or cancel the labels was begun after Mao's death.

Foreign Policy 1953–7

During the period of the First Five Year Plan and the various campaigns on the intellectual front, the People's Republic also had to continue to develop its international relations. Two major changes in 1953 coincided with the shift towards economic mobilisation – the death of the Soviet leader Stalin on 5 March, and the armistice in the Korean War in July, achieved after China's relaxation of its views on repatriation of prisoners of war. The death of Stalin permitted the Soviet Union to adopt a more equal approach to China, with senior Soviet leaders visiting Beijing for the first time in 1954 and there agreeing to the winding up of the joint-stock Sino-Soviet companies set up in 1950 and offering further credits. The ending of the Korean War enabled China to become a participant in international diplomatic conferences in Geneva during 1954, the first from April to mid-June on Korea, with no progress achieved, and the second from mid-June on the situation in Indo-China where the collapse of French colonial power had threatened major international involvement. The Chinese, led by Premier Zhou Enlai, sought to contain this involvement, so close to Chinese territory, and did not hesitate to pressure the North Vietnamese to accept a truce agreement which gained less than their immediate military position seemed to permit.

At the same time as this wider diplomacy in Europe, the Chinese signed an agreement with India in April 1954 which recognised Chinese sovereignty in Tibet. This included in its preamble five rules, later entitled 'the Five Principles of Peaceful Coexistence', at a meeting on June 1954 between Zhou Enlai and the Indian prime minister, Nehru. The principles were:

1. mutual respect for territorial integrity and sovereignty;
2. mutual non-aggression;
3. mutual non-interference in internal affairs;
4. equality and mutual benefit;
5. peaceful co-existence.

Some of these principles had been stated in earlier declarations by Mao, but the complete set became an important feature of Chinese diplomacy thereafter. In harmony with these principles was the Chinese position at the Afro-Asian conference of independent nations, held in Bandung in April 1955, where premier Zhou stressed the need for peaceful coexistence to allow the nations of Asia and Africa to progress. At the conference China also offered to open talks with the USA to reduce mutual tensions, an offer which resulted in a limited channel of communication being opened between Chinese and American ambassadors, first, in Geneva and later for many years at Warsaw, but resolution of major issues between the two nations proved impossible. A parallel improvement of relations with

Japan occurred, despite Japan's treaty arrangements with Taiwan, and by 1957 some two-thirds of the members of the Japanese Diet had visited China.

The general improvement in China's diplomatic position from 1953 was gradually threatened from 1956 by the results of the attack on Stalin by the new Soviet leader, Khrushchev, which called into question many of the principles and procedures of the socialist bloc. The CCP's first response, published on 5 April 1956 as 'On the historical experience of the dictatorship of the proletariat', was to urge a more balanced assessment of Stalin's achievements and faults, while asserting that Marxist–Leninist parties need leaders and that contradictions, such as that between the cult of the individual leader and the development of the socialist system, were possible under socialism. This last idea was removed from the translation of the article as it appeared in the Soviet newspaper, *Pravda*, on 7 April 1956. The impact of de-Stalinisation in Eastern Europe was dangerous for the Soviet Union, with unrest in Poland, over which the Chinese supported the new Polish leadership, and with the need for a military intervention in Hungary, which the Chinese wholeheartedly supported. In January 1957 Zhou Enlai visited Eastern Europe to seek to bolster support for the Soviet Union, but on a theoretical level the CCP argued that contradictions between leaders and the masses could be expected, even in Communist countries, a view which the Soviets had never accepted. This view led into the escalation and subsequent suppression of the Hundred Flower movement within China in May and June 1957, but by the time Mao travelled to Moscow for the fortieth anniversary of the Russian Bolshevik revolution in November 1957, it seemed that Sino-Soviet relations were still good, especially with a secret military agreement of 15 October which related to delivery of nuclear technology to China.

At the November meeting Mao began to urge the Soviet Union to take advantage of the new military technology available to the USSR, namely the ballistic missile and the first orbiting satellite, to be more assertive in the psychological battle between the socialist East and the capitalist West. He talked of US imperialism as a 'Paper tiger' and argued that a nuclear war should not be feared, since only capitalism would be destroyed by it, not the progress towards communism. Soviet attempts to play down the inevitability of war and to stress the possibility of a peaceful transition to socialism had to be tempered with Chinese assertions on the dangers of imperialism creating new wars and the likelihood of non-peaceful transitions to socialism. Nevertheless Mao did give strong support to Soviet leadership of the socialist bloc, but with an assumption that the USSR would act after consultation with its partners, not unilaterally.

Problems with the Soviet Model

The apparent closeness of relations between China and the USSR at the end of 1957 hid from view the growing disillusion in the Chinese leadership with the Soviet model of economic development, which had dominated the formulation of the First Five Year Plan. The issue had first arisen over the limited growth in agriculture in 1953 and 1954, which restricted both the revenues and grain supplies available to the government and the supply of raw materials for light industry. The late 1953 decision to monopolise grain purchases and the arguments over the pace of cooperativisation in 1955 had both been related to attempts to improve agricultural growth and gain security of grain supplies for urban areas. The overall agricultural growth rate of around 4 per cent per annum remained disappointing for China's leaders, who had hoped for 9 per cent growth both in 1953 and 1954. During the latter half of 1955, Mao urged the more rapid collectivisation of the countryside and a parallel movement snowballed in the cities, where the limited targets of the Five Year Plan were overtaken by an enthusiastic rush, begun in Beijing, which saw all cities completing socialist transformation of private businesses by the end of January 1956. In this atmosphere of organisational transformation, Mao proposed measures which were finally approved in January 1956 as a twelve-year programme for agriculture, with ambitious goals for increases in grain production. Targets for production for 1956 in industry and agriculture were raised well beyond those of the Five Year Plan, but very quickly the economic disruptions from such a 'leap forward' approach forced the Party to readjust these targets downwards.

During early 1956 Party leaders and leading economic officials held extensive discussions on the economic programme, which resulted in public modifications away from the Soviet model. The first issue was the scope of investment in heavy industry, where Mao, summarising the discussions in his speech 'On the Ten Great Relationships', argued that it was possible and better to develop heavy industry by increasing immediate attention to light industry and agriculture, which would satisfy the needs of the people and would lead to more rapid accumulation of funds for subsequent investment in heavy industry. As a result, the ratio of investment between heavy and light industry was reduced slightly in June 1956 and more investment was earmarked for agriculture in developing the Second Five Year Plan, although the planned level for state investment in agriculture was still very low, at 10 per cent of total state investment. The second issue concerned the methods of economic management. The Soviet model implied a highly centralised system with control in the hands of economic ministries which issued their orders directly to lower units, especially in the industrial sector. In addition, within the factories, authority should have been placed in the hands of one manager, although in practice the Chinese had never adopted the system fully, in part for lack of suitable personnel. Both these aspects of the model tended to reduce the control of the Party over the operation of the economy and to stress the role of economic and technical rather than political expertise. A parallel discussion occurred in the military, over the relative importance of modernisation as compared with the guerrilla tradition of the People's Liberation Army, with efforts from 1956 to intensify political training and Party structures in the military, without abandoning the goal of a modernised army.

In September 1956 the CCP met for its Eighth Party Congress, the first since taking national power, and its political report argued for an economic focus for future work, stating that the new primary contradiction in China was between the advanced socialist system and the backward social productive forces. The congress warned against the dangers of both rash advances and 'right conservatism', while Zhou Enlai's report on the Second Five Year Plan outlined a balanced development based on realistic targets. Thereafter the State Planning

Commission began to develop the specific strategies for the second plan, including the need to produce more chemical fertiliser to boost agricultural yields and the need to expand smaller-scale plants, rather than depend upon very large enterprises which tended to rely upon imported machinery. Smaller plants were also more labour-intensive and would soak up the non-agricultural unemployed, who were still numbered in millions by 1957. There was also a realisation that the earlier decision to encourage industrial development into the interior of China did not ensure the best results for the funds invested and that the coastal regions should be allowed to grow more, in line with their economic advantages.

Despite the limited improvements in rural strategy promised by the planners since mid-1956, the major hurdle facing China's economic growth remained agriculture. Climatically 1956 was a poor year and 1957 only average, with the result that agricultural production did not grow as required. At the end of 1956 many peasants withdrew from their cooperatives, dissatisfied with the returns from collective farming, and there was a major grain-supply crisis by mid-1957, which forced the Party to curtail rural free markets and to launch a rural socialist education movement portraying the superiority of socialism. Nevertheless, although the authority of the Party was thereby maintained, it was clear that some solution had to be found to boost agricultural production, either by greatly enhanced state investment in agriculture, which would mean unacceptably slower rates of growth in the rest of the economy or by some other mechanism yet to be devised. Given the limited economic resources available to the leadership and the enormous successes which the leadership felt it had achieved in its political and social campaigns, it is understandable that the new strategy should emerge as the mobilisation of the Chinese in a campaign style to overcome economic problems by organising mass enthusiasm, to make China take a 'Great Leap Forward', as the next chapter relates.

7 The Chinese Way: Mark One

The Chinese Communist Party under Mao's leadership decided to strike out in a new direction in 1958, largely as a result of concern over the effectiveness of the Soviet model for the development of China. The change was also occasioned by the tightening of general discipline in the wake of the Hundred Flowers movement of mid-1957. 1958 had been scheduled as the first year of the Second Five Year Plan, but instead witnessed a change of approach involving a Great Leap Forward and the creation of communes. This change placed enormous confidence in the aroused masses of China to achieve rapid economic advance at the behest of Mao, who may also have seen the communes as a way to bypass the Party bureaucrats in his bid for continued real authority in China. Although the Great Leap was disastrously unsuccessful in raising medium-term output, the institutions it spawned and the ideological problems its failure engendered were to be at the core of China's politics for a decade, while the nation looked steadfastly inwards for the sources of modernisation. The retreat from the Great Leap marked the first outright setback for the CCP since the events of 1927 and 1934, but whereas those setbacks had resulted in major personnel changes in the CCP leadership, 1959 saw the punishment of only the critics of the Great Leap, not its advocates.

The problems associated with the Soviet model have been outlined in the last chapter, especially with regard to the place of agriculture in economic development. In addition the credits provided by the USSR since 1950 had now to be repaid, largely through agricultural and raw material exports. This meant that China from 1957 at the latest had to maintain a balance of trade surplus with the USSR, at a time when there was limited agricultural production to satisfy Chinese consumers. In the military sphere, the Soviet offers of aid for army modernisation in late 1957 and the suggestions in 1958 on nuclear-sharing arrangements with joint-control systems apparently convinced Mao and others that the USSR was seeking undue control and that China must gain independent nuclear capacity.

The Great Leap Forward

The Great Leap Forward approach did not emerge as a coherently argued Party policy announced as a whole, but rather was a developing response to the problems of the Chinese situation from late 1957. In September and October 1957 at the third plenum of the Eighth Central Committee, Mao criticised the Eighth Congress report, in particular its opposition to 'rash advances', as having lowered mass enthusiasm and provoked the rightist attacks on the Party, while Deng Xiaoping reintroduced a modified version of Mao's Twelve-Year Agricultural Programme of early 1956, calling for a high tide in rural activity over the coming winter. Then in November 1957 in Moscow, Mao, probably without consultation with his Party colleagues, committed China to overtaking Great Britain economically within 15 years. Liu Shaoqi repeated this claim publicly in China in December, although the Chinese planners defined such catching up in absolute, not *per capita*, terms. The term, 'Great Leap Forward', although mentioned in the press as early as November 1957, only received full promotion in February 1958. Agricultural strategy was to be guided by the 'Sixty Points on Work Methods', also issued in February, which urged rapid increases in production and suggested that production targets urged at the local levels should be set above the targets actually required by higher levels, a procedure that could readily inflate targets and subsequently caused false reporting of success. In March 1958 at a CCP conference in Chengdu the slogan 'Go all out, aim high and achieve greater, faster, better and more economical results', was launched and this soon became the general line of the Great Leap.

The impetus for a more rapid and more suitable development programme for China drew on a number of experimental cases, which were then promoted nationally. In line with the desire for a rural high tide over the winter of 1957–8, the CCP had initiated a drive to expand irrigation opportunities, regarding better water supplies as a major factor to boost agricultural production. The centre claimed that 100 million peasants took part in this drive, which newly irrigated some 8 million hectares. Nevertheless the conflicts of interest over water rights and the small scale of projects achievable even by higher cooperatives forced the cooperatives to enter into associations for more efficient construction work by larger labour forces. These associations of cooperatives were inspected and approved by senior Party leaders, the first one with a published constitution being formed in Suiping county, Henan, in April 1958. There the resources of twenty-seven cooperatives were pooled, including the peasants' private plots, and members were to be paid a monthly wage and guaranteed free grain from public dining-rooms. At the second session of the Party's Eighth Congress in May 1958, Mao and Liu Shaoqi spoke enthusiastically of the large gains already achieved in the first four months of the year and called for further unleashing of mass energies, by the decentralisation of decision-making. This congress did not use the term 'commune' for the organisational developments in the countryside and although 'commune' was used in internal Party documents from June, it was not until August that the term was publicly promoted, especially after Mao's visits to rural areas endorsed the concept.

The Great Leap Forward, even before the creation of the communes, implied the comprehensive mobilisation of resources through the policy of 'Walking on two legs' – that is, by simultaneously developing local industry using labour-intensive cruder methods and centrally planned industry using modern, more capital-intensive methods. Industry and agriculture were to be developed together, with the demands of revolution and production equally met. The most obvious symbol of the development of local rural industry was the backyard furnace, the production of iron and steel in small furnaces using local materials. Several desired results were intended by this means, to involve the peasantry in industrial practice, thereby bridging the urban–rural gap, to promote the use of local resources, and to expand heavy industrial potential at the least cost to central finances. Although highlighted at the time, this rural industry activity was not so important as the huge increase in investment in larger state-owned units, with more projects started in 1958 than during the whole of the First Five Year Plan, as investment almost doubled the 1957 level. Although more capital-intensive than rural industry, these new state units still required labour and the non-agricultural labour force in state employ increased by over 20 million in 1958, as the urban population swelled by over 30 million, most of whom needed to be supplied with food through the state grain-rationing network.

The response to the call for a Great Leap Forward was very enthusiastic and in the context of excellent weather in 1958 produced a temporary surge in agricultural production. The mobilisation of labour on collective ventures was far more extensive than anything experienced thus far in the PRC, breaking down older habits of staying within the village to work, or, in the case of women, of staying within the home. Enormous managerial problems arose over the efficient use of this labour, but at the start there was tolerance of some waste. The backyard furnace campaign was carried through with immense drive, with in many cases the collection of all scrap iron, and even pots and tools, replacing the search for local iron ore. The furnaces faced major problems of construction materials, fuel supplies and quality control, but again mass enthusiasm seems to have silenced the growing realisation that the iron produced was inadequate for most purposes because of impurities. The creation of public kitchens freed many women for labour outside the home, but although public dining rooms were provided, many peasants preferred to carry food away to eat at home. The convenience to the peasant and the chance of a considerable supply of free food from collective reserves were offset by problems of wastage and later by fears that an automatic food-supply system failed to generate sufficient incentive for the continuing herculean labour efforts, which saw many peasants working through the night under artificial light.

The institutional climax of the Great Leap Forward in the rural areas was the people's commune, formally promoted by a Central Committee resolution of 29 August 1958. By December virtually all rural households had been incorporated into 27 000 communes, with an average population of 20 000 each. The commune offered not only the means to organise labour more extensively for larger water control projects, but also was of sufficient scale to run industrial and trading ventures. The communes took over from the existing townships as the political unit for rural administration. According to the August resolution, the communes were named as the fundamental policy to accelerate socialist construction, to complete the building of socialism ahead of time and to carry out the gradual transition to communism. The mention of the transition to communism was treated with great suspicion by the USSR, because it implied that China was claiming to be reaching communism more quickly than any other country led by a communist party. Such a claim was doctrinally unacceptable, given China's low productive capacity. Nevertheless, within China, talk of communes as basic units for communism led to an exaggerated euphoria among lower cadres who strove to create communes whatever the difficulties.

The Jinmen (Quemoy) Crisis

The August resolution on the communes occurred at a moment of high tension in China's international situation caused by the Jinmen (Quemoy) crisis. Jinmen was one of the islands close to China's coast which remained in the hands of the Nationalist government based in Taiwan, and it can be argued that the drive for the incorporation of the island at this stage was part of the Communist Party's desire for outstanding achievements on all fronts, economic, social and nationalistic. Nevertheless, the attack involved other factors, relating to the politics of the socialist bloc. During the early months of 1958, the Chinese had been much more vigorous than the Soviet Union in their attacks on Yugoslavia, partly over the issue of Yugoslav views on peaceful coexistence between East and West. Then in July, the USSR under Khrushchev had, in China's view, failed to react forcefully enough against US and British troop movements into the Middle East, in particular when he had suggested a summit conference excluding China but including India. Khrushchev paid a hurried visit to China from 31 July, but his talks with Chinese leaders on military cooperation produced only friction. The question of a possible attack on Jinmen was not raised, which led to later Soviet criticisms, but the Chinese leaders almost certainly felt that an attack on Jinmen was an internal issue for China.

The artillery bombardment of Jinmen began on 23 August 1958, followed by naval actions to cut the sea links between Jinmen and Taiwan. The USA, under President Eisenhower, promptly offered support to Jiang Jieshi and units of American forces arrived in the Taiwan Strait, preparing to escort Nationalist ships to Jinmen. Relations between the USA and the PRC had been deteriorating since December 1957, when ambassadorial talks in Warsaw were suspended because of Chinese refusal to talk with any official lower than the ambassador, even during changeovers of staff. Chinese anger over US moves in Lebanon in July 1958 had led to renewed public calls to liberate Taiwan, but the vigour of the US response over Jinmen surprised the Chinese leaders, who had previously been arguing a firmer policy by the socialist bloc against the USA. The crisis subsided during September with Premier Zhou Enlai calling for new ambassadorial talks on 6 September, but not before the Soviet foreign minister, Gromyko, had visited Beijing on 5 September to talk with the Chinese. On 7 September Khrushchev wrote to the US President that an attack on China would be regarded as an attack on the USSR, but privately the Soviet leadership began to review the links with her rather reckless ally, which later culminated in the June 1959 decision to end the nuclear assistance agreement of 1957.

The Slowing of the Great Leap Forward

Despite the failure of the attack on Jinmen, the Party pushed forward with the Great Leap, a policy that was supported by nearly all the Party leadership. Only Premier Zhou Enlai and the leading economic planner Chen Yun voiced concern among the civilian officials, because the Leap contradicted an orderly, centrally managed development strategy, while military opposition centred on Peng Dehuai, the Defence Minister, who objected to the need for the military to participate in civilian projects and to support local militia activities. These worries did not halt the Leap programme, but in accordance with CCP practice, Party leaders toured the country through the latter part of 1958 inspecting the achievements of the new campaign. These inspections soon revealed that the ambitious targets of the Leap were not being fully achieved and that in particular not all areas were experiencing agricultural abundance as the official statistics implied. Nevertheless the leadership remained supportive of the basic strategy of the Leap, but in November 1958 Mao convened two meetings to discuss and rectify the 'communist style', which had led to commandism by cadres as they forced the population to act ahead of its level of political consciousness.

The sixth plenum of the Eighth Central Committee followed, with a resolution warning against skipping the socialist stage and calling for revolution by stages, but with the expectation that these stages would flow one into another in an uninterrupted fashion. As befitted the current socialist stage, payments were to be based more clearly on work, which must be restricted to a maximum of twelve hours a day, with some private property still permitted. The plenum urged the use of the winter season to check up the communes and confirmed the role of the commune militia as an independent military organisation directly responsible to the CCP centre, with the militia coming to number 220 million by January 1959. The plenum also announced Mao's proposal not to stand as PRC chairman in the 1959 election, a decision previously communicated within the Party and to foreign visitors during 1958, but which nevertheless implied some acceptance of responsibility by Mao for Great Leap problems.

During 1959 the enthusiastic early mood of the Great Leap Forward was lost and China moved towards economic disruption, a trend heightened by the first of three years of exceptionally harsh weather for agriculture. The commune had resulted in managerial and leadership problems which threatened the viability of rural life. The 'communist style' of many cadres had led to the deployment of labour and capital without regard for individual or collective rights under the pretext of total equality. The extensive use of labour in commune construction and industrial projects and the large migration of labour to the cities had diverted labour away from basic food production, leaving some tasks such as weeding incomplete.

Moreover the peasants were expected to continue their efforts through the traditionally slacker winter period. The desire for quick results had provoked the use of 'blind' directives, issued from above without regard for specific local conditions, a major example being the excessive use of deep ploughing and dense planting. Equally serious from the viewpoint of the centre was the trend to boasting and exaggeration, which produced the submission of false inflated figures for output, with any local objectors being threatened with a rightist label. Not realising the extent of this problem, the centre in December 1958 announced the 1958 harvest as 375 million tonnes of grain, double the 1957 level, and worse still, went on to base its economic strategy for 1959 on this figure, calling for raised quotas of compulsory sales to the state by peasants, a 10 per cent cut in the area sown to crops, and greatly increased exports of grain. In fact the 1958 harvest was probably about 200 million tonnes, less than 3 per cent more than in 1957, but the centre took several years to admit such a pessimistic result.

The retreat from the Great Leap and the communes in the first half of 1959 can be clearly charted in the series of CCP meetings called to debate the problems experienced. At Zhengzhou in late February, Mao, while claiming success for the Leap, criticised the egalitarianism of the commune and urged the division of ownership and management among three layers, the commune, the brigade, roughly equivalent to the former higher cooperatives, and the production team, equivalent to the former lower cooperatives. He also argued that the state must accept that grain was being concealed by the peasantry, who wished to defend their consumption opportunities. In early April the seventh plenum of the Eighth Central Committee, meeting in Shanghai, urged that at least 85 per cent of commune labour be directed into grain production and ordered higher cadres to go down to rectify lower-level mistakes. The plenum spelt out the relationship among the commune, brigade and production team: the *commune* was to direct operations for industry owned by all the commune members; the *brigade* was to be the basic unit of account and audit for distribution of peasant income and was to own land, animals and tools, while running in practice most of commune-owned industry; the *teams* were to be responsible for agricultural production and welfare work. Individual households were to regain their private plots. The plenum also adopted the 1959 plan, with a grain target of 525 million tonnes, far beyond any achieved by China up to that time or since.

Concurrently with these events the Chinese leadership faced growing problems in Tibet, where Chinese rule had been reimposed in 1950. As part of their consolidation there, the Chinese had by 1958 completed the road between west Tibet and Xinjiang across the Aksai Chin plateau, an area shown on Indian maps as part of India, although the Indian government had been unaware of the construction work. Indian protests were met by proposals from Premier Zhou Enlai to maintain the *status quo* – that is, with China accepting Indian government in its North-East Frontier Agency area, claimed by the Chinese and with India accepting the Chinese presence in the Aksai Chin, claimed by India. No resolution of the issue had been achieved, when the discontent of the Khambas of east Tibet erupted into a full revolt, culminating in Chinese military suppression and the flight of the Tibetan spiritual leader, the Dalai Lama, to India in March 1959. India offered asylum to the Dalai Lama, provoking Chinese protests of interference in China's internal affairs, and tension mounted on the Sino-Indian border, as the Chinese Army sought to seal the frontier passes, with military clashes occurring in August and October 1959. During these clashes the USSR adopted a strictly neutral stance and Khrushchev deplored the clashes as stupid, a position which heightened ill-feeling between China and the USSR.

Having quelled the Tibetan revolt, the CCP leadership was again ready to focus on the economic situation within China, meeting at Lushan in July 1959 for an enlarged Politburo session, followed by the eighth plenum of the Eighth Central Committee in August. By this time Soviet irritation over the trends in China had resulted in the Soviet cancellation of nuclear aid on 20 June 1959, and in July Khrushchev publicly attacked the building of communes as displaying a poor understanding of communism. The main open opponent of the Great Leap strategy within China was Marshal Peng Dehuai, who had toured parts of China to discover production dropping and had addressed an open letter to Mao about this. Peng suggested at

Lushan that only 30 per cent of the rural crisis was caused by natural conditions and that 70 per cent was the result of man-made errors. These had been induced by subjectivism and petty-bourgeois fanaticism, in practice by the expectation that will-power and mass enthusiasm could overcome the restraints of the existing productive forces. Peng, as defence minister, had previously clashed with the Party leaders over the issues of military spending and the development of an independent Chinese defence system, and had weakened the CCP role in the army by downplaying the CCP committees in army units. He also objected to the militia build-up which had been part of the commune strategy. His criticisms of the Leap followed his visit to the USSR and Eastern Europe in June, a coinci-dence which led to suspicions that he had colluded with the Soviet leadership to attack the Leap.

Mao's response to these attacks was to call on the Party leaders to choose between himself and Peng and to threaten to launch a guerrilla war if he was rejected. Mao was aware that the majority of the leadership had turned against his policies, but he re-jected the claim that the Party had lost the support of the masses. The Party leaders, under Liu Shaoqi, rallied to Mao and agreed to purge Peng from his military posts with labels of right opportunist, careerist, hypocrite and conspirator, but only on condition that they could pursue their own policies with Mao in semi-retirement. Removed along with Peng were several senior army officers from the PLA central sections and the provincial Party secretary from Hunan, whose demotion resulted in the promotion, at Mao's request, of a junior cadre, Hua Guofeng, who was to emerge as Mao's successor in 1976. The Lushan plenum announced adjustments to the commune, including a reduction in the grain targets expected, but con-tinued to claim that the Three Red Banners, the Great Leap, the Communes and the General Line for building socialism, were a successful policy direction.

The impact of the Eighth Plenum was immense, because it relaunched the Great Leap Forward which soon collapsed into disaster, because it undermined the role of criticism as a policy rather than as a personal matter within the CCP leadership and because it turned the PLA under its new leader, Lin Biao, towards a vigorous political role as the upholder of Mao, while the Party moved away from Mao's direct authority. Since Peng had been removed as a right opportunist, implying his inappropriate resistance to the progressive policies of the Leap, it was inevitable that the Party would proceed with the commune, halting any suggestions of retrenchment and even moving in early 1960 to promote urban communes. Mass mobilisation of labour was again required through the winter months and in industry Mao supported the role of politics in management, by promoting in March 1960 the new constitution of the Anshan Iron and Steel Works, replacing a constitution based on Soviet models.

The Collapse of the Great Leap Forward

The collapse of the Great Leap during 1960 and 1961 devastated China, although at the time there was little appreciation of the scale of the problem. On the basis of figures made available in the 1980s, it is clear that the population of China dropped by over 13 million between 1959 and 1961 and that the total number of deaths beyond those normally expected from old age and infant mortality was more than 20 million. Such figures imply the most severe famine ever experienced in China and probably the greatest in the twentieth-century world. The impact of the famine seems to have been highest in rural areas, with Anhui province in central China as probably the worst hit. Urban areas suffered less harshly, because of considerable stocks acquired by the government procurement programme, the forced resettlement of urban dwellers to rural areas and, from 1961, massive imports of grain from overseas. Although bad weather was responsible for some of the drop in production of grains in the years 1959 to 1961, most of the responsibility for the famine must lie with government policies, which had diverted labour away from agriculture, promoted poor-quality irrigation schemes, reduced the sown area in 1959, continued high state-procurement and high exports on the basis of false production figures and encouraged serious problems in the organisation of agricultural activity by its insistence on the advantages of management by the leaders of the large commune unit.

Although the reduction in grain production had the most immediate impact on the lives of the Chinese, the downturn from the Great Leap affected the rest of the economy too. As peasants struggled to grow food, production of non-food crops plunged, forcing light industry to retrench between 1960 and 1962. Heavy industrial production was halved between 1960 and 1962, and the government, seeking to control considerable budget deficits which developed from 1958 to 1960, cut back on all state investment, until by 1962 the rate of accumulation fell to only 10 per cent of national income, less than half the figure of the mid-1950s. Industrial development was also hard hit by the withdrawal of all Soviet advisers from China in July and August 1960, after clashes between Khrushchev and Chinese delegates at the congress of the Romanian Communist Party in June over both the Great Leap policy and the role of war in advancing the growth of the socialist bloc.

The CCP's reaction to the problems of the Leap occurred gradually throughout the second half of 1960, but a comprehensive response to create a new direction for the future was only developed during 1961 and 1962. At a meeting at Beidaihe in north China in July and August 1960, it was proposed that agriculture be taken as the base, with industry as the leading sector, replacing the previous formula of simultaneously developing agriculture and industry, with priority to heavy industry. It was also agreed that consolidation, not rapid growth, was the order of the day, the final slogan launched formally in January 1961 being 'readjustment, consolidation, filling out and raising standards'. Following the low autumn harvest, the Party issued a twelve-article directive on rural work, which allocated basic ownership to the brigade, permitted private plots and family sideline activities, ordered more of collective income to be devoted to payments to members and restricted the amount of collective income that could be distributed as free supply without relation to work done. In addition, rural markets, under suitable supervision, were to be permitted, although a free market in grains was not allowed.

Further decentralisation in agriculture occurred with the publication of the Sixty Articles of May 1961. These ordered the reduction in the size of the communes, whose total number finally trebled to 75 000, and indicated that the production team, now of twenty to thirty households, was the basic unit. Land, labour, draft animals and farm tools were to be permanently allocated to the teams, who would guarantee output quotas to their brigades. The role of material incentives was encouraged, with a reduction in accumulated funds, and the communes were restricted to the use of a maximum of 2 per cent of brigade labour in commune enterprises. Private plots and free market trade after meeting state quotas were allowed, this sanction becoming the later basis for the *sanzi yibao* (three freedoms, one contract) policy, whereby private plots, free markets and enterprises with responsibility for their own profits and losses increased and output quotas were fixed on a household basis. The degree to which individual household farming reappeared varied greatly through the country, but some have argued that in some areas up to half the land returned to private control. Such trends were accepted as necessary to survive the immediate situation, for as Party secretary-general Deng Xiaoping repeated at this time, 'It does not matter whether a cat is black or white, as long as it catches mice, it is a good cat.' In addition heavy government pressures on rural grain-producers were reduced, by lowering the compulsory deliveries to the state, especially in terms of tax grain, and by raising the price paid to peasants for non-tax compulsory grain procurements.

Rebuilding after the End of the Great Leap

The wider issues beyond agriculture produced two responses within the leadership, one involving a renewed focus on political work as under Lin Biao in the military, the other involving widespread investigation of actual conditions and the formulation of more pragmatic documents to spell out specific programmes under the guidance of central Party leaders. Lin's approach, to combat demoralisation in the mainly rurally recruited army, stressed the study of Mao's works, often in a simplified form, culminating eventually in the creation of the 'little red book', *Quotations from Chairman Mao Zedong*, but his colleagues saw little use for this method outside the military. During 1961 and 1962 the other leaders, especially Liu Shaoqi, Deng Xiaoping and the economic expert, Chen Yun, created guidelines for many fields, such as education, industry and commerce, with a general stress on the role of experts and the importance of material incentives. Premier Zhou Enlai reconstituted the Finance and Economics small group to be the crucial policy-making body at the centre, with an increasing role for Chen Yun, who urged lower rates of investment, the increase of industry directly linked to agriculture, such as chemical fertilisers, and the allocation of resources to assist areas which were efficient producers, rather than insisting on regional self-sufficiency.

The major issue requiring assessment during 1962 was the degree to which China was recovering from the Leap-induced downturn and here the Party leaders were unable to agree. At a work conference for 7000 cadres held in January and February 1962, Liu Shaoqi argued that the economy was still in a critical condition, caused largely by political mistakes, while Mao indicated that the economic situation was more optimistic. All agreed that the inner life of the Party needed to be revitalised by more effective communication on the basis of the long-recommended principle of democratic centralism, but could not agree on how far to rehabilitate rightists who had criticised policy, including Marshal Peng Dehuai. Although Mao's views on the situation were temporarily to prevail because of a general reluctance to challenge the Chairman, by the end of February, with new reports on likely budget deficits, Chen Yun, Liu Shaoqi and others initiated a further period of readjustment before any new vigorous programme could be begun by the government. During the readjustment further de-collectivisation in agriculture would be permitted, while former capitalists and technical experts would be encouraged to aid the urban economy. Such an approach drew criticism from officials in heavy industry, who wished to return to the high targets for investment and steel production that had characterised the Leap mentality, as well as from those, like Mao, who pondered the impact of readjustment on the development of classes and socialism in China.

While the Party leaders sought to resolve the enormous domestic problems resulting from the collapse of the Great Leap, China was also faced with increasing isolation internationally. Such isolation may have promoted the ideal of self-reliance which had been urged in the Leap, but even after the Leap was abandoned, self-reliance remained, to culminate in the later 1960s in the extreme anti-foreignism of the Cultural Revolution. Antagonism towards the West was understandable and reached one of its peaks in mid-1962 when it was feared that there might be a Nationalist invasion from Taiwan, backed by the USA. Hostile relations with the socialist countries were a newer phenomenon, drawing partly on matters of interpretation of Marxism–Leninism and partly on longer-term national rivalries between China and the Soviet Union, as neighbours and states with wide ambitions. The mid-1960 withdrawal of Soviet advisers was followed in November 1960 by a bitter conference of world communist parties, where Deng Xiaoping led the attack on the Soviet leaders. During 1961 China's principal supporter in the socialist bloc was Albania, which was verbally attacked by the Soviet Union, had its Soviet advisers withdrawn and then in 1962 was expelled from major Eastern European organisations such as the military Warsaw Pact. Direct attacks by the Soviet Union on China were limited, but on the Xinjiang border tensions rose as migrants flowed across to the USSR to escape distress in China. In July 1962 all Soviet consulates in Xinjiang were closed and the border converted into a depopulated zone; later the Chinese were to accuse the USSR of seeking to detach Xinjiang. Soviet disapproval of China was matched by a growing military relationship between the USSR and India, which had received Soviet aircraft and helicopters by mid-1962. The USSR also underlined the weakness of China in the field of nuclear weapons, by informing the Chinese in August 1962 that the USSR was accepting an American initiative on the non-proliferation of nuclear arms, by banning nuclear-weapons-technology transfer to non-nuclear countries.

As an increasingly isolated China emerged from the darkest days of the depression which followed the collapse of the Great Leap, political attention was again focused by Mao upon the future course of the Chinese revolution. Although accepting that the short-term measures for economic recovery necessarily gave greater scope to private initiative, Mao insisted that the Party must avoid any weakening of commitment towards socialism. Such insistence stemmed in part from Mao's worries about the apparent turn away from socialism in the Soviet Union, which he feared might be repeated in China, and about the

subtle literary attacks being launched by some Party intellectuals against Mao's leadership and the Leap policies, attacks led
by Deng Duo and Wu Han of the Beijing Party committee.
These attacks used literary and historical allusions to criticise
Mao and to argue a greater role for intellectuals, even those
outside the Party. The circulation of these attacks in official
publications implied support for their views by those higher in
the Party who had permitted their publication, and therefore
indicated to Mao that the Party was in need of political rectification.

Mao's opinions carried the day at the tenth plenum of the
Eighth Central Committee, held in Beijing in September 1962,
as the climax of two months of top-level discussions. The plenum endorsed Mao's call to combat revisionism and never to
forget class struggle and also decided to launch a Socialist
Education Movement. Mao feared that the reappearance of
speculation, usury, exploitation of hired labour and corruption of government cadres in rural areas would lead to the re-
establishment of economic class lines within the peasantry,
allowing a comeback by classes suppressed by the land reform
process. Resolutions passed at the plenum also suggested that
the commune system should not be changed for at least thirty
years, but approved the existing practice of regarding the production team as the basic unit of ownership and accounting.

Before vigorous attention could be paid to the development
of the Socialist Education Movement, the international situation in the last months of 1962 again diverted the attention of
the Chinese leaders. Tensions along the Sino-Indian border
had escalated as the Indian government under Nehru pursued
a forward policy, seeking to establish outposts in disputed territory and finally sending patrols into indisputably Tibetan territory. In September 1962 the Chinese proposed talks without
preconditions, but in the absence of an acceptable Indian reply began a successful offensive against Indian forces on 20
October. This offensive halted within a week, as the Chinese
pondered the impact of the far larger crisis between the USSR
and the USA which arose that week over the issue of Soviet
missiles entering Cuba. As the Cuban crisis subsided, the Chinese continued their advance against Indian forces, until China
declared a unilateral ceasefire on 20 November, withdrawing
Chinese troops out of disputed territory in north-east India on

the basis of a demilitarised frontier zone. Thereafter China, having initially supported the USSR over the Cuban crisis, began to attack the Soviet actions, as adventurist for having tried to introduce missiles into Cuba and capitulationist for having removed them so promptly. The USSR replied by disputing the Chinese opinions on the origins of the Sino-Indian war, thereby widening the rifts between China and the USSR.

By early 1963 the CCP leadership was able to turn its attention to local experiments preparing for the launching of the Socialist Education Movement and on the basis of these local cases drew up national guidelines at two work conferences, dominated by Mao, in February and May 1963. These guidelines on 'Some problems existing in current rural work' were issued on 20 May 1963 and are often referred to as the First Ten Points. They spelt out Mao's view on the existence of class struggle in socialist society and called for reliance upon the poor and lower middle peasants. Cadres were urged to take part in productive labour and to promote the 'Four Clean-Up' campaign, checking the handling of accounts, inventories, workpoints and public property, to root out corruption. Although these Ten Point regulations had considerable theoretical potential for a new approach to rural issues through mass activism, in practice the document was lacking in specific detail on how to organise the peasants and how to conduct the clean-up campaign, besides a general directive to avoid public struggle rallies. Poor and lower middle peasant associations were formed during the summer of 1963, but their relationship to the local Party branch was unclear.

Given the imprecision of the May regulations, the Party centre issued a supplementary set of ten points in September 1963, which shifted priorities well away from Mao's earlier draft. These 'Second Ten Points', probably drafted by Deng Xiaoping, narrowed the focus towards questions of economic irregularities by lower cadres. Work teams from higher levels were to be despatched to the rural areas to investigate corrupt practices, but without mention of the role of peasant associations. The teams were also to begin the task of detailed class analysis of the rural population. The work team idea was well-established within the CCP tradition, but the methods used in the period, 1963–5, were later criticised for their reliance on setting aside local Communists and on secret investigation, techniques particularly favoured by President Liu Shaoqi's wife from her experiences at the Taoyuan brigade in Hebei. Use of the work team allowed the provincial and county Party members to control the movement, to restrict wider criticisms and to lead the masses, rather than reacting to proposals from the masses.

During 1964 the practice of the Socialist Education movement was criticised by Mao and President Liu Shaoqi, revealing considerable differences in approach. Mao in June 1964 proposed six criteria for the evaluation of the movement, stressing popular mobilisation and cadre participation in manual labour, with the implication that a movement directed by the Party authorities was inadequate. Liu, in the revised later ten points of September 1964, emphasised the role of the work teams and called for the re-registration of Party members and the reclassification of the class status of all rural dwellers. Lower level cadres were to be criticised by the masses under the guidance of the work teams and care was to be taken to avoid excessive leniency, thereby greatly widening the target for attack. Liu described the movement as a long-term struggle over five or six years, but the procedure he outlined ensured that the senior leadership of the Party was not called into question.

While the Party leadership during 1963 and 1964 debated the best mechanism for the rectification of the rural Party members, the nation as a whole experienced a rapid recovery from the severe setbacks in the economic sphere during the Great Leap. The production of grain rose sharply until the 1965 level was almost back to the pre-Leap peak, while non-grain production exceeded pre-Leap levels, with yields per acre improving markedly. Nevertheless the amount of grain available for consumption per capita was well down on the mid-1950s figures, because of continued population growth. In industry recovery was even more pronounced, with major items such as steel and cement reaching double their pre-Leap peaks by 1965. In addition China began to develop its crude oil production, with Daqing in the north-east as the main field, and a huge growth in the chemical industry occurred, both through the refining of oil and the creation of large fertiliser factories. Such industrial growth was achieved by raising the rate of accumulation back to levels above 20 per cent of national income as in the mid-1950s, but the share of this investment which was allocated to agriculture dropped away, as the Party again moved to focus on industry as the means for rapid growth, despite the slogan of agriculture as the base.

In the international sphere China's relations with the USSR continued to deteriorate during 1963 and 1964, with open polemics between the two sides over issues of theory, culminating in Chinese accusations against the phoney communism of Khrushchev in July 1964. Also at issue was the territorial question, with Beijing noting that all the northern borders of China with the USSR were defined on the basis of nineteenth-century unequal treaties imposed by Tsarist Russia, which implied that those boundaries might need to be readjusted in the more equal circumstances of the 1960s. China was, however, prepared to accept the unequal treaties as the basis for any such readjustment. The press polemics with the USSR were conducted by the highest levels of the CCP, and it seems that many of the articles were written by Mao, often with the aid of Kang Sheng, a former public security chief, who was well-versed in Soviet affairs. Talks between China and the USSR had been urged by other communist parties, but were suspended in July 1963, when the USSR signed a treaty with the USA banning atmospheric nuclear tests. China went on with its own nuclear preparations and achieved an atmospheric test on 16 October 1964, just two days after the dismissal of Khrushchev as Soviet leader. Zhou Enlai, the Chinese premier, hurried to Moscow, but found the new leadership under Brezhnev and Kosygin equally unwilling to compromise with China.

In its relations with the non-Communist world during 1963 and 1964, China achieved some successes, but faced the growing threat of US intervention in Vietnam, her southern neighbour. China sought to cultivate relations with the newly independent nations of Africa, achieving diplomatic recognition from several, but the Chinese, even after a tour by the eloquent Zhou Enlai, could not persuade African countries to turn against the USSR, in part because China had little economic aid to offer the Africans. During 1964 China began to develop a closer relationship with Pakistan, as a result of a common enmity against India, and unexpectedly China achieved diplomatic relations with a major Western country, France, whose leader, General de Gaulle, was keen to demonstrate the independence of French diplomacy from US dictation.

It was, however, in Indochina that the Chinese faced their greatest immediate threat. Agreements resulting from the Geneva conference of 1954 had established four states in the area, North and South Vietnam, Laos and Cambodia, with subsequent Geneva accords seeking to define the status of Laos as a neutral. China offered support to Prince Sihanouk in Cambodia, but the major problem arose from the continued weakness of the South Vietnamese governments in the face of rural Communist insurgency assisted by North Vietnam, a situation which increased the US air force presence into Thailand. In August 1964 US planes bombed North Vietnamese naval bases for the first time and China responded by offering strong verbal support to North Vietnam and by making aircraft available to it. The situation in Vietnam was to become more critical as the USA increased its military presence on the ground over the next few years. China continued to voice support for North Vietnam but sought to avoid full involvement in the Vietnam War. Revelations in the late 1980s imply that Chinese troops did fight in that War, but officially the Chinese left the Vietnamese to fight their own battles, in part because, as defence minister Lin Biao argued in 1965, people's war and self-reliance are the only guarantee of a meaningful victory over aggressors.

1964 ended on a confident note for the Chinese leadership. At the Third People's Congress Premier Zhou Enlai affirmed that China was ready to begin a Third Five Year Plan in 1966 and that the need was for stability to allow the modernisation of China. Economic prospects were excellent with a full recovery from the post-Leap depression. These economic hopes were indeed justified through 1965 results, but politically 1965 presented major problems, in two areas in particular. The first was over the effectiveness of the Socialist Education Movement, which a work conference under Mao in January sought to broaden from a focus on relations between cadres and peasants to a wider debate on socialist and capitalist approaches within the Party. Nevertheless, the movement seems to have generated little real change in cadre behaviour by the end of the year. The other area was foreign policy. China faced the escalation of the Vietnam War, with its corresponding requirement to allow the transit of Soviet goods to Vietnam and with the underlying question of how far Sino-Soviet enmity hurt the world socialist cause. The Chinese failed disastrously in their efforts to build long-term relations with Indonesia, when the Indonesian Communist Party's coup failed in September, while China proved unable to influence the 1965 war between India and Pakistan. China, despite its new nuclear status, was still a weak nation, unwilling to break its diplomatic isolation and facing the possibility of US attacks on south China. While such foreign issues were of importance, it was to the internal questions that Mao turned his attention as he prepared to launch the Cultural Revolution.

The Cultural Revolution

The Cultural Revolution, although initiated by Mao Zedong with a number of specific aims, can be viewed as a striking example of how, even in a tightly organised state, directives from the centre cannot completely control mass activity, if the centre is itself divided over policy. The chaos which ensued from the activities of Red Guards and from factionalism within the community forced the surviving government leaders to call in the army as the final arbiter of law and order, thereby nullifying many of the intended aims of the government, such as greater popular participation in government and the eradication of bureaucratism. Although the Cultural Revolution period came by 1979 to be spoken of as ten wasted years (1966 to 1976, the year of Mao's death), it is more usual and more meaningful to highlight the period from 1966 to the Ninth Party Congress in April 1969 as the main stage of the Great Proletarian Cultural Revolution, with the period 1969 to 1976 as a time of relative calm, during which policy debate did not regularly extend to include mass mobilisation and open violence. Indeed some of the policy shifts of these latter years, such as the opening to the West from 1971, have a greater continuity with events since 1976 than with the supercharged atmosphere of extreme radicalism which characterised the period, 1966–9. Nevertheless, the leaders who emerged during this period of intense activism sought to ensure that their interpretation of the Cultural Revolution and its successes was not neglected, as the task of reconstruction of the Party and state was attempted.

Mao's role in the initiation of the Cultural Revolution was a decisive one, made possible by his unassailable position as Chairman of the CCP and popular symbol of China's revolution. Although Mao's reasons for promoting a cultural revolution drew upon Marxist–Leninist argumentation, there is little evidence to suggest that the economic and social contradictions in China at that time would have produced such an upheaval, without the direct intervention of the CCP chairman in challenging the established authority of many leading Party and government figures.

Mao's argument for a cultural revolution brought together a number of ideological worries, which can best be summarised as concern over the future of China, even under the guidance of a supposedly Marxist–Leninist party. Such concern arose in part from Mao's analyses of the Soviet Union, which he argued had not only failed in its internationalist duties towards China but had also abandoned revolutionary foreign policy in favour of peaceful coexistence with the Western powers. Tracing such changes to their domestic causes within the USSR, Mao believed he had detected a capitalist restoration within the socialist heartland, created by party rulers who favoured revisionism – that is, inappropriate non-revolutionary interpretation of Marxism–Leninism – to ensure the preservation of their power and privileges. Mao's views were spelt out in the polemics with the Soviet leaders in 1963 and 1964, with the intention of justifying China's divergence from the USSR to the world communist movement.

The same opinions, when applied as a possible scenario for future development in China itself, implied the creation of policies to prevent the emergence of such revisionism and party privilege. Such prevention required the preservation of the revolutionary purity of the Chinese and especially of the younger generation, who had not experienced the pre-1949 period. Youth had to be taught revolutionary ways, thereby implying an educational or cultural input, since the economic revolution had been completed; hence the term 'Cultural Revolution'. Mao also realised that the Party in China might turn to revisionism, especially if the policies of the early 1960s came to be seen as the norm, rather than as a temporary retreat from the methods of the late 1950s which Mao designated as more socialistic. Indeed Mao had discovered during the Socialist Education Movement that many of the CCP leaders were not attuned to his vision for China and that his position as chairman did not guarantee adequate execution of the policies he advocated. Hence the Cultural Revolution would also serve to re-establish the effective leadership of Mao, by appealing to the mass of the population over the heads of the Party bureaucrats, who had become accustomed to their privileges and distrustful of revolutionary enthusiasms.

There was widespread Party opposition to Mao's thrust towards more revolutionary policies stressing the continuation of class struggle in society and the purging of capitalist and revisionist tendencies in the Party, and this forced Mao to adopt an indirect approach, rather than open assault upon those he viewed as his greatest opponents. Mao was able to prepare his position in two areas of society, the army and the cultural sphere, where respectively Lin Biao and Mao's wife, Jiang Qing, provided vital allies, even if their espousal of Mao's cause was sometimes excessive in its fervency. Lin Biao had overseen renewed campaigns for ideological training in the PLA, which since 1960 had stressed the need to study Mao's writings and the importance of political and ideological awareness for effective military work. Various selections of Mao's works were circulated in the PLA from 1961, culminating in the 1964 edition prefaced by Lin Biao, which was to be printed by the hundreds of millions after August 1966 and publicly brandished by all as the proof of their loyalty to Mao. As the authority of Mao's thought was re-established in the PLA, the PLA began to be promoted as a model for other parts of society, with PLA officers transferred to guide economic enterprises from 1963 and, in 1964, a nationwide call to 'learn from the PLA'. One famous model chosen by Mao from the PLA at this time was Lei Feng, the idealised version of the young selfless soldier who sacrificed his life for others, while asserting his absolute commitment to Mao.

The cultural sphere presented both opportunities and pitfalls for the advancement of Mao's cause. Debates in the philosophical field confirmed the ascendancy of Mao's view on the universal tendency for contradictions to arise in all phenomena, the so-called 'one divides into two' position, in contrast to the view that 'two combine into one', which was depicted as revisionist and likely to lead to neglect of class struggle. In the educational and literary fields, however, Mao's effective power was unclear. In the schools and universities, although Marxism–Leninism was still taught, greater attention was devoted to achievement in academic subjects, as the nation sought to train technical experts to assist in the economic development of China, an emphasis which tended to disadvantage the children from peasant and worker families. In literature, although the wave of subtly critical writings of such as those of Deng Duo and Wu Han in 1961–2 had ceased, these writings had not received appropriate condemnation in Mao's view. Concern was also expressed at the absence of high-quality socialist literature being written in China. This absence occurred despite clear guidelines being issued by the Party on how to present literary characters, including the rejection of middle or ambivalent characters, so as to promote a more uplifting socialist realism. The major area where new directions were being achieved was in Beijing opera, where Mao's wife, Jiang Qing, led the reform to remove feudal or traditional themes and to create revolutionary operas drawing on themes from the Party's history. Nevertheless the leadership in the cultural field remained largely with the Party's propaganda department and the Ministry of Culture, whose senior officials were in many cases personal enemies of Jiang Qing since the 1930s.

Thwarted in his efforts to drive home Party reform in rural areas through the Socialist Education Movement and secure in the support of the military through Lin Biao, Mao decided to launch his new campaign for a Cultural Revolution essentially in the cities of China. This marked a major shift for Mao, whose previous efforts to redirect Party aims against a generally accepted Party position had all involved rural initiatives. Whereas earlier urban initiatives by the CCP such as the three and five antis campaigns of the early 1950s had drawn on the wide experience of the leadership, the Cultural Revolution was launched by part of a divided leadership directed by Mao, whose suspicion of cities had been expressed on many occasions. Mao's links with the urban working class were limited, however strong they were supposed to be in theory, and hence it is not surprising that Mao turned principally for support to a group in city life with which he felt comfortable – the students – both in higher education and in the senior parts of secondary schools. These allies gave the Cultural Revolution much of its particular character, such as its destructive attack on aspects of older China, its scorn for intellectualism, its reduction of debate to quotations from Mao and its gloating pleasure at humiliating authority figures in the community.

Although the opening events of the Cultural Revolution can be presented relatively clearly and succinctly, the flow of events from August 1966 to mid-1968 is too complex to allow more than a general outline of the major trends to be explored here. This complexity arose from the loosening of central direction of policy as the Party began to lose authority and as a result each region of China experienced different combinations of power seizures, chaos, interventions by the military and restorations of some stability, as the different groups among the population jostled for leadership. Our greatest knowledge of regional events comes from South China as a result of the flight of some of the participants to Hong Kong, where they were interviewed by Western officials and scholars. Other sources of information for the period, in addition to the official Beijing Party press, include a wide range of publications by Red Guards – that is by organisations set up principally by students to promote the Cultural Revolution.

Although the Great Proletarian Cultural Revolution was formally announced on 1 May 1966 by Premier Zhou Enlai, it is usual to trace its immediate origins to an article of November 1965 by the Shanghai literary critic, Yao Wenyuan, on the subject of Wu Han's historical play, 'Hai Rui dismissed from office'. The portrayal of Hai Rui, an official in the sixteenth century who had been wrongly sacked by an evil emperor, was viewed by Mao as a thinly veiled reference to the dismissal of Peng Dehuai in 1959. Although Mao had spoken out against the play within Party circles at a central work conference in September and October 1965, his efforts had been ineffective, because Wu Han was protected by his political superior in Beijing, Peng Zhen. Peng had earlier been named as the head of a five-man Party group to spearhead cultural reform, a group on which Mao had only one close supporter, Kang Sheng. Yao's

article was printed in the Shanghai and army press, where Mao
had influence, but only later in the *Beijing Daily*, with editorial
comment that the problems of the play were academic, not
political. Nevertheless Wu Han did publish a self-criticism for
his errors and Peng Zhen's five-man group produced an outline report in February 1966 for circulation within the Party.
This report restricted the debate on Wu Han to questions of
interpretation of historical figures. Mao immediately counterattacked by criticising Peng Zhen for suppressing attacks on
Wu Han and for distorting the direction of the cultural revolution. Meanwhile a new set of guidelines for literature and
art in the PLA was drawn up under Mao's wife, Jiang Qing,
with strong criticism of a 'black line' in cultural work. These
attacks culminated in the dissolution of Peng's five-man group
and in May his dismissal from his post as mayor of Beijing.

Even before Peng Zhen's dismissal, the Great Proletarian Cultural Revolution had been announced after several meetings
of senior Party leaders, but the later scope of the movement
was not immediately apparent from Premier Zhou's call to wipe
out bourgeois ideology in all fields. To implement the Cultural Revolution, a new group of eighteen was created at a
mid-May Politburo meeting, under the leadership of Chen Boda,
Kang Sheng and Jiang Qing. This meeting also denounced
representatives of the bourgeoisie who had sneaked into the
Party. The most immediate result came in Beijing University,
where on 25 May a group led by Nie Yuanzi, a lecturer in the
philosophy department, put up a big-character poster accusing
the university and city authorities of restricting the Cultural
Revolution by their insistence on strengthening the leadership.
The authorities replied by suppressing the poster, but Mao
arranged for the broadcast of its message on the radio on
1 June and its publication in *The People's Daily* on 2 June, which
forced the departure of the University's president and opened
the way to widespread student activism. This was further enhanced by a Central Committee decision to postpone examinations for a semester.

The criticism of school authorities by students forced the
school Party committees to seek help from higher Party levels,
help achieved by the dispatch of work teams, authorised by the
state chairman, Liu Shaoqi, who was in daily charge of Party

organisation. The work teams, although initially welcomed by the students, quickly revealed that they were intent on suppressing the student activists, in defence of the school authorities. Very soon the campuses became divided over attitudes to the work teams, with a tendency for support for the work teams to come from those students who were from families of Party cadres or otherwise advantaged by the system, while opposition often arose from those unable to advance easily under the class preferences of the Party, such as children from families classified as bourgeois. The work teams, backed as they were by the authority of the Party organisation, were largely successful in suppressing opposition in June and the first half of July, but the reappearance of Mao in Beijing on 18 July, after a famous swim in the Yangzi River on 16 July, marked a change from finding targets among the students to a refocusing of the attack upon Party leaders opposing the Cultural Revolution. Some of the trends visible in June and July were to develop greatly over the coming months, the use of public or big-character posters, the call to sweep away the old, the promotion of loyalty to Mao Zedong Thought as the proof of revolutionary character, the efforts of senior Party leaders to deflect attacks or to step up conflicts among the masses, and the efforts of the young to challenge many of their elders.

With the return of Mao to Beijing, a central work conference was held for central and regional Party leaders, followed by the eleventh plenum of the Eighth Central Committee, 1–12 August 1966. This plenum was unusual in that it was attended by only two-thirds of the regular committee members, while revolutionary teachers and students also attended, thereby ensuring the passage of resolutions largely favourable to Mao's view. As the plenum opened, Mao wrote a letter in support of student wall-posters and then on 5 August wrote his own wall-poster entitled 'Bombard the Headquarters', which attacked the work teams and indicated Mao's dissatisfaction with many of his senior colleagues, although without naming them specifically. The plenum, after heated debate, passed a sixteen-point resolution, published on 8 August, which provided initial guidance to the expanding Cultural Revolution. The focus was to be urban, with the creation of cultural revolutionary groups and congresses as permanent mass organisations to help to achieve the revolutionary goals. The campaign was not to interfere with production nor to involve the military whose own cultural revolution would be internally handled. The resolution was imprecise on the targets of the Cultural Revolution, naming three – capitalist roaders in the Party, bourgeois academic authorities and non-socialist aspects of culture – without a clear order of priority, but it was clear that the main vanguard in the attack on these targets was to be revolutionary youth. The plenum also demoted Liu Shaoqi from second to eighth place in the Party and raised Lin Biao to be Party Vice-chairman, while readjusting membership of the Politburo and its Standing Committee to increase support for Mao.

The Central Committee's call for a vanguard role for revolutionary youth gave full sanction to the formation of the Red Guards, the most famous innovation of the Cultural Revolution. Although the term had been mentioned as early as May 1966, it became sanctified when Mao donned a Red Guard armband at the first mass rally of Beijing youth on 18 August. At the second Beijing rally on 31 August, Premier Zhou Enlai encouraged the Red Guards to seek 'great exchanges of experiences', which resulted in millions of young Chinese travelling throughout China, often without paying for their train tickets. At the start membership of Red Guard groups was restricted to students, particularly those from the five revolutionary backgrounds, the children of workers, poor peasants, revolutionary cadres, soldiers and martyrs, but increasingly other students from more politically suspect backgrounds sought entry. In addition Red Guard units were later created outside the educational field. The activities of the Red Guards during August and September focused on attacks upon 'bourgeois intellectuals' who were to be humiliated in public parades and meetings, and on the search for evidence of attachment to traditional culture, which often involved the forcible entry into homes and the subsequent destruction of undesirable items found.

By October 1966 Mao and the Cultural Revolution Small Group which supported him had come to realise that the Red Guard movement was not achieving the desired impact upon the Party and therefore sought to extend the target more clearly to power-holders taking the capitalist road within the Party. To achieve this, the Party press in early October talked of the manipulation of the Red Guards by the 'bourgeois reactionary line' and demanded that individuals decide whether commands from above were in accordance with Mao Zedong Thought, thereby denying the automatic authority of superiors in any organisation. Recruitment to the Red Guards was to be open to all activists, regardless of their family background, a decision which released much hatred towards the earlier Red Guards chosen from cadre families, and all the files from the mid-1966 work team investigations were to be destroyed. Violent confrontations arose between radical and conservative factions within the Red Guard movement, with the radicals initially as the victors, and wall posters began to appear that named Liu Shaoqi and Deng Xiaoping as the leaders of the bourgeois reactionary line. A central work conference during October attempted unsuccessfully to define the scope of the mistakes of Liu and Deng and revealed a division between Defence Minister, Lin Biao, with his call for revolutionising one's ideology and the Cultural Revolution Small Group's desire to struggle against powerholders in the Party. After the work conference the Party press stressed revolutionising one's ideology and a major campaign was pushed to study Mao's writing, with Mao described by Lin as the greatest genius in the present era.

By mid-December the Cultural Revolution was spreading rapidly, with calls for Cultural Revolution groups to be formed in factories and communes, and the first public struggle meetings against senior Party leaders such as Peng Zhen, Beijing's former mayor, were organised by the more radical Red Guards. The addition of factory workers to the activists greatly increased the potential for large-scale action, but the workers were divided in their objectives. Workers with permanent jobs tended to defend the existing situation, although keen to push for higher wages, whereas workers on contract or temporary workers used the opportunity to air their grievances against factory and Party bosses who had taken advantage of their poorly protected positions. As Party committees sought to defend themselves from radical attacks, they began to offer wage increases or handouts to workers and in rural areas communal funds were sometimes divided up among the peasants. This rise of 'economism', the use of economic incentives to deter workers from seeking deeper political goals, severely disrupted the Chinese economy, bringing much of industry to a halt as workers left their posts either in series of strikes or to travel at factory expense. Since the original goals of the Cultural Revolution had included promoting production, this new situation required a vigorous response.

This response came in January 1967 with the call for power seizures from below by the masses, as the Maoist leadership despaired of the revolutionary possibilities of most Party leaders. The developing situation in Shanghai provided the main inspiration for this central initiative. Conflicts in Shanghai between factions of Red Guards from December 1966 had culminated in the seizure of the local *Wenhuibao* newspaper by the radicals and open attacks upon the Municipal Party committee, which actions were endorsed by the national newspaper, *The People's Daily*. There followed the takeover of factories and transport by mass organisations which ousted the established Party leaders. This process of power seizure from below was adopted as Maoist policy on 22 January 1967 and spread slowly to other areas of China. Within Shanghai the mass organisations announced the creation of the Shanghai People's Commune on 5 February with Zhang Chunqiao, a local Party cadre, as the principal leader; it was modelled on the direct participatory democracy of the Paris commune of 1871. The process of power seizure which occurred at both provincial and ministerial levels often resulted in chaos, since there were no effective guidelines to determine which groups ought to seize power, and this was not clarified by the vague instruction to the PLA regional units to support the left of the broad masses.

By February Mao and his colleagues at the centre had realised that the programme of power seizures and the attempt to govern without any input from former cadres were not applicable to most of China. Hence a more moderate policy was pursued, later dubbed by the radicals as the 'adverse February current', which repudiated the idea of the Commune and preferred the creation of provincial and municipal revolutionary committees drawn from three sources, the former cadres, the PLA and representatives of the mass organisations. The centre also sought to re-establish order through bans on the exchange of revolutionary experience and the control of materials published by the Red Guards. The role of the PLA was very important from this time onwards in the Cultural Revolution, for it was the principal national organisation that was left intact during the Cultural Revolution. Thus it remained available to impose law and order when other groups were in conflict and it also tended to give support to those mass organisations which were willing to accept superior authority, a practice which did not often result in support of the left.

By March 1967 the intervention of the PLA regional units had reduced the role of the mass organisation leaders, and the Red Guards sought to counteract this trend with the support of central leaders. The role of the masses was again stressed in the Party press and in early April the Army's Cultural Revolution Group was reorganised to improve support for Mao. In addition regional units of the PLA were instructed to step aside from the merging of mass organisations, and units of the PLA's centrally commanded Army corps were deployed to ensure that local commanders did not act arbitrarily or allow any shooting to pressure the masses. To provide a clear focus for Red Guard activity, the Party centre began in early April an official, open attack on the former state chairman, Liu Shaoqi, but although this identified the top target for criticism, it did not fully solve the factional problems within the Red Guard movement, particularly over the choice of lesser targets for attack. The events of the first three months of 1967 had created considerable Red Guard dissatisfaction with senior government ministers and with the PLA, but open challenge to the PLA or to the government's head, Premier Zhou Enlai, was not sanctioned. Hence Red Guard attacks were mounted against ministers and vice-premiers and against individual PLA local commanders, but with limited effect because the central leadership was unwilling to offer its vigorous support and the attackers were opposed by other factions within the Red Guards.

Between April and July 1967 factional fighting among Red Guards occurred over much of China, with many hundreds killed, as attempts were made to create great alliances of the masses in preparation for effective operation of revolutionary committees. The level of violence was probably greatest in Sichuan and Inner Mongolia. Underlying the factional tensions were tensions within the elite, especially between the Cultural Revolution Small Group and the leaders of the government and the PLA. The Small Group was determined to spread the search for bourgeois power-holders as widely as possible and was frustrated at the limitations on exposing capitalist roaders in the PLA. An offshoot of the Small Group, called the May 16 Group, developed a programme for the manipulation of radical Red Guard activity, with the ultimate aim of deposing Zhou Enlai and discrediting the regional PLA. The May 16 Group consisted largely of intellectuals with connections to the media, who hoped to gain by a complete shake-out of the existing authority structures.

A major shift against the PLA and in favour of the Small Group resulted from the Wuhan incident of 20 July 1967. In Wuhan the local PLA had offered support for the more conservative faction of the Red Guards by disbanding the radicals' headquarters in March. Arguments between the radicals and the local PLA had led to conference in Beijing, which failed to resolve the radicals' grievances. Conflicts persisted and the disruption more than halved the industrial output of the city. A fact-finding mission from the centre, including Wang Li, a leading member of the Small Group, arrived in Wuhan in mid-July. After investigation it indicated that the PLA leaders had acted wrongly in supporting the conservatives and that the radical organisation must be re-established. On his return to his hotel, Wang Li was kidnapped by the conservative Red Guards and the local PLA refused to step in, claiming that this was a spontaneous action by the masses. Peking replied promptly by despatching centrally commanded troops to the Wuhan area. Wang was able to escape and the conservative Red Guards organisation disintegrated. The Small Group interpreted this event as proof of the existence of capitalist roaders in the PLA and persuaded the centre to authorise the masses to drag out the power-holders in the army. Jiang Qing, Mao's wife, told Red Guards on 22 July to 'defend with weapons and attack with words' and this provoked Red Guard attacks on PLA arms depots. The PLA, still under orders not to shoot the masses, replied by aiding conservative organisations to attack the more radical Red Guards. The result was an August of urban civil war, which even included the takeover of the Foreign Ministry and the raiding of the British Embassy, parts of which were burnt down.

This level of chaos was clearly unacceptable to the majority of the Chinese leadership and calls for moderation began during

August, with the revelation of the existence of the ultra-leftist
May 16 Group and opposition to dragging out the PLA power-
holders. A directive from Mao spoke of the PLA as the Great
Wall defending the revolution and the PLA was also instructed
to use force against any attempt to seize its weapons. The Party
press began to attack ultra-leftism and two members of the
Cultural Revolution Small Group, Wang Li and Guan Feng,
were purged. Efforts were made to promote Premier Zhou Enlai's
image as a mediator between the rival factions throughout China.
The role of the students in the Cultural Revolution was played
down, with the reopening of schools, although without restart-
ing formal academic study, and with further attempts to stop
students travelling to exchange experiences. As the students'
role was reduced, so the role of workers was praised as the
leading force in the Cultural Revolution, a position which was
likely to reduce the radical mood of the movement, since workers
tended to be less disruptive than the students.

In parallel with the attack on ultra-leftism was a renewed
push to establish revolutionary committees as the new form of
authority throughout China. This push required the collaboration of the rival mass organisations in accepting suitable mass
candidates for the committees and also in deciding which Party
cadres had proved themselves worthy, either by their pre-
Cultural Revolution careers or by their recent acts. Such collaboration was not easy to achieve, and discussions involved the
local PLA and the intervention of the centre, with a key role
for Zhou Enlai. The establishment of preliminary committees
was followed by study classes in Mao Zedong Thought, which
were intended to build solidarity among the groups represented.
New revolutionary committees were formed in eleven provinces
between November 1967 and mid-March 1968, to join the seven
committees already in existence by November. Although the
mass organisations, the cadres and the PLA were to be equally
represented on these committees, in practice rivalries within
the first two groups meant that the PLA representatives usually
dominated the committees.

Nevertheless, the increasing role of the PLA was not viewed
with favour by the whole of the central leadership and in March
1968 the purge of the chief of staff, Yang Chengwu, for 'serious
mistakes', launched the last radical phase of the Cultural

Revolution. Yang Chengwu had attempted to use the attacks against ultra-leftism as a way to discredit the Cultural Revolution Small Group, and hence his purge coincided with a reversal of the official line in a new campaign against rightist trends, especially against the 'rightist reversal of verdicts'. These reversals referred to efforts to change the labels which had been placed upon those criticised in the first two years of the Cultural Revolution. The Small Group took this opportunity to promote again the view that one's class was determined by one's recent performance during the Cultural Revolution, rather than to one's family's class background, thereby allowing a renewed legitimacy to many of those students who had been active in the early period of the Cultural Revolution.

The result was renewed conflict between radical and conservative mass organisations, with armed struggle in many areas by June and July 1968. On this occasion the PLA's unity and ability to maintain control was severely compromised, as on occasions units of the PLA lined up on opposing sides in the local factional disputes. Hence the centre was obliged to stress the need for stability in the army, despatching special army units under direct central control in June to all areas to seek negotiated settlements of factional disputes. When this failed to produce order, the centre in July announced that anyone engaging in armed struggle was a class enemy, thus denying specific legitimacy to either radicals or conservatives among the mass organisations. Although this approach largely brought a halt to open fighting, since the PLA could intervene without the need to investigate the claims of the fighting groups, it could not resolve the many conflicts within society. This task was clearly given to new Worker-Peasant Mao Zedong Thought Teams who operated not only in factories but also in schools to arrange cease-fires, and to build grand alliances. There was considerable resistance by students to this worker intrusion into educational institutions, but Mao's support for the worker teams was clearly expressed by his symbolic gift of mangoes to a worker team at Qinghua University in Beijing in early August. In addition Yao Wenyuan, whose article against Wu Han's play had opened the Cultural Revolution, wrote in August that the working class must exercise leadership in everything, thus reconfirming the opinion which had been voiced in mid-1967 that workers were more important than students in the revolutionary process.

The principal task to be undertaken by the Worker-Peasant teams was the campaign to purify class ranks, an attempt to begin the rebuilding of the Party with only genuine supporters of Mao included. The Party leadership, although relying in part upon criteria of class background, also noted that perform-ance in the Cultural Revolution was important and tried to reduce the number of cadres to be purged by softening the categories for attack. Thus, for example, instead of purging all bourgeois power-holders, the guidelines called for only the elimination of stubborn bourgeois power-holders. Although the mass of the population was to be involved in the judgement of each case, the higher authorities reserved the right to approve or disapprove any decision.

As part of the consolidation process the remaining provin-cial revolutionary committees were all formed by early September 1968, but the creation of the revolutionary committees at lower levels was still beset with problems left over from the rivalries of the Cultural Revolution. The problem of how to deal with the student Red Guards in the cities was resolved, at least as far as the cities were concerned, by sending the Red Guards to rural or border areas where they were to take part in produc-tion. It now seems that the Red Guards were not very welcome in the rural areas and that their integration with rural produc-tion was for the most part minimal. Sending to the countryside was also used as a remedy for errant cadres, who attended 7 May cadre schools. Although announced as opportunities for study and remoulding by contact with the peasant masses, in practice these schools tended to keep the cadres working in isolation from ordinary peasants: in addition most cadres con-tinued to be paid their urban salaries whilst working rurally, although unable to draw upon these funds while in the 7 May schools.

The formal conclusion of the active phase of the Cultural Revolution came with the enlarged twelfth plenum of the Eighth Central Committee, held in Beijing from 11 to 31 October 1968. This plenum was attended not only by the remaining committee members who had not been purged during the Cultural Revolu-tion, but also by representatives from the PLA and the revolu-tionary committees. The plenum approved a new draft Party constitution for circulation within the Party, including the formal naming of Lin Biao as Mao's successor. The plenum also confirmed the correctness of launching the Cultural Revolution and publicly named Liu Shaoqi as the primary traitor within the Party, who was therefore dismissed from all his posts and from the Party. No public statement was issued about the number two target, Deng Xiaoping. The plenum foreshadowed the calling of a Ninth Party Congress, which would allow the full consolidation of the victories of the Cultural Revolution within the Party.

The foregoing discussion has focused upon the Party and political aspects of the period 1966 to 1968, but it is necessary also to note the impact of these events in other spheres. Given that the Cultural Revolution involved massive disruption of urban life at times, it was inevitable that industrial production was reduced, with 1967 production well below 1966 levels, but 1968 saw a return to nearly the levels of 1966. Agricultural production was less severely hit by the political situation, reacting more to climatic variations which allowed some small improvement in 1967 and a slight decline in 1968. The desire to weed out capitalist roaders led to greater stress upon moral, rather than material incentives as the motivation for work. There was a renewed stress on the brigade in agricultural organisation and some communes sought to abolish private plots, a policy the centre described as premature. The differences between the better-serviced urban communities and the more-deprived rural areas were attacked by Mao, particularly in the medical field, which saw the growth of a rural para-medical service of 'barefoot doctors', who could offer simple care directly to the peasants in their villages. Some scientific work at a more complex level was also promoted during this period, culminating in the explosion of China's first hydrogen bomb in 1967.

In the foreign affairs field, the Cultural Revolution produced a severe contraction of all China's foreign relations as most ambassadors were recalled. China continued to support the North Vietnamese in their escalating war against the USA, but without direct involvement. Relations with Britain were particularly badly affected by the events of the Cultural Revolution, with the detention of Britons in China, with the burning of part of the British Embassy and with the spread of mass violence to the British colony of Hong Kong in 1967, inspired by events across the border in China. Relations with the socialist bloc countries remained strained, except for Albania, and China denounced the Soviet invasion of Czechoslovakia in August 1968 as an act of social-imperialism, comparable in behaviour to that of the USA in Vietnam. That Soviet invasion had been justified by the Soviet leader, Brezhnev, through the argument of limited sovereignty for nations in the socialist bloc and hence China faced the possibility that she too might be attacked by the USSR, especially for the purpose of destroying China's nuclear facilities before they became too sophisticated. Many have argued that the decision to wind down the Cultural Revolution in 1968 was related to the deterioration in relations with the USSR, although few anticipated at that time that there would be large-scale military conflicts on the border.

The winding down of the Cultural Revolution continued during the first two months of 1969, with a general stress on order and stability, and this mood was enhanced by the fighting between Chinese and Russian soldiers along the Ussuri River at Zhenbao Island in March. The conflict centred on a river frontier, where the position of islands in relation to the main river channel was a possible subject for dispute, especially given that the maps attached to nineteenth-century treaties were very small-scale: in addition the river froze over in winter. The Chinese claimed that the Russians had entered clear Chinese territory and had finally been driven out by force, this 2 March intrusion coming after more than fifty border incidents in the area in the previous two years. A further battle occurred on 15 March, with the Chinese retaining the island. Large public demonstrations were held throughout China to denounce Soviet actions and smaller anti-Chinese demonstrations occurred in some Russian cities. These incidents in the Chinese north-east reinforced the antagonism which had been growing for a decade between China and the USSR and resulted in a coldness between the two powers which lasted into the late 1980s. In the short term other incidents occurred during 1969 in the Yili area in the Chinese far west, where tensions had been previously high in 1962 and where clashes on a small scale had happened hundreds of times annually since 1964.

The Ninth Party Congress and After

The events on the frontier were not allowed to interfere with
the main political event of 1969, the convening of the Party's
Ninth Congress from 1 to 24 April, and indeed may have given
greater importance to the Congress as an opportunity to display unity. The Congress spent most of its time discussing a
political report prepared by Lin Biao and refining the Party
constitution. It was later revealed that Mao had been dissatisfied with the early draft of Lin's report, but there was no open
evidence of this at the time of the Congress. Lin's report detailed the reasons behind the Cultural Revolution, stressing the
struggle between the two lines of Mao and Liu Shaoqi since
1957, and outlined events up to mid-1968, without officially
stating that the Cultural Revolution was over. The report called
for leniency in the treatment of those who had made mistakes
and asserted that the Cultural Revolution would allow a more
rapid economic advance because of its arousal of the masses.
The longest section in the report dealt with China's foreign
relations, with strong criticisms of both the USSR and the USA
and an optimistic assessment of the prospects for world revolution. The general mood of the report was sober, with an
acceptance that the final victory of the revolution in China
was a long way off.

The new Party constitution was a much shorter document
than that of 1956 and failed to clarify some important issues,
such as the relationship between the Party and the new revolutionary committees. Mao Zedong Thought was proclaimed
afresh as the current guide for the Party, being claimed as the
contemporary form of Marxism–Leninism, and Mao's leadership was praised. Lin Biao was formally named as Mao's
close comrade-in-arms and successor. Party membership was to
be specifically open to workers, poor and lower-middle peasants, and soldiers, but there was also a vague category of 'any
other revolutionary element'. The Party members were encouraged to unite with those who had wrongly opposed them, a
call to put aside the conflicts of the Cultural Revolution. The
constitution stressed that the army and the mass organisations such as the Red Guards must accept the leadership of
the Party. Power within the Party was concentrated in the Po-

litburo and its Standing Committee, with no mention of a Party secretariat.

The Ninth Congress also elected a new large Central Committee, of 270 members (full and alternate), only forty-eight of whom remained from the Eighth Central Committee. Over 40 per cent of the Ninth Central Committee were serving military men, reflecting the major role of the army in the re-establishment of order in China in 1968 and 1969. The trend was even more clear at the Politburo level, where ten of the sixteen new members were military men, but the Standing Committee of the Politburo had only one specifically military figure, Lin Biao, alongside Mao, Chen Boda, Zhou Enlai and Kang Sheng. The new Central Committee also had some model workers and representatives of mass organisations, but very few prominent Red Guard leaders, an indication that the new line of unity and stability was intended to be pursued by the Party without undue radical interference. Although the Congress was interpreted at the time as proof of military dominance within China, subsequent events including the fall of Lin Biao in 1971 have led analysts to note the limitations of Lin's power, including his inability to confirm the continuation of the Cultural Revolution Small Group, which was last mentioned in the official press in December 1969.

Throughout the remainder of 1969 the political focus was on the rebuilding of the Party organisations at the lower levels, but this programme proved difficult to implement because of rivalries left over from the Cultural Revolution. Party rebuilding was initially based on a model developed in Shanghai, which stressed maximum popular participation with non-Party members attending meetings, recruitment linked to activism in the Cultural Revolution and delayed rehabilitation of erring cadres until after prolonged education, but this approach was abandoned in early 1970, with a much-reduced role for the masses and greater leniency over rehabilitations. Reports still emerged of areas, such as Shanxi province, where anarchy was said to reign on occasions, as different factions sought to ensure supremacy in the new revolutionary committees. The first county-level Party committee was re-established in November 1969, but even by a year later less than fifty such committees had been achieved. The Party's main call was for unity, but this was contradicted in part by reminding Party members to be vigilant and avoid relaxing in the belief that the victory of the Cultural Revolution was secure. During 1970, there was a further campaign against disruptive elements, called the 'one-hit, three antis' campaign, which resulted in the imprisonment of thousands, who were released after Lin Biao's death.

With the gradual return of less-disrupted political conditions throughout China, the government was able to turn its attention to economic issues. Several provincial conferences were held in later 1969 on agricultural and economic matters and there was even some talk of creating a 'flying leap' in agricultural production. The 1969 harvest saw record grain production, which has been taken as evidence that the Cultural Revolution caused only limited dislocation in rural areas. One problem created for the rural areas in the winding down of the Cultural Revolution was the absorption of urban youths who had been sent down to the countryside. Although much propaganda talked of the revolutionary enthusiasm of these rusticated youths who probably numbered over 10 million, in practice many resented what they saw as banishment, and proved uncooperative with the demands of their new peasant leaders. In the industrial field production continued to grow, with particular success in the expansion of China's oil production, but it is not clear how far activity fell within the intentions of the Third Five Year Plan which had theoretically begun in 1966.

The events of 1970 and 1971 revealed how fragile was the superficial unity which had resulted from the apparent Maoist victory in the Cultural Revolution. As with previous divisions in the Party, the policy issues and the personality questions were tightly interwoven and the fall of Lin Biao resulted in a flood of personal attacks upon Lin and his senior military colleagues. Although some of these attacks were ridiculous, for example, claims that Lin had been consistently opposing Mao for at least forty years, the general shape of the conflict between Mao and Lin is clear.

There were at least four areas where conflict appeared, concerning the relations of the army and the Party, the need to persevere with institutions and ideas from the Cultural Revolution, the question of how to break out of China's diplomatic isolation and the issue of leadership in China, but it was the last of these which proved the main problem at larger Party meetings. Lin Biao wished to restore Mao to the post of state chairman and to promote Mao's reputation as an extreme genius, both of which schemes Mao interpreted as preparing improperly for Lin's own advancement. At the second plenum of the Ninth Central Committee, meeting in late August and early September 1970, Lin had repeatedly urged Mao to accept the state chairmanship and finally Mao had responded by persuading the committee to alter the state constitution to remove the possibility of the post even existing. Mao also initiated attacks on Lin's colleague, Chen Boda, who had previously been Mao's secretary. Chen was associated very closely with the Cultural Revolution Small Group and with the more radical aspects of ideology in the Cultural Revolution.

The second plenum also initiated a modification in the method of Party reconstruction, changing the focus from creating county Party committees to the rebuilding of provincial Party committees. In nine months from December 1970 provincial Party committees were achieved all over China and this achievement can be seen as a threat to the authority of the military as exercised in the provincial revolutionary committees. Nevertheless the public impression generated at the time was of a unified Party seeking to reconstruct, rather than of a process which Lin Biao and some of this military colleagues sought to obstruct.

The details of Lin Biao's moves against Mao in 1971 are clouded with uncertainty, with the most extreme versions indicating a fully fledged plan for a military *coup d'état* under the title of The 571 Project. The name was a pun in Chinese implying armed uprising. The prime mover in such a plot may have been Lin's son, rather than Lin himself. Even if such a formal conspiracy did not exist, Lin Biao and some of his senior military colleagues, including the chief of staff, Huang Yongsheng and the air force head, Wu Faxian, did come to feel by mid-1971 that Mao was seeking to undermine their authority by appointing his own choices for major military posts, especially in the Beijing military region. During August 1971 Mao toured the provinces, speaking against splitting the Party and urging prudence, while voicing his own criticisms of Lin. This open pressure from Mao confirmed to Lin that Mao was determined to restrict Lin's power and Lin reacted by preparing to move against Mao. Whether a full military coup was attempted at this point or whether, as seems more likely, only some pre-paratory planning was undertaken, the result was totally unsat-isfactory for Lin and his colleagues. Fearing the discovery of their plotting, Lin and his wife may have attempted in mid-September to flee the country but, if so, their escape plane crashed in Outer Mongolia on its way to the USSR. Inspection of the wreckage was carried out very limitedly and this has raised suspicions that the two were dead before they entered the plane and that the crash had been stage-managed to give the impression of Lin as a traitor fleeing the country.

The question remains of why Lin Biao should have fled towards the USSR, either in reality or in the stage-managed version of events, and this relates directly to the international aspects of the Lin affair. As China's main spokesman for people's war and revolutionary diplomacy in the mid-1960s, Lin proved unwilling to accept the shift in Mao's diplomatic tactics arising from the 1969 open conflict with the USSR. For Mao the threat of facing the USSR unaided required the acquisition of diplo-matic friends in the classic united front pattern, rather than the continuation of Cultural Revolution isolationism.

With opposition to Soviet 'hegemonism' as the new centre for China's policy, there was room for accommodation with countries of the West, whose support for the internal policies of the CCP was limited or non-existent. The USA, under its new president, the Republican and vigorously anti-Communist Richard Nixon, had signalled a willingness to relax its line on China by its mid-1969 reduction in the restrictions on visits to China, even while still prosecuting its war against Vietnam. Edgar Snow, Mao's biographer of the 1930s, was employed by Mao and Zhou Enlai in late 1970 to relay the message that China would welcome the restart of USA–China discussions and a possible visit by Nixon to China. 'Ping-pong diplomacy' in April 1971 saw the Chinese table-tennis team inviting a US team playing in Japan to visit China, and in July it was announced that Henry Kissinger had spent two days secretly in Beijing with Zhou as Nixon's special envoy. The results were spectacularly success-ful for Mao and Zhou, with the People's Republic regaining its seat at the United Nations in September 1971, as the US realignment became clear, followed by the visit of Nixon to China in February 1972 and the opening of wide-ranging diplomatic and economic contacts with the West and Japan. Nevertheless, for Lin this shift must have represented a betrayal of the anti-capitalist claims of the Cultural Revolution and an unacceptable preference for the blatantly bourgeois West as against the nominally socialist USSR. Hence a flight to the USSR is understandable, as a rejection of Mao's nationalistic approach of seeking the best international environment for China's development, regardless of its counter-revolutionary impact in other ways.

Although it is understandable that foreigners should want to think that external events have been more important than internal ones in determining China's development, the diplomatic shift in 1971, with its accompanying internal affirmation of the leadership of Mao and the Party over the temporarily ascendant military, does mark a crucial change. The first version of Chinese self-reliance had meant exactly that, a sense that China could achieve anything with its own expertise and labour, but 1971 began the acceptance of foreign advice, not in the spirit of socialist internationalism as in the 1950s, but from a view based strictly on economic advantage. 1971 allowed the Party to begin the criticism of ultra-leftism and to adopt more overtly economic criteria for judging the value of industrial projects, even though the full flowering of the opposition to empty revolutionary rhetoric did not occur until after Mao's death in 1976. Although the Party later looked back on the period, 1966–76, as the wasted years of the Cultural Revolution period, the period 1971–6 was more ordered and more productive than the period, 1966–71. The later years allowed the re-emergence of leaders who had been condemned in the active phase of the Cultural Revolution, notably Deng Xiaoping, and this mellowing of the Party's line on the value of revolutionary veterans links this later period clearly with the time after Mao's death.

8 The Chinese Way: Mark Two

Chapter 7 outlined the history of the period from 1958 to 1971, a time when the Chinese sought to find their own way to achieve socialist development, after the rejection of Soviet economic models. This search began with the overtly economic programmes of the Great Leap Forward and the retrenchment after its failure, but culminated in the much broader political and social programmes of the Cultural Revolution. These conceived socialist transformation in terms of ideological purity and social equity and gave rise to several policy thrusts. These included anti-intellectualism, greater egalitarianism, popular involvement in economic affairs and attacks on bureaucracy. Underlying the whole period lay the principle of self-reliance, both on a national scale and also on a region-by-region and ideally a commune-by-commune basis. This self-reliance policy stressed the importance of strategic defensive concerns, as against economic calculations based on the comparative advantages of different areas for different economic tasks. Self-reliance also appealed to the nationalism of Chinese leaders, who had led their revolution to achieve a China independent of foreign influence, except for guidance from the originally Western theory of Marxism–Leninism.

Nevertheless the chaos which had been induced by the Cultural Revolution between 1966 and 1968 and the continued political difficulties between the army and the Party culminating in Lin Biao's fall led many of the Chinese leaders, with Zhou Enlai as their principal spokesman, to question the value of Cultural Revolution approaches for the betterment of China. With the death of Lin, Zhou moved to initiate a vigorous programme of policy specification, through the convening of central policy conferences on different topics. Such conferences implied formal venues for the creation of policy, very remote from the mass mobilisation of the Cultural Revolution. In late 1971 conferences were held on economic planning, science, public security and education. The emerging goal for policy became modernisation, implying rapid economic growth, with a political stress on unity and stability under Party leadership.

Such a goal required an expansion in trained scientific and technical personnel and the existence of an experienced administrative group to oversee the programme. Given the reassertion of Party authority since the Ninth Congress and especially since Lin's death, and given also the highly politicised atmosphere emerging from the Cultural Revolution, there was only one possible source for these needed administrative cadres. They had to be from the politically educated veteran administrators who were Party members. Since these had formed the major target group in the Cultural Revolution, it was necessary to rehabilitate these veterans and to claim that their behaviour had been altered by their re-education. This claim has been challenged several times since, both within the Party as in early 1974 and mid-1976 and later from outside, as evidence of corruption and abuse of power has been revealed. A further change in rehabilitation policy occurred in late 1971, whereby veterans were to be rehabilitated into their original work units at their pre-1966 rank, rather than sending them to new units at lower ranks, as had been the practice. To reduce tensions in work units somewhat, many new cadres in leading positions, that is those who had risen rapidly in the Cultural Revolution, were assigned back to grassroots levels, nominally to prevent them from becoming divorced from production.

The emerging new programme, finally codified in 1975 as the Four Modernisations, directly challenged the 'newborn things' which had appeared from the Cultural Revolution, by placing economic importance above political value. As indicated in Chapter 7, the most obvious feature to outsiders was the shift in foreign policy, which allowed vigorous economic relations with the advanced capitalist countries of the Western world, based on a realisation that China was still backward technologically, however advanced its political system might be. Contracts were placed in the West and Japan for the construction of ninety-five complete industrial plants, with a value of at least US$ 2 billion. These purchases over a two-year period were paid for in part by medium-term overseas credits and the total was only a little less than the entire complete-plant import programme of the 1950s from the USSR and Eastern Europe. The plants included a major expansion of the Wuhan steel complex, twenty-six factories to double China's nitrogenous fertiliser capacity from modern equipment, and a range of petrochemical installations. Part of the cost was also to be met by increased exports of Chinese raw materials, especially oil, whose production had leapt since the early 1960s.

Although the opening to the West had clearly been endorsed by Mao through his meetings with Western leaders, it was much less clear how far Mao approved of the rest of the new programme, for which he never publicly indicated his support. Thus the attempts under Zhou to modify policies in industry, agriculture and education were met with resistance by those who regarded these modifications as rejections of the Cultural Revolution, with in some cases the apparent support of the aging Mao, whose ability to lead decisively and consistently had largely disappeared.

The search for a nominally new course, reflecting some aspects of practice between 1953 and 1966, and the desire of some to maintain strict conformity with Mao's more recent policies since 1966, lay at the heart of the Chinese political process from 1971 to 1976. It was given greater intensity because the outcome would determine not only the direction of China, but also the leadership after Mao's death. Mao had already failed with the nomination of two successors, Liu Shaoqi and Lin Biao, and hence was understandably reluctant to name a third. There were two possible options, to entrust leadership to another veteran revolutionary, whose time in power would be limited by age, or to select younger activists from lower down the Party, who would have to make up for their lack of administrative experience by their energy and ideological zeal. In practice Mao prevaricated, allowing the advancement of the major Cultural Revolution target – the veteran Deng Xiaoping – in government work, and the promotion of Cultural Revolution activists, notably a Shanghai worker, Wang Hongwen, who emerged as number three in the CCP in 1973. The situation was further confused by the unexpected emergence of a middle-aged Party member, Hua Guofeng, as first vice-chairman of the

Party in 1976, with what was said to be Mao's full support. Although Hua survived for a time to lead the post-Mao Party, the final resolution was the claiming of leadership by the Party veterans under Deng and the repudiation of the Cultural Revolution. Even after these veterans began to retire from executive posts in the 1980s, their power remained and was firmly reasserted in 1989, during the bloody suppression of large public demonstrations in Beijing.

Politics in 1972 and 1973

The fall of Lin Biao in 1971, described in the last chapter, was admitted to foreigners by Mao and others in July 1972, but no official announcements were issued in China. Nevertheless, the absence of Lin and his close military colleagues was obvious, as were calls for the army to follow the Party. In 1972 the Party began a national campaign to criticise revisionism, which was used to criticise ultra-leftism as practised by 'swindlers like Liu Shaoqi'. Ultra-leftism included, for example, the promotion of democracy without the necessary centralism and the weakening of productive capability by destroying labour discipline, trends clearly reminiscent of Cultural Revolution excesses. Its criticism permitted such pre-1966 phenomena as labour emulation campaigns with material rewards for advanced producers to reappear. Such covert attacks upon the Cultural Revolution heritage were unacceptable to those who had gained politically by the Cultural Revolution, in particular the remaining three survivors of the Cultural Revolution Small Group, Jiang Qing (Mao's wife), Zhang Chunqiao and Yao Wenyuan. From their power base in Shanghai they launched in October 1972 a new view of Lin Biao as a rightist. Such a re-evaluation would protect the Cultural Revolution from direct criticism and at the same time would follow Communist preference for rightism as the major term of abuse, but it is not clear that the re-evaluation was approved by the central authorities, even if Mao may have favoured it. Although criticisms of ultra-leftism were reduced, by March 1973 half of China's provinces were still silent on the re-evaluation and it did not become definite policy until approved in Zhou Enlai's report at the Tenth Party

Congress in August 1973. That report claimed that Lin had wished to turn the CCP into a revisionist, fascist party and to restore capitalism in China.

The Tenth Party Congress of August 1973 was supposed to represent a new unity after the problems of the Lin affair, but below the superficial unity were clear indications of new conflicts. Rehabilitation of veteran cadres had proceeded rapidly in 1972, ending in the reappearance of Deng Xiaoping, the number two capitalist roader of the Cultural Revolution, as a vice-premier in April 1973. The balance between newcomers and veterans was revealed at the congress. At least fifty cadres who had been removed from office in the Cultural Revolution were elected to the Central Committee, while at the Politburo level several newcomers with recent revolutionary achievements were elected, such as two textile workers, an engineer-worker and the peasant leader of China's most famous agricultural model, the Dazhai brigade in Xiyang County, Shanxi.

Only two speeches from the five-day congress were publicly distributed – Zhou Enlai's general report and the new second vice-chairman Wang Hongwen's report on revising the constitution. Zhou spent most of his time on the Lin Biao question, spoke little about the Cultural Revolution, and asserted the need for a Leninist party with centralised leadership and clear rules. He also stated that the USSR was a greater threat than the USA. Wang argued for the continued relevance of large-scale political conflict, with the constitution stating that cultural revolutions would have to occur several times. He described the Party as one unusually open to the masses, which had been restructured to guarantee a role for Cultural Revolution activists and he defended the new constitutional article allowing 'going against the tide', which implied no unconditional obedience of Party superiors if they were perceived to be in error. He also indicated that the USSR and the USA were equal threats.

Politics in 1974 and 1975

The further repudiation of Lin Biao after the Tenth Congress gradually became linked with a campaign to criticise Confucius, which had begun quietly with a superficially academic article in *The People's Daily* in early August 1973. Confucius was described as a reactionary who had wished to preserve and restore the slave-owning society against the forces of progress. In parallel with criticisms of Confucius came approval of his opponents, the Legalists, and in particular praise for the first Emperor of Qin, who has traditionally been reviled as excessively cruel. Attempts to link criticisms of Lin and Confucius were at first unsuccessful but the 1974 New Year Editorial did spell out the link and in February Mao confirmed that a joint campaign was necessary. The results were twofold, the intense study of China's early texts by the mass of the population with the help of specially trained theorists, and the spread of chaos, as the campaign turned to wall posters and great debates. There were regional reports of factional fighting, production sabotage and loss of Party control. The central authorities tried to restrict the campaign in April, but failed because the Party did not appear united. The campaign, although serving to attack Lin, appeared also to be an attack on premier Zhou, especially over the issue of recalling to office those who had retired into obscurity. A Central Committee directive in July 1974 redefined the campaign as one of study and criticism and denounced factionalism, which brought the active campaign to an end over the next few months.

It was during the Lin Biao–Confucius campaign in July 1974 that the first known rebuke by Mao of a faction of four occurred. These four, known after Mao's death as the Gang of Four, were Jiang Qing (Mao's wife), Zhang Chunqiao, Yao Wenyuan and Wang Hongwen, all Politburo members. All had emerged as prominent figures in the Cultural Revolution and had striven to retain the gains from that revolution, both from ideological commitment and on behalf of those who had gained access to power-holding positions between 1966 and 1969. The Gang had relied heavily upon Mao's support in the late 1960s, but in the 1970s this support became less dependable as Mao retired more and more from detailed policy-making. Hence the four came to build their own network of support, which included a regional base in Shanghai, an intellectual base in groups in Qinghua and Beijing Universities and a propaganda base involving the creation of very active writing teams. Opportunities for this last-named were expanding rapidly in the

1970s, with the publication of at least eight new journals, the most famous being *Study and Criticism*, and by the almost complete capture of the country's main newspaper, *The People's Daily*, in 1974, as its staff were reshuffled in punishment for wrong accusations of Lin Biao as a leftist in 1972. Accusations of factionalism arose from the actions of Wang Hongwen in calling two major meetings of 10 000 cadres in January 1974 without Politburo consultation. There Wang and Jiang Qing criticised leaders who were lukewarm in the Lin Biao–Confucius campaign and also tried to add 'going through the back door' as a major part of the campaign. This referred to the corrupt practices of cadres who gained privileges for themselves and their families. Mao forbad the circulation of tapes of the speeches from these unsanctioned meetings and a Central Committee document was issued removing 'the back door' as a campaign issue. Other topics on which the four criticised the new trend under Zhou included attacks on Western music, on the export of traditional arts and crafts and on changes in cultural policy which threatened the supremacy of the revolutionary operas which Jiang Qing had championed.

Despite the Tenth Congress rhetoric about further cultural revolutions and the attempt by some to keep Cultural Revolution ideals alive, the general social and economic mood from late 1971 had been one of seeking to return to pre-1966 normality and a less overtly politicised life style. Public commitment to Maoist slogans was still necessary, but the chaotic energy of the divided society of the late 1960s was much less in evidence, although many still suffered from the memories of the accusations raised in those years. In the economic sphere agriculture was deeply affected by the campaign begun in late 1970 to promote grain as the key link. Although understandable in terms of the primacy of food production, the campaign was often approached mechanically, with a ban on the planting of crops other than grain and with the strong suggestion that resistance to the campaign and its goal of local self-reliance was equivalent to political resistance to Mao. Grain production did grow slightly in the early 1970s, but this was at the expense of industrial crops such as cotton whose production stagnated. The rural areas were also the subject of continual attempts by the more radical wing of the Party to push for restriction on private plots and the preference for brigade rather than team-level accounting, both being features of the 'Learn from Dazhai' approach. Although the radicals never commanded full authority to insist on agricultural changes, they were able to mount local campaigns pushing for a more collective approach, by whipping up fears of peasants and local leaders being accused as capitalists.

One major area of contention in the early 1970s was education. Although some higher educational institutions had opened a few experimental classes from 1969, it was not until 1972 that universities and colleges were reopened extensively across China. Selection of students was to be mainly from those recommended by the masses after at least two years of practical working experience, but even so judgements of academic worth by examination gradually came to be involved. Opposition to the latter was shown by the case of the much-applauded exam script of Zhang Tiesheng, published in *The People's Daily* in August 1973. It was claimed that Zhang had not answered any questions, but had written a note to the examiners explaining that after being sent down to the countryside he worked so hard in the commune that he had no time for study. The newspaper queried whether book knowledge should be the criterion for university entry, preferring ability to learn. At the lower levels schooling had reopened sooner, but there were important changes in the style of school activity, with less stress on examinations and more opportunities for combining study and labour, as in school farms and workshops.

1975 opened with the first meeting of the National People's Congress in more than a decade. Zhou Enlai came to the Congress from hospital to launch the call for the Four Modernisations and the new national constitution was introduced by Zhang Chunqiao. Zhou's speech stressed the need for unity in building an independent, relatively comprehensive industrial and economic system before 1980 and achieving comprehensive modernisation before 2000, in agriculture, industry, defence and science-technology. Zhang spoke of the need for struggle and noted how the constitution confirmed Cultural Revolution gains, such as revolutionary committees, three-in-one leadership and the four greats of mass action. These were: to speak out freely, to air views, to hold great debates and to write wall-posters.

Nevertheless the constitution also confirmed several rights to which the radicals objected, such as private plots, sideline production and accounting at the production-team level. The Congress also ratified ministerial appointments on the State Council, most importantly placing Deng Xiaoping as first deputy premier. This promotion confirmed the rising prominence of Deng, who had been fulfilling more and more of the sick Zhou Enlai's roles through 1974, including meeting foreign dignitaries and representing China at the Sixth Special Session of the United Nations General Assembly. Deng was also promoted to the standing committee of the Party's Politburo and apparently put in charge of day-to-day work in the Party, replacing a somewhat inadequate Wang Hongwen.

The remainder of 1975 witnessed an increasing confrontation between Deng's desire to pursue the Four Modernisations and the attempt led by the four Cultural Revolution leaders to resist the shift of national energy away from political issues towards economic goals. As Zhou Enlai had done from late 1971, Deng sponsored a wide range of fact-finding investigations into the problems of the economy and called many national conferences between March and October 1975, with Deng speaking at least five of these. Only two of these conferences – on the coal industry and on learning from Dazhai in agriculture – received any publicity at the time, partly as the result of the control of the media by agents of the four. Deng tried to overcome the problems of factionalism in productive units by experimental programmes in the rail and steel industries, which had been badly affected by disruption in the Lin Biao–Confucius campaign. These programmes championed the role of managerial expertise, the need for disciplinary rules and the use of material incentives with unevenly distributed wage rises. On the basis of these experiments and of the conferences, Deng supervised the preparation of three planning documents, on Party work, on industrial development and on the Academy of Sciences, and towards the end of 1975 started work on a fourth, on education and culture. These documents, which were not published in the press, sought to define the acceptable political category in China as all patriotic Chinese working for modernisation, rejecting all earlier political labels. The documents also challenged most of the Cultural Revolution approaches, for example, by demanding clear lines of authority, an end to factionalism and a rejection of the conditional obedience of the 1973 Party constitution.

Responding to Deng's push to legitimise the modernisation programme, the four Cultural Revolution leaders sought means to sidetrack this process, by keeping alive the highlighted cleavages of the Cultural Revolution such as rebel and conservative or proletarian and bourgeois. To an extent they were supported in this by Mao, but again as in 1974 he was to criticise them as a gang in May 1975 for their disregard of Party norms. The major mechanism for the Gang of Four's resistance was the media, whose political stridency through 1975 and on into 1976 deceived many foreign observers as to the effective power of the radical faction.

The Gang of Four almost immediately disrupted the call to study the documents of the Fourth People's Congress (January 1975) by a campaign to study the theory of the dictatorship of the proletariat, with major articles by Yao Wenyuan and Zhang Chunqiao. This campaign argued for the need to continue political struggle, because of the tendency of political authorities to become bourgeois in their habits, by ideological degeneration and by corrupt opportunities. The economic seeds of the appearance of a new bourgeoisie lay in the remaining bourgeois rights in society, such as inequalities in distribution and exchange, in ownership systems and in relations between people. Hence these bourgeois rights must be restricted, implying attacks on wage reforms, private plots, etc. The campaign also suggested that a degenerating political leadership could affect the class character of productive units – that is, that bourgeois elements at the top could overturn the socialist economic base, a reversal of the usual Marxist view. The campaign began with demands for prompt restriction of bourgeois rights, but was gradually toned down, until it petered out in July with explicit endorsements of the Four Modernisations. At the lower levels, however, its impact was considerable, with factional violence and economic disruption continuing into late August, requiring the use of the army in Hangzhou to reestablish order in some factories.

The second 1975 campaign launched by the Four was one to criticise the popular old novel, *Water Margin*. This arose from a mid-August private conversation of Mao with a literature professor, which was relayed to Yao Wenyuan. Yao immediately began to organise a campaign, which had not been sanctioned by the Politburo. Mao's new view on the novel was that the normally accepted hero was in fact a 'capitulationist', that is one who had pushed aside a more revolutionary leader and had accepted the amnesty of a reactionary government. The analogy of Deng usurping the leadership of Mao and stopping the revolution halfway is quite clear, in hindsight, although the campaign baffled many observers at the time. The campaign received full publicity in *The People's Daily* in early September, but was not the subject of any formal Party directive. Hence it was only pursued locally in Shanghai and Liaoning, where the Four had bases of support. When Jiang Qing addressed the Dazhai agricultural conference to promote the campaign, her speech was not permitted to be circulated with the conference documents, apparently at Mao's command.

The third campaign mounted by the Four in 1975 was the Great Debate in Education and arose from Deng's moves towards a public criticism of Cultural Revolution ways in education. Deng realised that to promote a return to academic values in education so as to create the technical specialists for modernisation, it would be necessary to challenge Beijing and Qinghua Universities, the main academic strongholds of the radicals. Hence in August and October 1975, probably at Deng's prompting, letters were sent by Party members at the universities to the Central Committee, spelling out abuses of power and demanding investigations. In early November Mao urged the universities to solve the problems internally and there followed a month of meetings and wall-posters, which revealed full control of the campuses by the radicals. In early December the national media announced that the challenge to the universities had been an attack on the Cultural Revolution and urged other campuses to take up the challenge. In an unprecedented move in late December, foreign journalists were invited into the two campuses in the capital to photograph wall-posters, presumably in the hope that foreign press would lend its publicity to the campaign. The 1976 New Year Editorial spoke of a 'rightist deviationist wind to reverse verdicts' and quoted Mao to the effect that the call for stability and unity did not end the importance of class struggle. Finally in early February 1976 it was claimed that Mao had inaugurated the campaign and that the right deviationist wind was an all-out attack on the proletariat by capitalist roaders, an attack which threatened a full return to the language of the Cultural Revolution.

The Death of Zhou Enlai and Politics in 1976

This widening of the Great Debate in Education into a general counter-attack against the 'rightist wind to reverse verdicts' was closely related to the death of Premier Zhou Enlai on 8 January 1976 and the need to create a new leadership below an aging Mao. The rising criticism of Deng prevented his rise to the premiership, but unexpectedly Mao turned not to the next vice-premier, Zhang Chunqiao, but to the relative newcomer at the centre, Hua Guofeng, who had caught Mao's eye much earlier by his administrative efforts in Mao's home province of Hunan. In the absence of any clear public documents to guide the new campaign against the rightist wind and with Deng's 1975 reassessments out of favour, it was necessary to inform the Party of the leadership's thinking. Hence two overlapping meetings of provincial Party leaders were held in late February and early March in Beijing. Hua Guofeng addressed the assembled cadres with Mao's views that the Cultural Revolution had been 70 per cent achievements, 30 per cent failures; that the Party opposed a full purge for Deng and his supporters; that the Party must not reject the whole 1975 reassessment, even if the radical line in education and culture was correct, and that leadership must be by Party committees, not through mass action groups and other mass mobilisation. Mao wished class struggle to be retained as the key link and seemed to imply that older veterans risked becoming capitalist roaders. Hua's interpretation of Mao's views was challenged by the actions at the conferences of Wang Hongwen and Jiang Qing, who sought to condemn Deng more vigorously, especially over foreign trade policy, where it was claimed that Deng had gone too far in selling Chinese raw materials to buy Western goods. Meanwhile in late February Yao Wenyuan ordered the national media to spread the campaign against the rightist wind into agriculture and industry, while Zhang Chunqiao, using his 1975 appointment to high military post, sought information to challenge the 1975 army leadership reshuffle, which had benefited Deng.

In March the national press highlighted a so-called 'recent statement' of Mao, indicating that the bourgeoisie was inside the Communist Party, and in Shanghai two articles foreshadowed a possible attack on the late Zhou Enlai, as a capitalist roader who helped an unrepentant capitalist roader back to power. This latter accusation was too much for the general population. Wall-posters appeared in Nanjing against the radical Zhang Chunqiao and were echoed in at least half of China's provinces, but the major response occurred in Beijing.

Traditionally the Qingming festival, due on 5 April in 1976, had been an opportunity to honour the dead and as it approached, the Beijing population took it as an excuse to pay homage to the memory of Zhou Enlai in Tiananmen Square in the centre of the city. By 4 April an estimated 2 million people had paid their respects, including laying wreaths and pinning up poems. The active central leadership under Hua Guofeng persuaded the ailing Mao that the popular actions were instigated by counter-revolutionaries and on 4 April plainclothes police entered the Square, taking photographs and making a few arrests. That night police lorries cleared the Square of its wreaths and poems, but on the 5 April the crowd swelled to 100 000, angrily demanding the return of the wreaths. In the evening the police and units of the new urban militia moved in to clear the crowd by force, making more than 200 arrests. The Politburo met without Mao on 7 April, declared the demonstration counter-revolutionary and stripped Deng of all his posts, implying that he had fomented the unrest. Hua Guofeng was named as first vice-chairman of the Party and confirmed as premier. At the end of the month a top-level reception was held in Beijing for the public security men who had suppressed the demonstration, but significantly the top military figure in the Politburo, Ye Jianying, did not attend.

The ousting of Deng provided the opportunity to attack further his supporters and the 1975 approach, and the radicals exploited this to the full. A double pursuit and investigation movement was launched to identify those active in the early

April demonstrations. The urban militia, a body created earlier under Wang Hongwen, patrolled the streets of Beijing. Attacks on powerholders were sanctioned by the radicals' ideological line that there was a bourgeois class within the Party, developing out of earlier capitalist roaders, and that leaders like Deng had never been Marxists, only bourgeois democrats. At a June meeting of Public Security Bureau chiefs, Wang Hongwen announced that the Bureau's principal work in the future would be against the bourgeoisie in the Party, not against counter-revolutionaries in society. A July conference on economic planning failed to achieve any results, as the radicals attacked most of the attenders as pro-Deng and by implication unworthy to speak. Clearly an attempt was being made to redirect society back to the political intensity of the Cultural Revolution, and economic disruptions were reported as productive units returned to factional struggles over local leadership of enterprises. At the same time it was clear that Mao was nearing his end, since the leadership had announced in mid-June that he would meet no further foreign statesmen.

The political struggles within China were rudely interrupted by a massive earthquake on 28 July which wiped out the mining town of Tangshan in north China, causing at least a quarter of a million deaths. Although superstitiously interpreted by some as a portent of Mao's death, the earthquake drew a rapid response from around China, especially from the military, in a rescue effort spearheaded by Hua Guofeng. The radicals meanwhile announced that the anti-Deng campaign was still the focus and demanded an intensification of that campaign. In particular in August the campaign was spread into the army, with attacks on the military modernisation programme developed in 1975. In order to discredit Deng further, his three documents of 1975, which had been described as poisonous weeds, were issued in pamphlet form for study, with criticisms attached, but the results were the opposite: the documents indicated themes which were of popular concern, such as wage rises and a call for an ordered society. Thus although the unrest in China in August 1976 was probably unequalled since the height of the Cultural Revolution, the radicals, from their power base in the media, maintained their attempt to destroy Deng's programme. This action had generated two fatal enemies – most

of the Party and military elite, threatened by claims of the
presence of the bourgeoisie in the leadership; and much of
the general population, which saw more reward for itself in
Deng's programme than in that of the radicals.

The Death of Mao Zedong, and the Party, 1976–8

Mao Zedong died on 9 September 1976, bringing to an end
the longest period of stable leadership in China since the collapse of the Qing dynasty in 1911. Although Mao had been in
declining health for several years, there was no question that
major issues of policy still had to be sanctioned by him and
that access to him provided an important criterion for power
among the Party leadership. The major shifts discussed above,
such as the turn to the West, the Lin Biao–Confucius campaign and the campaign against bourgeois rights can all be
traced back to Mao, even though his subordinates differed among
themselves about how to achieve policy goals and used the
developing situation for their own interests. In the last months
of Mao's life the rise of Hua Guofeng owed much to Mao's
blessing, but having failed in the choice of two successors, Mao
was unable to ensure the success of any further choice, especially in the short time available.

Mao's death allowed major questions to be raised again within
the leadership over the direction for China and it was inevitable that the resulting debate should also involve the removal
of the losing side from active politics. Mao's own position on
most issues tended towards an optimistic stress upon the opportunities for advance rather than upon the obstacles and
problems, a position which gave him much greater patience
with leftist options than with rightist caution. A firm belief in
the power of the aroused people under suitable Party guidance, a definite preference for politics over economics and a
desire to establish a strong China as rapidly as possible had
resulted in two decades of national life in which leftism had
come to be seen as the norm and rightism had become the
standard term of attack. Nevertheless there were plenty of
Chinese who were willing to question whether the Maoist approach had advanced China as far as possible and whether the

continuation of such policies promised an effective method for the future. In particular it was deemed necessary to question whether the actual situation in the country was as rosy as the official media claimed.

Although a facade of unity was maintained for nearly a month after Mao's death, the underlying jockeying for power climaxed with the arrest of the four top leaders who had been so prominent in the first years of the Cultural Revolution, and the arrest of over twenty of their subordinates on 6 October 1976. The Central Committee's announcement of Mao's death spoke of his great achievements and indicated the continuation of the anti-Deng campaign, which the official press recommenced after the formal mourning period. Nevertheless the central directives, in the face of economic dislocation and the Tangshan relief operation, called for order and the down-playing of the struggle against capitalist roaders. The Gang of Four reacted to this call for restraint, by ordering provincial Party committees to route upward communications direct to them rather than to the Party's General Office under Wang Dongxing and by launching a press campaign that Mao's last instruction had been 'Act according to the principles laid down', when other Politburo members knew this to be untrue. In addition Jiang Qing, Mao's wife, removed some of Mao's papers and only returned them under pressure from vice-chairman Hua Guofeng, after she had tampered with them. It was clear to other members of the Politburo that the Four were manoeuvring for further power, beyond their existing media control. Several versions of the subsequent events exist, but it is clear that Wang Dongxing, who headed unit 8341, the Party centre's guard unit, as well as the Party's General Office, offered his support to *de facto* Party leader Hua and military leader Ye Jianying, allowing the arrests to proceed smoothly. There was some fear of an uprising by the urban militia in Shanghai, but this was avoided by summoning the Shanghai leadership to Beijing.

Public information about the arrests was gradually made available, in a typical exercise of preparing the Chinese public for a new policy. On 10 October it was announced that Hua had been made Party chairman at a Central Committee meeting on 7 October, although probably no full meeting had been held. More importantly it was announced that a mausoleum for Mao and the editing of more of Mao's writings would be major national projects. The large public meetings which followed all took this as their theme. Meanwhile the press, while retaining some anti-Deng articles, added a vigorous series on Mao's instructions, 'Three Dos and Three Don'ts', opposing Party splitting, revisionism and conspiracy. By 20 October there was official talk of tampering with Mao's directives and then on 21 October full release of the news of the arrests. Massive rallies occurred all over China to celebrate the downfall of the Four. Although these were organised by the victorious leaders of the Party, foreign observers present in China at the time all agree that there was genuine popular relief at the departure of the Four, as evidenced for example in unofficial cartoons lampooning the behaviour of the Four, especially of Mao's wife. The Four were eventually placed on trial in 1980, alongside the survivors of the 1971 military action against Mao, and received heavy sentences.

The arrest of the Gang of Four confirmed the leadership of Hua Guofeng, but could not immediately resolve three major issues facing the Party, the evaluation of the Cultural Revolution, the future role of Mao and his cult, and the recall of Deng Xiaoping. Since the Gang had been major activists in the Cultural Revolution and in the anti-Deng campaign and had claimed close links with Mao, any attack on them was liable to affect public views on these three issues and therefore required careful handling. Since Hua's rise was at the expense of Deng and highly dependent upon Mao's favour, it was not in his interest to recall Deng quickly or to attack Mao's heritage, while the Gang-led suppression of the demonstration in Beijing on 4 April 1976 had received support from several of the new leadership. Nevertheless Deng and parts of his 1975 programme were well-respected within the senior levels of Party, government and military, so that his rehabilitation could add strength to the post-Mao leadership. Hence Hua followed a policy of retaining Mao's cult, with a positive view of the Cultural Revolution, while allowing a gradual re-examination of Deng's case, although anti-Deng articles appeared up to the end of 1976.

To indicate further its continuation of the Mao cult, the leadership under Hua issued a major editorial on 7 February 1977, committing the Party to uphold whatever policy decisions Mao made and to follow whatever instructions Mao gave. This line, later dubbed the 'Two whatevers', was not in practice a very clear guideline for policy, since Mao's decisions and instructions had varied enormously over the decades of his rule, but it did preclude major innovations beyond the policy approaches of 1949 to 1976. In addition, efforts began to create a cult of Hua, through the issue of portraits of Mao and Hua together and by extravagant personal praise of Hua in the press. Calls for the return of Deng persisted, however, including the appearance of wall-posters in Beijing in January, and a work conference of the Central Committee in March 1977 agreed to reinstate Deng at the next formal plenum of the committee. With this unofficial rehabilitation, Deng returned to Beijing and began to attack the 'two whatevers' policy, on the grounds that no leader is infallible and that even Mao had admitted some mistakes.

The major political event of 1977 was the Party's Eleventh Congress, held in August, with a preceding plenum of the Tenth Central Committee held in July. The plenum confirmed Hua as Party chairman and reinstated Deng as number three in the Party, after Hua and the military leader, Ye Jianying. It also approved the expulsion of the Gang of Four from the Party. These decisions were upheld at the Congress, nominally representing a party of 35 million members, about half of whom had joined since 1966. Hua Guofeng addressed the Congress at length in his political report, which praised Mao effusively, claiming that the Cultural Revolution's victories were Mao's, as was the success against the Gang. The Cultural Revolution was officially proclaimed as finished, but no criticism was made of it, except as regards the activities of the Gang. Over a third of the Tenth Central Committee were not re-elected to office, their places being taken by pre-1966 Party veterans. Although the Cultural Revolution was over, Mao's slogan of taking class struggle as the key link was retained, which implied that divisions within society, rather than the potential for unity, would play the major role in political life, even permitting a second Cultural Revolution to be justified. In contrast, at the plenum Deng had proposed Mao's 1942 call for seeking truth from facts as the basis of Mao Zedong Thought, but this view was not formally endorsed at the Congress.

With the Gang ousted and the Cultural Revolution over, the
new leadership required to state the new immediate goals for
the Party and the nation, and given the political excesses of
the previous decade it was clear that the best goals to choose
would be economic. Hence Zhou Enlai's Four Modernisations
re-emerged as the preferred target, with Hua Guofeng vigorously promoting extensive economic programmes during 1977,
which culminated early in 1978 as a Ten Year Plan. The aim
of this plan, nominally 1976–85, was to achieve at least as much
capital construction as had been achieved between 1950 and
1976, including 120 major projects. The plan was based on a
return to the Stalinist-style centrally controlled economy of the
1950s, but with the key modern projects provided by capitalist
economies, especially Japan, through the use of loans. Nevertheless it rapidly became clear that China could neither sustain such a rate of capital construction with its existing level
of resources, nor did China possess enough trained personnel for such a programme, because of the educational losses
since 1966.

Issues of the mechanisms for sustainable economic growth
now moved to the centre of the political agenda, with increasing criticism of irresponsible planning. The debate covered two
principal areas, first the ideological debate on taking practice
as the sole criterion of truth and second economic debates on
the problems of socialism. The former debate was spearheaded
by Deng during the spring of 1978 in order to create some
flexibility in the interpretation of party policy, by indicating
that theory must change as conditions change. Although its
slogan of 'seeking truth from facts' may sound banal, its impact in a country where quotes from great leaders were defini-
tive could be devastating. One fact that would have to be
considered would be the backwardness of China and the limited economic successes achieved in nearly thirty years, especially
in agriculture. Just such 'facts' were at the heart of the second
debate, where the economist, Sun Yefang, and the theorist,
Hu Qiaomu, were active. Sun, while in prison, had prepared
in his head a book on Marxist economics and on the role of
the market under socialism, while Hu wrote of the disregard
of economic laws when politics had been placed in command,
resulting in stagnation. To redress the situation, China's leaders

needed to evaluate China's economic experience, to study the management methods of capitalist countries, which were achieving higher productivity than socialist methods, and to ensure that economic laws were obeyed.

The Third Plenum of the Eleventh Central Committee

These debates were resolved by a political victory for Deng's view at the Party meetings at the end of 1978, a central work conference beginning in November and the justly famous third plenum of the Eleventh Central Committee in December. The slogan of socialist modernisation replaced class struggle as the key link, with a clear call to seek truth from facts. The official verdict on the 1976 Tiananmen demonstration was reversed, making it into a heroic act and many senior Party leaders were rehabilitated from their Cultural Revolution accusations, several posthumously, although not the top target, Liu Shaoqi. Mao was still praised, but it was noted that he had made mistakes. A new Discipline Inspection Committee was created to oversee the purification of the Party under the chairmanship of the Party's veteran expert in economic affairs, Chen Yun, who increasingly came into conflict with Deng through the next decade. Such a purification was intended to root out those unsuitable members who had joined since 1966, but the actual purification process seems to have been half-hearted at best, with very few members expelled.

Although these political issues were of importance at the Third Plenum, much more immediate in effect were the economic decisions, which reflected the sense of China's backwardness internationally and of the lack of enthusiasm in domestic agriculture. The Plenum gave full support to an Open Door policy, whereby China would vigorously seek to adopt foreign technology and also some foreign methods to achieve greater economic growth. Although self-reliance was still mentioned, the new policy was intended to achieve this by cooperation with foreign interests rather than by isolation from international trends. The economic impact of the Open Door has been great, especially in the coastal areas of China, but the policy has had much wider results, in part linked to the extensive travel of individuals, Chinese as students and delegates to the rest of world and non-Chinese as tourists and experts to virtually all parts of China. Although the policy has drawn Party criticism for its non-economic results, variously called 'spiritual pollution' (1983–4) and 'bourgeois liberalisation' (1987 and 1989), the Open Door has remained as a centrepiece of Deng's approach and was the basis of much of Deng's wide reputation outside China. The immediate diplomatic viability of the Open Door approach had been made possible by negotiations with Japan and the USA, which resulted in the Sino-Japanese peace treaty, signed in Japan by Deng in October 1978, and the December 1978 announcement to normalise US–China relations from January 1979. Both these agreements had been reached without China insisting on a total break in Japanese and US relations with Taiwan, thus indicating that China was willing to subordinate its long-term goal of national reunification to its more urgent economic and diplomatic needs.

Changes in Agricultural Policy

The domestic equivalent of the Open Door was the new policy in agriculture, publicly revealed by raising the state purchase price for crops by 20 per cent for compulsory quota sales and 50 per cent for above-quota sales. Such price increases were intended to raise peasant enthusiasm for production through the use of material incentives. Their effect was less important than the issues raised in two unpublished drafts passed by the plenum: *Decisions* on some questions concerning acceleration of agricultural development, and *Regulations* on work in rural people's communes. These documents had arisen from debates among agricultural cadres, concerning the value of the early 1960s approaches to agriculture and the existence of various local initiatives, first in Anhui and Sichuan, to reorganise income distribution to peasants. By late 1977 there was some criticism of the Dazhai model, which abolished private plots, eroded team rights in favour of the larger brigade and tended to level all incomes through the work-point allocation. During 1978 discussion centred on the socialist principle of payment by labour and the direct link between income and output, both challenging the use of the work-point, which pooled individual effort in collective achievement.

The plenum documents stated that peasants' reward must be proportional to the labour performed and that responsibility for tasks could be given to small work groups, whose reward would be proportional to the yield achieved. This latter ruling did not specify the size of small work groups, but the peasants, especially in poorer areas, increasingly saw the household as such a group, implying a return to household farming. In addition the class enemy labels which had attached to about 4 million rural dwellers were removed and in practice this had put an end to the use of the 1950s class labels as a device to divide the countryside and to provide automatic targets for political campaigns.

The limited initiatives for agriculture discussed at the third plenum rapidly became the basis for a major transformation of the forms of agricultural organisation over the next five years, culminating in a return to household farming. This shift was not explicitly directed by the Party, but arose largely from below, as peasants sought ways to raise their incomes in a social environment which, with Party endorsement, stressed economic achievement over time-consuming demonstrations of political correctness. Throughout the shift the position of the production team as the collective owner of most rural land remained in place, but the control of the inputs applied to the land gradually moved from the teams to the individual household. In the initial stages, teams signed contracts with households, allocating a fixed amount of land to the household in return for a targeted output from that land, with the team providing tools and other inputs. Very rapidly this was superseded by a contract whereby all inputs were the responsibility of the household and any surplus production achieved from the land belonged to the household, after payment of taxes and collective dues. Such a surplus would only be valuable if it could be traded legally and as early as November 1979 the government had permitted sales of grain and oil-bearing crops on the free market after state quotas had been met. By the end of the autumn harvest of 1981 more than a third of rural households were operating under full household-responsibility contracts, and two years later almost all rural households were.

In addition, the ability to contract for land for special areas of production led to the appearance in 1982 and 1983 of specialised households who produced almost entirely for the market, repaying the collective with part of the money thus earned. Many specialised households, by identifying profitable market opportunities in, for example, fruit or flowers, emerged with enormously increased incomes, leading to official acclaim of the 10 000-*yuan* rural household as the model for the future, this at a time when many rural households still failed to reach 100 *yuan* of annual income. Party theorists argued that such disparities in income were not divisive but were necessary on the basis that some must become rich first before economic growth had benefited everyone.

Such organisational changes in agriculture could only be justified politically by economic success and this was strikingly achieved, as grain production reached 400 million tonnes in 1984, with gross value of agricultural output growing by nearly 5 per cent per capita per annum between 1978 and 1986. Nevertheless the Party recognised the danger that short-term increases of production might be gained at the expense of soil fertility, where land was contracted to households on a yearly basis. Hence in 1984 fifteen-year leases of land were sanctioned, with provision for transfer of such leases to other cultivators. Peasants were to be allowed to hire wage labourers to work their leased land and were given greater freedoms to invest their capital in rural non-farming enterprises. Moreover during 1982 and 1983, the communes which had been formed in 1958 were disbanded as the large-scale managers of agricultural activity, their general administrative role being taken over by township authorities.

The rapid growth in agricultural output can be largely attributed to three factors, but when the immediate gains resulting from these three had been realised, output growth slowed and other problems became obvious. The three factors were the material incentives offered to households by the household-responsibility system, the wide range of collectively built projects in, for example, water conservancy which had not been used to their full economic capacity, and the greatly increased availability of chemical fertilisers, made possible by the industrial investments of the 1970s. By 1986 it was clear that agriculture could not continue to grow at rates of 5 per cent per year, especially in the absence of state or collective investment in major land reclamation or irrigation projects. In addition the return to household farming had revealed the level of under-employment in the countryside, as the small plots available, however intensively worked, could not occupy the available labour which was now working directly for personal income, rather than earning work-points whose value was determined by the total output of the team.

Two possible outlets existed for surplus rural labour, to move around China in search of employment or to remain locally in a range of non-agricultural rural enterprises. In practice both occurred. The floating population of peasants, who lacked for-mal residency rights in the cities, grew through the 1980s, with some analysts estimating their numbers in the tens of millions, a major problem for the maintenance of law and order. Com-munes and brigades had been entitled to organise rural enter-prises on the basis of collective ownership, but initiative had usually come from county or commune cadres. With the ar-rival of the household-responsibility system and criticisms of commune structures, the way was open to the devolution of enterprise management to lower levels and in many cases indi-viduals or small groups contracted to use the collective assets in return for a set payment.

The result was the emergence of what rapidly became the most dynamic sector of the Chinese economy, rural industry, which by 1984 was producing 24 per cent of China's industrial output. The rural enterprises had major advantages over ur-ban collectives in tax terms and over state enterprises in that they were not required to provide housing and social services for their workers. Also being outside the formal state plan, they were more flexible in responding to markets and less con-cerned over health and pollution issues. Capital for rural en-terprises was generated from existing rural savings and increasingly from the state banking system which was granted an increased role in economic management through greater flexibility in the granting of credit.

Party Leadership 1978–87

Although the third plenum of December 1978 can be viewed as the moment when Party attitudes to the peasantry began to change towards more flexibility, the plenum was less successful in resolving the other immediate economic and political issues facing the Party. Although some criticism of the Cultural Revolution had been allowed since 1977, the Party leadership had still not agreed on the issue of Mao's role in China's recent history, even though many of his purged opponents had been rehabilitated. The question of why the country had plunged into the chaos of the Cultural Revolution while led by a Communist Party provoked discussion of the need for greater democracy and stricter controls on personal power. Such discussion happened within the Party, especially linked to Hu Yaobang, a leading figure at the Central Party School from March 1977, and outside the Party, in a burgeoning movement to post wall-posters in Beijing, especially at what came to be known as 'Democracy Wall'. Many of those writing posters were former Red Guards who had been disillusioned by their experiences after 1966 and the most famous, Wei Jingsheng, argued by early 1979 that the Four Modernisations would fail without a fifth one, democracy.

At the time of the third plenum, it had suited Deng Xiaoping to offer some support to the Democracy movement, since it lent weight to his attempts to isolate Hua Guofeng and others who had been close to Mao, but in early 1979, as the Democracy movement became more audacious in its criticisms, Deng turned against it, stating his case most clearly in a speech in late March 1979 on the four cardinal principles. These upheld Marxism–Leninism–Mao-Zedong-Thought, Party leadership, the socialist road and the dictatorship of the proletariat as the unchallengeable tools for China's progress. Wei Jingsheng was arrested, ostensibly for leaking military secrets to foreigners during China's attack on Vietnam in February 1979, and later sentenced to fifteen years in jail. Democracy Wall was moved to a less-frequented part of Beijing and closed down in late 1979.

In the economic sphere the Party had been committed by Hua Guofeng to the very ambitious Ten Year Plan announced in February 1978, but by late 1978 the targets for investment, especially in heavy industry, seemed excessive. Formal criticism could not begin at the Third Plenum, since Hua's position as chairman was too strong, but by April 1979, on the basis of 'seeking truth from facts', a Central Committee work conference called for a policy of readjustment, entailing the lowering of many heavy industry targets and the cancellation of many foreign contracts, even at the cost of penalty payments. This policy was then forwarded to the mid-year session of the National People's Congress, where copious statistics on China's economic situation were revealed. Despite the cancellation of much development investment, the national budget was unable to be brought into balance and 1979 saw the reappearance of limited inflation, for the first time since the Great Leap Forward era. Thereafter the Party faced considerable conflict over issues of budgetary control and of the appropriate balance between investments in heavy industry and light industry, and between investment for production and investment for non-productive purposes, such as housing. While all in the Party agreed with the goal of the Four Modernisations in the long term, the means for economic growth were more open to debate from 1979, as the problems of a centrally planned command economy became more apparent.

Over the next two years the power of Deng Xiaoping rose markedly as he ousted his rivals from early 1976 including Hua Guofeng, but Deng did not seek to take the top Party and government posts for himself, although he did occupy the chairmanship of the Military Affairs Commission. The fourth plenum of the eleventh Central Committee was held just before the thirtieth anniversary of the PRC and allowed the description of the Cultural Revolution as a catastrophe. The fifth plenum in February 1980 removed four top leaders associated with unquestioning following of Mao's statements in the post-Mao era and fully rehabilitated Liu Shaoqi, the Cultural Revolution's prime personal target. This plenum also recreated a Party secretariat, under Hu Yaobang, and appointed Zhao Ziyang to the Politburo Standing Committee, these being two Party leaders who in Deng's 1980 view shared his vision for China.

Hu Yaobang, who became chairman of the Party's Central Committee in 1981, had been involved with Party events as far back as Mao's 'Autumn Harvest' uprising of 1927, and had risen to be head of the Communist Youth League before being attacked in the Cultural Revolution. Hu was rehabilitated before Mao's death and served as Party secretary for the Academy of Sciences, where he earned a reputation as a defender of science against political mishandling. He was disgraced along with Deng in mid-1976, but returned to favour after Mao's death.

Zhao Ziyang, who became premier by September 1980, had a vigorous provincial career in Guangdong after 1949 and achieved national repute with his success in energising China's most populous province, Sichuan, after his transfer there in 1975 as Party secretary. Sichuan, which was Deng's native province, had been a rice-surplus area, but the effects of radical policies had turned it into a rice-importer by the mid-1970s. After Zhao's arrival, a vigorous programme of promotion of peasant sideline activity and of widening possibilities for production on private plots resulted in a rapid turnaround of this situation, even before the reforms advocated by the third plenum in December 1978 had taken effect.

In November 1980 the Party leadership felt ready to place the Gang of Four and the remnants of the military associates of Lin Biao on public trial for their crimes in the period, 1966–76. The trial was an opportunity to reveal a host of information on the persecutions suffered in the Cultural Revolution, but care was taken to show that the crimes had been personally motivated, rather than caused by the Party. Meanwhile the new Party secretariat had been drafting a detailed resolution on the history of the Party since 1949, which was widely discussed within the Party in the last part of 1980 and formally adopted at the sixth plenum in June 1981.

The Resolution on certain questions in the history of the Party since the founding of the PRC defined the Party's 1981 view on the role of Mao and also presented an analysis of events since 1949. A short section described Mao's successes before 1949 and indicated that he had been only the most prominent among many important leaders of the Party. Mao's activity after 1949 was divided into three periods, the early and mid-1950s when his achievements outnumbered his mistakes, the late 1950s and early 1960s when achievements and mistakes were evenly balanced and after 1962, when mistakes predominated. Principal responsibility for initiating the Great Leap Forward and Cultural Revolution lay with Mao, although others had a lesser responsibility, especially as regards the excesses of the Cultural Revolution, which was seen in total as a severe error.

Care was taken to distinguish between Mao as a leader capable of mistakes and Mao Zedong Thought which was seen as the refined collective wisdom of the Party and as an important guide to the application of Marxism–Leninism in China. According to the Resolution one reason for Mao's later mistakes was the change in his work-style which no longer conformed with the methods advocated by Mao Zedong Thought. The Resolution also contained some judgements on the post-Mao period, with criticisms of the mistakes of Hua Guofeng. When the Party's Central Committee Plenum adopted the Resolution, it accepted Hua's resignation from his chairmanships of the committee and of the Military Affairs Commission, jobs taken by Hu Yaobang and Deng Xiaoping respectively.

With Deng's position secure and the Party's view of recent history codified, the leadership could now proceed to call the 12th Congress of the Party, which met in September 1982. A new Party constitution was adopted with no provision for a Party chairman, but only a general secretary, this post falling to Hu Yaobang who delivered the political report to the Congress. A Central Advisory Commission chaired by Deng was devised to offer help to the Central Committee from those who had been more than forty years in the Party, and this institution was seen by many analysts as a first move to remove elderly veterans from the day-to-day running of the Party. This proved inaccurate, as lines of real power continued to emanate from the oldest veterans, including Deng.

In his political report Hu stressed the socialist modernisation of the economy with a goal of quadrupling output by the year 2000 on the basis of four Five Year Plans, the plan for 1981–5 (the sixth plan) having been adopted by the National People's Congress in late 1981. Economic development was to occur mainly through a planned economy, but with a supporting role for market regulation. Self-reliance was to be the basis, but with a continuing expansion of links with foreign countries. While attaining its economic goals, China must also achieve a socialist spiritual civilisation through improvements in education and the cultural activities of China's intellectuals. Within the Party, improvement of the socialist spirit would require a programme of rectification of Party members to begin in 1983, under the control of the Central Commission for Discipline Inspection chaired by Chen Yun. This programme was completed over the next four years, initially in urban areas and then in rural areas, with 650 000 members being punished for violation of Party regulations.

The Twelfth Central Committee remained stable in its membership until September 1985, when at its fourth plenum one fifth of the members sought leave to retire, principally on grounds of old age. This plenum was followed by a conference of Party delegates, not formally a Party congress, but nevertheless able to make appointments to Politburo to introduce leaders in their fifties and sixties to that body. By this time the achievements in agricultural growth were clearly visible and the Party had begun its tentative efforts to spread the reform programme to the urban sector. Deng Xiaoping spoke optimistically of the potential for rapid growth, while Chen Yun spoke of the need for less speed in economic growth and reform, for fear of lowering ideological standards and of disrupting the socialist economy with an excessive use of market mechanisms. Such differences between the Party elders were inevitable, given the lack of precision in Marxist writing about the development of socialism in a country that lacked an extensive industrial base, but did not directly affect the position of Hu Yaobang and the Party secretariat.

The next shift in leadership occurred in early 1987, with the fall of Hu Yaobang following a period of student unrest which began in November 1986. The student protests had been both over immediate issues of concern such as services to students and over broader issues of political reform, including demands for more democracy. By early 1987 the student protest, which was claimed to be affecting only a tiny fraction of all students, had been brought under control, but the Party began an attack on bourgeois liberalisation, that is the negation of the socialist system in favour of the capitalist one. Several prominent intellectuals, including the astrophysicist, Fang Lizhi, the writer, Wang Ruowang, and the journalist, Liu Binyan, were dismissed from the Party in early January. Hu Yaobang was forced to make a self-criticism in mid-January over his handling of criticism of bourgeois liberalisation and over his decisions in dealings with Japan. Hu was replaced as Party general secretary by Premier Zhao Ziyang, but Zhao made it clear by March 1987 that the campaign against bourgeois liberalisation must only be within the Party and must not spread into society to create any kind of second Cultural Revolution.

Zhao Ziyang's pre-eminence was confirmed at the Party's Thirteenth Congress held in October 1987, where he presented the keynote address. In this the Party defined China as being in the 'initial stage of socialism', a formula which implied continued use of the language of socialism in Party documents about the long-term aims of the Party, but with extreme flexibility possible for short-term measures. Since there was no authoritative writing from the father-figures of socialist theory on such an 'initial stage', the Chinese leadership was able to argue that any means leading to the development of China could be justified, even ones which in other contexts might have been dismissed as unduly capitalist. Zhao's elevation to Party general secretary entailed his resignation as premier. Li Peng, a new member of the Politburo's standing committee, was appointed as acting premier in mid-November, a choice confirmed by the National People's Congress of March 1988. Li had been technically trained in the USSR and had become the adopted son of the deceased premier, Zhou Enlai. Zhao Ziyang's work style relied heavily upon the use of 'think-tanks' or research bodies which sought to develop more effective ways of modernising China, but the general approach they adopted has been characterised as neo-authoritarian. Zhao and his supporters wished to expand economic reform, by government and Party orders, rather than by any widespread consultative process.

Foreign Relations and the Open Door

In adopting the slogan of socialist modernisation and the Open Door in late 1978, the Party leadership had hoped that the advanced economies of the West would wish to share in China's economic development as the Party moved to distance itself from the political excesses of the late Mao era. Western doubts about China's strategic value to the West in its struggle against the USSR were largely overcome as a result of China's response to two events in 1978 and 1979, Vietnam's invasion of Kampuchea and the USSR's invasion of Afghanistan. China's actions confirmed that China was still vigorously anti-Soviet and allowed the USA to begin low-level military cooperation with China as a strategic partner, whose economic advancement should be encouraged.

In late December 1978 Vietnam, China's southern neighbour, overran its smaller neighbour, Kampuchea, to remove the China-supported Khmer Rouge government under Pol Pot. Vietnam had previously stiffened its treatment of overseas Chinese residents of Vietnam, which had resulted in a large-scale exit of refugees, some as boat people towards South-east Asia, more by land into south China. Vietnam had also entered into a friendship treaty with the USSR in October 1978, including rights of naval access. China responded with condemnations of Vietnam over Kampuchea, overseas Chinese and border violations, dating back to 1974. China then proceeded to launch what it called a 'self-defensive counter-attack' on 17 February 1979 and, after advancing to the provincial capital of Lang Son, withdrew by 16 March. China's intention had been for a limited and overwhelmingly victorious campaign, as against India in 1962, but the advance was slow, in part because of spirited Vietnamese resistance, in part because of military problems within the Chinese army. Vietnam was not effectively cowed and its forces remained in Kampuchea for ten years, while its relations with the USSR flourished. During those years China remained not only a firm supporter of the Khmer Rouge, to which it supplied arms, but also a diplomatic sponsor of the Kampuchean government-in-exile, a stance which was bound to perpetuate hostility with Vietnam, while it won favour with the West.

In December 1979 Brezhnev, the USSR leader, ordered the Soviet Army into Afghanistan to protect the pro-Soviet government – in place since a coup in April 1978 – from Muslim nationalist insurgents and from its own factional in-fighting. China's response was immediate condemnation and the suspension of talks with the USSR. These had begun again after China had given formal notice in April 1979 that it would not be renewing the 1950 Sino-Soviet treaty when its thirty-year term expired. China feared the Soviet advance as a sign of a long-standing Russian desire for southern access to the sea and as a direct threat to China's ally in south Asia, Pakistan, which bordered Afghanistan and now faced a major refugee and security problem along its northern frontier. In China's view, which was officially announced in 1982, major improvement of Sino-Soviet relations during most of the 1980s would require three changes: withdrawals of Soviet troops from the Chinese border and from Afghanistan and the withdrawal of Vietnamese troops from Kampuchea. At this time the USSR had approximately 1 million troops stationed near the Chinese borders or within its satellite state of Outer Mongolia.

With China's anti-Soviet status confirmed and with its public commitment to modernisation and the Open Door, it still remained to be seen what practical measures would be taken to promote profitable investment in China by foreign capitalist businesses. Obvious problems to be overcome included the lack of clear economic and tax legislation, the deficiencies in China's transport and energy infrastructure, the legacy of suspicion attached to contact with foreigners, and the possible challenges of capitalist to socialist practices in enterprise and labour management. At a deeper level lay memories of imperialistic exploitation of China before 1949, the problems for China's socialist identity in allowing the return of capitalist activity on any large scale and the risk that undesirable Western ideas and habits might damage Party control and Chinese society.

The most obvious innovation made to attract foreign capital was the establishment of four special zones for export in mid-1979, the name being changed to Special Economic Zone (SEZ) in 1980. These coastal zones, all in South China, could be isolated from the rest of the country, in theory at least, while the teething problems of the Open Door policy were faced. In order to allow the zones to operate, the government had to extend the categories of permitted enterprises beyond those allowed since the late 1950s – that is, state or collectively owned. Joint ownership by foreigners and Chinese was sanctioned in 1980, but the same year also established the legality of joint state–collective enterprises and individual enterprises in the cities and of joint collective–individual enterprises in rural areas. This retreat from socialist forms arose in part from a realisation that state-controlled Chinese industry was inefficient, with often inappropriate outputs for consumer needs. A shift to wider ownership forms would also enhance employment possibilities, especially in urban areas where there were public security problems with youths 'awaiting work' which was unavailable at already overstaffed state enterprises.

The SEZs did enjoy rapid economic growth, especially Shenzhen north of Hong Kong where some US$840 million of foreign, mainly Hong Kong, capital had been invested by late 1985, but this was at considerable cost to China as a whole. The government was required to create the modern infrastructure of roads, power supplies, etc., at a cost which far exceeded all original estimates. The zones also proved not to be net exporters, with imports as much as five times exports in some years. Indeed over half the production of the zones was consumed in China. Also the technology introduced was not as advanced as the government had hoped.

Nevertheless, the relative economic opportunities of the zones had drawn the envy of other coastal parts of China which sought to share in the Open Door possibilities. The government was persuaded in late 1979 to grant expanded authority over trade and investment decision to Shanghai, Tianjin, Beijing and the provinces of Guangdong and Fujian. In 1984 fourteen coastal cities and Hainan island were able to offer tax incentives to foreigners and the Pearl, Min and lower Yangzi river areas were declared trade and investment promotion zones. By then the SEZs were attracting about a quarter of the direct foreign investment in China and this proportion dropped further through the remaining 1980s, but Guangdong province as a whole took over half of the funds directly invested into regional China by foreigners in the 1980s. In 1988 288 counties in eleven coastal provinces were declared open, to attract foreign investment even more widely.

The viability of the policy of economic reform and opening to the world depended not only on the political situation within China, but equally upon China's attractiveness to countries with technology and markets to offer. In this respect the early 1980s offered particular opportunities to China, which were to some extent lost in the later 1980s. With the Soviet invasion of Afghanistan in December 1979, the trend towards détente between the USSR and the USA was halted and therefore the importance of China as a co-partner in the control of the USSR was enhanced. In addition China's role as opponent of Vietnam which had overrun Kampuchea strengthened China's acceptability in South-east Asia. Two issues could have clouded the image of China as a new, more attractive nation in its post-Mao form – human rights, and China's handling of the unification process with Hong Kong, Macau and Taiwan. Fortunately for China, although some human rights abuses were reported by international groups such as Amnesty International, the principal focus of Western concern was upon abuses in the USSR as revealed by its political dissidents who received wide coverage in the Western media, in a way which China has never experienced. The issue of unification was handled sensitively by the post-Mao leadership, with a realisation that the process must be spread over many decades.

The immediate issue was Hong Kong, where the Anglo-Chinese treaty of 1898 provided for a 99-year lease on the so-called New Territories – that is, land inland from the harbour area of Kowloon and a number of islands surrounding Hong Kong island. Most observers agreed that modern Hong Kong could not effectively exist if this territory and its population were detached from the colonial territory of Hong Kong Island and Kowloon, gained by Britain from China in the treaties of 1842 and 1860. Moreover given the role which Hong Kong played as the major port for south China and as a major earner of foreign exchange for China, it was essential to maintain its viability in the lead up to 1997, especially since major investments to maintain economic growth there would require confidence in the long-term opportunities for profit. Many argued that long-term investments needed at least fifteen years to ensure adequate returns and hence that such investments would slow from 1982 onwards, unless Hong Kong's future was more clearly defined.

With these factors in mind both Britain and China sought to negotiate a settlement which would preserve Hong Kong's economic viability while removing the British colonial presence from China. In a military sense China could at any time in the 1980s have overwhelmed Britain in Hong Kong, as India did with the Portuguese presence in Goa, but the British did not expect China to act recklessly, given China's restraint over Hong Kong even during the Cultural Revolution and China's insistence that the decolonisation of Hong Kong was not a matter for international impatience and concern. Successful negotiations were concluded on the basis of the formula 'One nation, two systems', said by many to be Deng Xiaoping's personal solution to the problem. By this Hong Kong as a whole and not just the New Territories, would return to Chinese sovereignty in 1997, but the Chinese government guaranteed that Hong Kong's existing capitalist system would be retained for fifty years, despite the rest of China being socialist.

The Anglo-Chinese agreement was signed in 1984 and besides specifying the transfer in 1997, also allowed for some preparatory procedures, such as a Sino-British Joint Liaison Group and a Basic Law Drafting Committee. Since 1984 disputes have arisen over the degree to which China has a role to play in Hong Kong before 1997 and over how far Britain can alter Hong Kong's political institutions to increase elected representation before 1997. In general the resolution of these disputes has favoured China's views, both politically and over such economic issues as the funding of the new international airport for Hong Kong, leading some observers to accuse Britain of abandoning its responsibilities to Hong Kong.

With the Hong Kong agreement in place, the Chinese were only too ready to grant a similar arrangement to Portugal over Macau, which would return to Chinese sovereignty in 1999. This later date was chosen to allow the prior incorporation of Hong Kong, even though Portugal had offered to return Macau to China immediately after the dissolution of the rest of the Portuguese empire in the mid-1970s.

Resolution of the divide between the Chinese mainland and Taiwan has proceeded even more slowly. China has objected to requests from the USA which have urged China to renounce the use of force for reunification, stating that such requests are an interference in the internal affairs of China, but in practice China has not pursued a military path towards reunification since 1976. Signs of a new Chinese Communist approach to the Taiwan question were revealed in official statements from late 1978 onwards. These urged the reopening of people-to-people relations even while the official party-to-party relations were still frozen, but such proposals were treated with grave suspicion by the Guomindang authorities in Taiwan, who had memories of the united front experiences of the pre-1949 era. Nevertheless the gradual growth of China's overseas trade, especially from the south-eastern provinces, led to a rising indirect trade between the mainland and Taiwan via Hong Kong, as Taiwan's manufacturers sought to share in the new economic opportunities. Finally in 1988 the Guomindang relented on the possibility of visits to allow family reunions in Taiwan, after it became clear that residents of Taiwan were visiting the mainland from Hong Kong.

Since that time unofficial relations have flourished, with telephone and mail links between the mainland and Taiwan via Hong Kong and a growing investment by Taiwanese capitalists in manufacturing plants in Fujian province. Guomindang confidence in allowing dealings with the mainland increased markedly in the late 1980s, because of the worldwide difficulties of the socialist bloc and the realisation that standards of living in the mainland were now well below those in Taiwan. Officially the Guomindang maintained a policy of no contact with the Communist Party, but did come to accept that Communist China existed, an acceptance most clearly signalled by the end of martial law in Taiwan in 1987.

Political Reforms in the Early 1980s

Although the economic reforms of the early 1980s revealed a willingness to break away from the rigidities of the socialist forms of the early People's Republic, the political rate of change was much slower. The reasons for this difference lay in part with the political convictions of the veteran leaders who still held power through the Party and in part with public disinterest in political activity after the excesses of the campaign politics of Mao's era. Whatever the policy debates between the veterans over such matters as the existence of alienation in a socialist society, they could all agree that the Party must control the debate through its control of the media and through its status as the source of orthodoxy in a socialist country. Moreover even in the absence of any stress upon class struggle within

China, the Party was able to portray certain ideas as contrary to Marxism–Leninism and their upholders as suspect citizens, although the punishments were less harsh than in Mao's time.

Nevertheless the pace of economic change and the consequent influx of foreigners and foreign information did force consideration of the issue of political reform. To the conservatives among the veterans, such debate of Western political methods amounted to 'spiritual pollution', a tainting of the socialist ideals of China by the bourgeois values of the West. These values could be most easily criticised not in the political sphere where the shared ideal of democracy did not clearly separate China and the West, but in other manifestations of Western society, such as pornography, modern fashion and individualistic literary values, which came under attack in late 1983. This attack was quickly cut short by Deng and his supporters, who realised that such an attack threatened to escalate into a rejection of all things foreign, at a time when China desperately needed Western technical support to modernise its economic base. The conservative attack shifted against 'bourgeois liberalization' in late 1986, but again was defused although with more difficulty than in early 1984. As previously noted, one casualty of this later conflict was the Party's general secretary, Hu Yaobang, who was ousted in reprisal for his more liberal stance over student demonstrations, which had hit major cities in late 1986.

The areas of political reform that were raised included the nature of elections, the relationship of the party and the state and the role of the veterans in the political process. Electoral reform had begun with the 1979 Election Law which required the use of secret ballots and the presence of more candidates than the number of available positions being contested. Under the 1979 law, direct elections were held for county and township people's congresses, with higher-level congresses elected indirectly by lower levels. The representative nature of the elections was restricted by law, in that rural candidates were chosen by far larger electorates per candidate, four times larger at the county level elections. Such inequality was justified on the need to guarantee working-class leadership and the desire to ensure that congresses could represent as wide a range of interests as possible, since the Chinese argue that each representative can only represent one interest. The requirement for multiple candidacy was also restricted by law, in that although any number of candidates could be nominated to stand for election, the final election would be held after reducing the number of nominated candidates to a small figure, often only two per position, through a process of consultation and administrative guidance. Nevertheless, the post-1979 elections did allow for some non-Party members to be elected and for the defeat of some Party-supported candidates. Such electoral reforms even spread to the Party where, in its Thirteenth Congress in 1987, more candidates were proposed for committee seats than were able to be elected, resulting in the failure of some candidates to achieve election, as with the conservative propaganda expert, Deng Liqun, who did not reach the Central Committee.

Reform of the relationship of Party and state was a harder task to achieve. In theory it was possible to indicate that the Party took the lead in political and ideological work, while the state officials organised the daily supervision of the government's work, especially in the economic sphere. In practice, after three decades of zigzagging political lines, state officials refused to take responsibility for decisions which might lead to the risk of political criticism in the future. The leadership's desire to achieve more dynamic leadership for state enterprises clashed directly with the long-established practice of Party committees and Party secretaries demanding the right to initiate and review policy. In non-economic ministries such as education and culture the desire of Party members to dominate was even more ingrained, given both the traditional role of the Chinese state in fixing cultural norms and the Leninist ideas of a vanguard leading in the development of socialist consciousness. Despite these obstacles, there was some progress in establishing the authority of individuals whose first acknowledged loyalty was to their unit of work rather than to the Party, such as managers in state enterprises, some of whom were now elected by the workers rather than appointed by the Party. Similarly intellectuals began to challenge openly the authority of Marxism–Leninism–Mao-Zedong Thought as the orthodoxy on all issues – for example, in scientific research and literary creation.

The position of Party veterans proved the most intractable reform issue in the 1980s, culminating in the effective rejection after 1989 of all the reforms attempted in the previous decade. Given the enormous respect attached to those who had been in the Party before 1949 and especially before the Long March, it was inevitable that these veteran members would expect a leading role in the Party, but these same members, by virtue of their age, were unlikely to offer the dynamic leadership required in exploring the new economic ideas of the post-Mao era. Deng Xiaoping and those close to him faced this problem head-on, especially in the three-year period after 1982, by calling for the retirement of veterans and the reduction of the proportion of those over 60 years old in major positions: one call by Hu Yaobang in 1985 was for over 70 per cent of those in leading positions to be under the age of 60. 900 000 veterans are said to have retired between 1982 and early 1985, with an expected 47 000 veterans to retire from the military office in 1985. The leading core of the Party still remained elderly but gradually Deng and those near him in age shed the formal posts of state and Party power to men a decade or more younger, such as Zhao Ziyang and Hu Yaobang. As compensation for those retiring at the very top of the system, the Party had created a Central Advisory Commission in 1982, which offered an opportunity for some input on overall policy to those who had helped to establish the Party as the leading political force in China.

Urban Reform in the 1980s

The policy of economic reform in agriculture from 1979 had generated such a clear improvement in the total output of agriculture and of rural enterprises that it was inevitable that the Party would seek to attempt a similar success in the urban sector of the economy. Yet such an improvement could not be achieved without major adjustments. The rural success had been generated by individual and collective initiative outside the planning structure, whereas China's industrial sector as of 1978 and later was tightly controlled by planning requirements. These specified targets and also set the prices of many inputs into the production process. As a reform idea it was possible to say that factory managers would be judged on the basis of profit without Party interference, but it was hard to penalise such managers where their flexibility was negligible in terms of pricing and application of labour. Urban economic reforms would require a move towards a market economy, in which state enterprises would have to compete for resources and sales with the new dynamic collective sector. Given that many state enterprises were running at a loss and survived only through government subsidy, the government would have to accept that such enterprises might fail and close if government resources were to be used to their maximum economic effectiveness. Such enterprise failures would have profound effects, given that the social fabric of workers' lives was built around the work unit, which supplied housing, medical care and welfare services.

The moves towards urban economic reform were signalled by preparations in 1983 for replacing the automatic remission of enterprise profits to the state by a system of taxation of net income and by regulations issued by the State Council in 1984 granting greater autonomy to state-run enterprises, including powers to appoint factory heads and to dismiss or promote workers. Full implementation of the profit tax system was to be delayed until after full price reform, but even so by 1990 remitted profits from enterprises had dropped by more than 60 per cent, as a shift to taxes gradually occurred. Yet the problems of price reform remained too complex to be tackled effectively, with the result that the wider role for the market within a socialist economy could not be achieved. In particular the prices of energy and raw materials were not clearly related to the costs of production. In addition an increasing amount of government funds was being devoted to subsidies to maintain low prices for food in the cities. Nevertheless, even with state involvement in urban price fixing, inflation proved a major problem, fuelled in part by the government's budget deficit. In 1988 retail price inflation was officially said to be 18.5 per cent, the first double-digit figure since early in the People's Republic, and in practice inflation in general prices was even greater than the official figure.

The state planners were also deeply concerned at the rate of industrial growth which threatened to become overheated as uncontrolled investment raised the pace of construction and economic activity. Although the general trend between 1978 and 1990 was one of rapid growth in gross industrial output, the government had felt obliged to call for retrenchment and consolidation after the cancellation of Hua Guofeng's projects in 1979 and again after growth rates of over 20 per cent in 1985 and 1988. Yet the ability of the government to control the economy directly by planning was being restricted by the weakness of the state sector. Reforms designed to promote production in state enterprises resulted in practice in the growth of the collective sector, whose output expanded five times over between 1980 and 1990, compared with a doubling of state-controlled output. By 1990 state enterprises were producing just under 50 per cent of China's industrial output, compared with more than 75 per cent in 1980. Moreover the centre was finding it increasingly difficult to insist that areas of rapid economic growth such as Guangdong and Fujian remain within the centre's investment guidelines, since these areas now directly controlled substantial funds of their own.

Crisis in the late 1980s

Throughout the 1980s the calls for economic reform and an open door to the outside were the central features of Chinese political life, even though some leaders argued for caution. The result of these policies was a marked relaxation in the political constraints imposed upon the ordinary citizens of China, who were no longer required to become involved in endless political campaigns and who were allowed to pursue personal goals without immediate criticism from the Party. The limited freedom which ensued implied a weakening of Party power and a growing sense that the Party's ideology had only a limited role to play in carrying China to future prosperity. The Party contributed to the latter feeling by its own vague definition of China's condition as the initial stage of the change to socialism. This was a period for which the Party had no preordained directives, because its earlier claims of having achieved socialism under Party guidance had been revealed as inadequate. Since China was in a period of flux where much was experimental and pragmatic, it was inevitable that the role of Marxism–Leninism should be challenged, but the Party remained firm in its assertion that this ideology was the basis of intellectual and political life in China, even while borrowings from the capitalist West were necessary.

As the People's Republic approached its fortieth birthday in 1989, the results of ten years of reform and open door were becoming very apparent. China was now a major trading nation, with its overseas trade worth more than US$80 billion in 1988. Contacts with foreigners and with things foreign were extensive in the cities of China. Diplomatically China was now ready to accept high-level state-to-state relations with the USSR, a shift which offered a Communist China its first opportunity to be on friendly terms with all major nations after four decades of enmity against one or both superpowers. The economic situation in China was one of a booming rural industry, of state enterprises beset with difficulties and of a persistent inflation which the government attempted to control unsuccessfully. Politically the Party had lost its ability to guide the nation by ideological argument, and membership of the Party was more of a door to wealth and power than proof of activism in the cause of the revolution.

The contrast between economic dynamism at the level of individual and collective enterprises and the difficulties of state enterprises, some of which survived only by huge government subsidy, revealed the need for further reform, but such reform was extremely unwelcome for a Party committed to unquestioned power through Party leadership of the economic life of the state. With an increasing emphasis on productivity and economic results judged by profitability, management would have to pass into the hands of technical experts, rather than remain with veteran Party members with great political skill but limited economic understanding. Thus despite the government's call for urban reform from 1984, the changes had been limited, mainly related to the loosening of price controls, which only fuelled inflationary pressures.

The political and economic tensions created by the reform process reached their first peak in 1989 and were at first represented by student demonstrations. The immediate focus for the student organisation was the seventieth anniversary of the May Fourth movement, but just as that famous event occurred a few days before it had been planned to commemorate the May Seventh National Humiliation Day in 1919, so the 1989 demonstrations began early after the death of one of the top Party leaders, Hu Yaobang. Hu had been sacked as Party general secretary early in 1987 for his apparent sympathy with students who had demonstrated late in 1986 over their conditions of study and over issues arising from reform, such as inflation and rising Japanese imports. Therefore his death and funeral in April were regarded by the students as an appropriate occasion to criticise the government over a similar range of issues, which had not been resolved by the leadership since Hu's sacking. Thus inflation and study conditions were of concern, but more dangerously there were attacks on corruption in Party and official circles and calls for wider consultation in the making of decisions. These latter points had been expressed in the later 1980s by a number of prominent intellectuals in China, the most famous of whom was the scientist, Fang Lizhi.

Students were active in many Chinese cities, but world attention was focused upon Beijing, where students were demonstrating in Tiananmen Square in the city centre, just as China was preparing to receive the Soviet president, Mikhail Gorbachev, in a final reconciliation with the USSR. The Party's response was a vigorous condemnation of the demonstrators in the official press in late April, but this only encouraged the students to protest more at what they perceived as unjust criticisms of their actions. It soon became clear that the Party's top leadership was divided over the best way to handle the demonstrations, with Party general secretary, Zhao Ziyang, offering some sympathy to the students, and Prime Minister, Li Peng, firm that public demonstrations must cease. Throughout May the demonstrations continued in the square, despite the declaration of martial law in parts of Beijing on 20 May, and students were joined by other citizens of Beijing, until there were times when hundreds of thousands were gathered in central Beijing. Several hundred students went on hunger strike, promising to continue until the government withdrew the criticisms of late April, and the whole mood of the demonstrators began to shift from issues of corruption and economic concerns to calls for democracy and wider freedoms. This was most clearly expressed by the erection of a copy of New York's Statue of Liberty in the Square by art students. All the activity in the Square was relayed to the world by television crews from many nations and details of the Beijing events were transmitted to the rest of China by student networks, by foreign broadcasts such as Voice of America and by extensive use of faxed messages sent into China from Hong Kong.

As the scale of the protests escalated, the Party leadership had to discover an effective response to retain control of the capital and to the dismay of the Western world that response was military. Soldiers had been brought into the outer suburbs of Beijing in late May, but failed to make progress towards the centre in peaceful confrontations with the citizens of the area who argued with the soldiers against attacking unarmed civilians. As a result it seemed that the army rank-and-file might be unreliable in any showdown, but the Party leadership solved this problem by transferring troops from outside the Beijing region to the capital. These troops were less likely to fraternise with the general public, either linguistically or temperamentally, since they would be jealous of, rather than sympathetic towards, Beijing and the privileged position of its inhabitants. Although the details are still sketchy, it is clear that the Party leaders debated possible actions through late May after the departure of Gorbachev, whose visit had been a diplomatic success and a public relations embarrassment. The decision for a military crackdown came from the very top, from Deng Xiaoping and from the Party veterans who supposedly had relinquished power in the retirements of the mid-1980s. Tanks and other armoured transport began moving towards the centre of Beijing in the night leading to 4 June. Although there was some firing in Tiananmen Square and the foreign press rapidly broadcast news of a 'Tiananmen massacre', the main killings occurred away from the Square as the military sought to clear streets of blockages. Exact numbers of dead may never be known, but a figure in the hundreds seems probable, well above immediate official figures, but well below the figures of 7000 or more circulated by the Western press.

The results of 4 June were all-embracing. Diplomatically China became isolated from the Western nations which had been such supporters of the Open Door and reform policies and of Deng as their architect. Economically China faced an abrupt cut in foreign investments and in tourist arrivals, with the threat of even more trade sanctions as China's human rights record came under scrutiny. Politically the Party veterans were revealed as determined to retain power by whatever means. Those with a softer line on the students such as Zhao Ziyang were purged of their government and Party posts, while the whole reform programme was thrown into doubt, as attacks on bourgeois liberalization mounted rapidly. The place of the military in China's political structure suddenly jumped to a level not seen since 1969, with Yang Shangkun as its top spokesman. Yang was the last active member of the Stalinist 'Twenty-eight Bolshevik' group that had taken over Party direction in the early 1930s before the rise of Mao.

Nevertheless the limitations of Party power to control the Chinese were revealed clearly in the weeks after 4 June. Student leaders who had been active in Beijing and who had been accused of plotting counter-revolutionary rebellion began to appear in Hong Kong, having been protected and hidden by ordinary citizens as they made their way south through the country. Among the Chinese overseas, and especially among those who had only recently left China for study in the West, organisations arose to call for democracy in China and to reject Communist Party leadership as discredited by the events in Beijing. Such rejection did not stem from pro-Guomindang feeling nor from direct Guomindang manipulation, but expressed a need for a new style of political life in China. Within China itself the Party issued study materials on the June events, with particular use of Deng Xiaoping's speech of 9 June, but the public's response was lukewarm, with limited interest in the old exercise of labelling some as counter-revolutionary. For the urban dwellers beset by inflation and evidence of official corruption, the May protests had focused on issues where their sympathy was with the protesters, while for peasants the whole event was too remote from their concerns for making money in the individualistic economy of the countryside. Thus the Party's ability to dictate political activism had been lost, as many had suspected through the evidence of the limited campaigns of the 1980s, but which 1989 proved. The Party held control by military power, by force of habit and by restricting access to information, but it could only retain that control by offering continuing economic opportunities to a general population grown cynical about empty revolutionary promises.

The Party leadership's forceful response to the demonstrators in Beijing had been duplicated in a few other centres in China such as Chengdu, but in many cities the demonstrators had been dispersed without serious bloodshed, as in Shanghai. Thus it was from Shanghai that Deng Xiaoping now chose his new Party head, Jiang Zemin, who, while no challenge to the veteran leaders politically, could be seen as symbolising the reformist line economically. It was clear, however, that vigorous calls for more openness to the West and for further economic reforms would not be welcome to leaders who had seen the capital virtually taken over by groups whom they regarded as corrupted by Western bourgeois values. The veterans therefore demanded a slowing of reform and a closer adherence to earlier, more socialistic policies, a view strongly endorsed by the Prime Minister, Li Peng. Economically the wish to curb inflation and the cut in foreign investment led to a period of retrenchment, as the government struggled to control the budget deficit, but it soon became clear that the centre's ability to dictate economic life in the regions was limited, especially in South China. Protracted negotiations to reorganise the tax burdens of the provinces to reflect the new post-1978 levels of economic activity were largely unsuccessful, as the coastal regions refused to pay higher proportions of the national tax revenue.

Internationally the isolation of China proved short-lived. Within weeks of the Beijing events, US officials were secretly visiting Beijing, supposedly to warn China of the consequences of its actions, while the administration of President Bush urged other nations to halt credits and investments. Major loans from international agencies were frozen, but after a brief pause investment continued from Hong Kong into South China, as the British colony pursued its drive to take advantage of cheaper labour and land across the border in Guangdong. Fuller rehabilitation arose out of the desire to make the United Nations an effective agency for peace as the enmities between the USA and the USSR declined. Since China held a permanent seat on the Security Council and could thwart UN initiatives by the use of its veto, the other powers had to involve China in diplomacy over areas of concern, such as Cambodia or Afghanistan. Nowhere was this more obvious than in the developing situation in the Persian Gulf, after Iraq overran Kuwait in August 1990.

Since the Western powers wished to restrain Iraq by the application of world pressure and later by international military forces, it was essential that China be fully involved in the diplomacy at the United Nations leading to the dispatch of multinational forces to drive out Iraqi troops. The USA, under President Bush, had also assumed that more could be gained by retaining some contacts with China, as for example in granting most-favoured-nation trading status, rather than in isolating China and thereby arousing patriotic support for China's leaders whose other internal claims to legitimacy were weak.

China in the 1990s

China by the mid-1990s was thus reintegrated into the world community at least as much as pre-1989, with a clear indication that it wished to become further integrated, as in its desire to join GATT, the General Agreement on Trade and Tariffs, and its successor, the World Trade Organisation, and in its acceptance of international copyright and intellectual property rights agreements. The struggles within the Party leadership over the pace of economic reform have been won in the short term by Deng Xiaoping, who vigorously supported the Open Door during a tour of South China in January and February 1992 and whose view on wider economic reform carried the day at the Party's Fourteenth Congress in October 1992. Nevertheless the future for China remains uncertain. The Party is still beset with problems of corruption and with the difficulty of defining its role in a period of mixed economy. The Party's leadership is firmly in the hands of those over 80 years old and there is no guarantee that their chosen successors will survive them. Among intellectuals there is a general disgust with the Party, both for its corruption and for its role in 1989, but there is no clear movement to replace the Party. At the provincial and local levels, there is a desire by cadres to continue with more parochial economic projects and to avoid political control from the centre. Inflation is limitedly under control, but it seems likely that population growth is not. The original Four Modernisations targets of 1200 million Chinese in the year 2000 has been revised upwards to 1300 million by the government, in part because the one-child family policy was no longer effectively operating because of numerous exemptions and of peasant willingness to pay financial penalties for extra births.

Life for the ordinary population in China has generally improved since Mao's death, but this general improvement is not collectively shared as in the past, so that there are many for whom conditions have deteriorated. The population is still clearly divided, in residency terms, into urban and rural dwellers, with extreme difficulty in changing registration. Rural dwellers now have the opportunity to contract for farms from their teams and to run them as they see fit, even employing labourers. They may use their wealth to build new houses or in other forms of display such as relating to marriage. Nevertheless the evidence of millions of migrant peasant labourers implies that particularly in the interior there have not been wealth-creating opportunities sufficient to retain villagers in their home places, even with the growth of township collective enterprises. Some would argue that a new class division is arising in the countryside between the inhabitants of areas able to take advantage of rapid economic growth, especially in the coastal regions, and those from areas where economic opportunities are few, who, if they choose to travel as guest workers to more prosperous areas, often suffer extreme living conditions and considerable discrimination. In rural areas the political role of the Party and the economic role of the old collective institutions such as the production team and the brigade have been greatly reduced, granting the individual much greater freedom for decision-making within the village. Nevertheless the shift has involved a rise in petty crime, the reduction in welfare support for the unfortunate, and considerable problems in maintaining the infrastructure necessary to allow successful household farming, such as dykes and irrigation systems. Further progress in rural areas will depend upon the continuing viability of township enterprises and the ability to maintain and raise agricultural yields on a gradually reducing stock of arable land.

In the cities, which under current definitions contain at least 25 per cent of China's population, the situation is different, although not for the farmers within the defined city areas, still over 50 per cent of the 'urban' population in the 1980s. The non-farming urban population rely heavily upon their employment units (*danwei*), which supply wages, define rank, and control housing, education and welfare arrangements. Although a small proportion of urban dwellers is now involved in individually owned or collective enterprises, the vast majority fall under state-operated units, with Party secretaries as the principal officers. The units have immense powers over the individual worker, for whom transfer between units is difficult. Although the system creates an 'iron rice-bowl' – that is, permanent guaranteed employment – this is at the price of pervasive control by the unit leaders, including control over such issues as marriage, travel and the birth of children, as well as the maintenance of a personal file which is the basis of one's political standing with the leadership. The unit system is unlikely to be challenged because of its usefulness to the Party leadership, even though its original socialist ideals have been severely eroded. Urban dwellers have access to food both through official shops and through the free market, while consumer goods are widely available, although not always of good quality.

China thus presents itself as a society which in eighty years has advanced, but not without many problems remaining. Territorially the China of 1911, with the exception of Outer Mongolia, has been retained, although the cost, especially in Tibet, has been high. Internationally it has risen from the weakling of 1911 to the independent power of the 1990s, with nuclear weapons, a developing navy and a leading role at the United Nations. Yet it is still only a developing country, with a low GNP per capita and urgently in need of foreign loans, to bolster its development and to balance its budget deficit. The economic system has moved from the limited market involvement of the peasants of 1911, via vigorously capitalist and socialist phases, to a highly mixed economy in the 1990s, in which local enterprise is the dynamic sector. Equally importantly the economy has expanded away from total dependence upon agriculture and the size of the annual harvest for its viability, a shift which must surely ensure greater stability in the future. Ultimately, despite more than doubling in population, China is wealthier *per capita* now than in 1911. This achievement has been at considerable cost, as the political means to gain the desired atmosphere for economic development have been argued over, either on the battlefield or in the higher levels of the Party, often with scant regard for the immediate impact upon the people. Politically the CCP has retained control for more than forty years, yet its current mandate to rule is based more on inertia than on faith in its ideology or the ability of its leaders. Socially the scholar-elite of the late Qing has been replaced by the cadre elite of the Communist period with its base in Marxist–Leninist ideology, but the effectiveness of this ideology may be as eroded by market forces as was the late Qing Confucianism by the challenge of the West. Culturally China has suffered considerable loss in its high culture, for although some of the past has been preserved as in cuisine and visual arts, in many areas such as literature and philosophy the past has been repudiated and no comparable achievements have been produced to match those of the past. Nevertheless, even after eighty years of attacks on the past, the Chinese of the 1990s still possess sufficient of their general cultural heritage to be clearly related to their fellow-countrymen of 1911.

In the lifetime of Deng Xiaoping China has striven to match its enemies and to take charge of its own destiny. This goal is now within reach but the question that remains is 'who in China will decide what that destiny should be as China approaches the twenty-first century?'

9 Other Parts of 'Greater China' since 1911

The preceding outline of the history of China since 1911 has been dominated by the events, personalities and trends in what is often called Mainland China. This was the administered area and population bequeathed to the Chinese Republic by the Qing Dynasty at its demise, excluding the Mongol lands in the north which in 1945 became the Mongolian People's Republic, also known as Outer Mongolia. Yet clearly there is a need for some representation of the history of other areas where ethnic Chinese have dominated the population, areas which today are claimed by the People's Republic as inalienable parts of China. These areas are Hong Kong, Macau and Taiwan with its associated offshore islands, and from the early 1990s they and the People's Republic of China together have often been described as 'Greater China'.

The purpose of this final chapter is to comment briefly on the history of these areas, while providing some cross-reference to the events in the mainland. The main focus will be upon Taiwan, since this passed back into Chinese control in 1945 after fifty years of Japanese rule, whereas Hong Kong and Macau have remained under their foreign colonial administrations.

It could be argued that there is a need for a far wider geographic scope than just these colonial fringes of China, because the Overseas Chinese have played important roles in south-east Asia and beyond, including forming the majority of the population in one state, Singapore. It is known, for example, that their financial contribution has been vital to China, in that remittances from overseas Chinese to their China-based families have been a major factor in allowing China to run a substantial negative trade balance without severe economic repercussions, especially during the Republican period. In addition there were at least four moments in the twentieth century, when the activities of the wider overseas Chinese community enhanced existing trends in China: their support of active revolutionaries before and during 1911, their anti-Japanese fervour during the Resistance War, the patriotic return of many to help in the reconstruction of the motherland in the 1950s and their willingness to invest in China after the Open Door policy was announced in the late 1970s. Yet the overseas Chinese have not been the dominant factor in any aspect of the twentieth-century history of the geographic area known as China, and hence the full history of these more scattered communities of ethnic Chinese must lie beyond the scope of this book.

The historical experience of the colonised areas of Hong Kong, Macau and Taiwan has been quite distinct. The island of Hong Kong became British territory in 1842, with later expansions in 1860 and 1898, the latter technically a lease rather than a full cession of territory by China. Macau was under the control of Portuguese officials by 1557, but was only fully accepted as Portuguese territory by treaty in 1887. Taiwan was theoretically ceded to Japan by the Treaty of Shimonoseki of April 1895 between the Qing Government and Japan, but in practice the Japanese Army had to occupy the island forcibly after a declaration of an independent republic by local leaders protesting against the peace settlement. Chinese armed resistance to Japanese rule continued in the interior for a decade and the Japanese also faced later rebellions by non-Chinese aboriginals who lived in the mountainous areas.

The history of Taiwan from 1911 to the present can be seen in two waves, both leading to a relatively high standard of living for the non-aboriginal population, while providing little by way of political freedom until very recently. Although a Japanese colony, Taiwan experienced considerable economic growth before 1941 and it has been claimed that the residents of Taiwan had the second highest standard of living in Asia in 1941, after Japan. The second wave of development occurred after 1949, when members of the Nationalist government, its military and some of its supporters fled to Taiwan and initiated economic programmes which by the 1990s had made Taiwan into the second-largest holder of international reserves, again after Japan.

The first wave of growth was initially based on the expansion of agricultural production to meet the needs of the Japanese market, especially in rice, sugar, bananas and pineapples, and the population more than doubled between 1895 and 1945, when over 6 million lived on the island. From the start of the world economic crisis in 1929, more emphasis was placed by Japan on the industrialisation of Taiwan, so that by 1939 it is estimated that industry and agriculture contributed equally to Taiwan's economy. While pursuing this economic growth, the Japanese also conceived of Taiwan as a colonial laboratory, in which the best possible techniques used by other colonial powers would be tested and improved upon. Hence the Japanese had detailed programmes for education, health and other social services, as well as developing the economic infrastructure through the building of roads, railways and communication networks.

The Pacific War severely damaged Taiwan's economy, both by reducing safe access to Japan and by physical destruction through bombing raids from late 1943. The status of Taiwan, as a part of the post-1895 Japanese empire, was discussed at the Cairo Conference of the leaders of the USA, Britain and China in 1943. It was decided that Japan would be stripped of all its territorial gains since 1895, which meant that Taiwan would be removed from Japanese control. It was assumed by the Chinese leadership that Taiwan would automatically revert to Chinese control, but some have argued that the status of Taiwan became unclear as a result of Japan's surrender, a view which has not been accepted by either the Chinese Nationalist or Communist governments. To handle the formal aspects of the Japanese surrender in Taiwan from August 1945, the Japanese commander-in-chief in Taiwan was ordered to consider himself under the authority of the Japanese commander in China and Japanese officers from Taiwan were present at the official surrender ceremony in Nanjing in early September. The Nationalist government at Chongqing appointed Chen Yi as the new governor for Taiwan, but he did not reach the island until late October, after more than 10 000 Chinese troops had been delivered to the island by US ships in mid-October. Repatriation of Japanese troops from Taiwan was completed by early April 1946, thus leaving the island in Nationalist Chinese hands.

The Chen Yi governorship was a time of great hardship for Taiwan, since the incoming administration and especially its military had little respect for the Taiwanese and wished to enrich themselves from the considerable assets left by the Japanese in the island. Tensions between the mainlanders and the Taiwanese climaxed in late February 1947, when an incident related to the operation of the tobacco monopoly exploded into a period of disorder, especially in Taibei. Military repression gradually restored order, but the memory of the events of early 1947 helped to poison relations between mainlanders and Taiwanese for several decades. Chen Yi was sacked by the mainland government for his handling of the situation, but this failed to appease the Taiwanese.

As the military and political position of the Nationalists deteriorated in mainland China, the necessity of using Taiwan as a last refuge became more likely. China's gold reserves and art treasures were being moved there by early 1949 and martial law was declared in the island in May 1949, even though there was no direct threat of Communist action on the island. Martial law remained in force until July 1987, while normal operation of China's 1947 constitution was restricted through the temporary provisions of April 1948, granting emergency powers to the President. In addition, by a constitutional interpretation of the Council of Grand Justices in January 1954, the members elected in 1947 and 1948 to the National Assembly, the Legislative *Yuan* and the Control *Yuan* were to continue to serve, pending a new election. This could not be held because of the 'Communist rebellion', so that the formal political leadership in Taiwan was frozen.

The government on Taiwan after 1949 claimed to represent the whole of China, using the title 'The Republic of China' and was recognised as such by a majority of the world's nations until the 1970s, when, as discussed in Chapter 8, the USA and the People's Republic both found reasons to end their mutual isolation. The Nationalist Party and the Nationalist Government's military held total dominance up to the late 1980s, with Jiang Jieshi as President up to his death in 1975 and his son, Jiang Jingguo, as President shortly thereafter.

Political domination over the Taiwanese through emergency powers and military monopoly needed to be complemented by measures to ensure that local resistance to the Guomindang remained limited. These measures were essentially economic and social in their superficial appearance, but also served the Guomindang's political needs. The most immediate need was to control rapid inflation, largely achieved by 1951 through the curbing of government spending. The most important measure, however, was land reform, a programme pursued on the mainland against the Guomindang by the Communists, but now, in a different context, pursued by the Guomindang against the only group with any potential power in Taiwan, the local landlords.

The land reform occurred in three stages up to 1953, an initial ceiling on rent levels, then the sale of lands confiscated from Japanese owners, and finally the sale by each landlord to the government of any landholding of more than approximately 3 hectares in paddy rice areas or 6 hectares in dry areas. The landlords were paid in a mixture of ten-year bonds and of stock in four government corporations. The government resold the land to the existing tenants with payment over ten years, reducing pure tenant farmers from 38 per cent of all farmers in 1950 to 15 per cent by 1960. The reform process was assisted by a Chinese and American Joint Commission on Rural Reconstruction, and to promote subsequent agricultural development 33 per cent of US aid between 1951 and 1965 was directed at agriculture. Much of the political credit for the success of the land reform went to Chen Cheng, the Nationalist governor of Taiwan, who went on to become vice-president of the Republic of China, before his death in 1965.

To retain the support of the Taiwanese and to maintain its claim to superiority over the Communists, the Nationalist government had to deliver economic improvement. This task was eased by the existing infrastructure created in Taiwan by the Japanese, including an educated work force, and by the limited geographic area of the island which could be firmly controlled by the government, unlike the mainland before 1949. The government also benefited from the outbreak of the Korean War and the freezing of relations between the USA and the People's Republic, which facilitated the regular delivery of US aid up to 1965. Nevertheless it was government policy which ensured that Taiwan would move from its economic situation of the early 1950s to that of the late 1980s. In the early 1950s Taiwan was heavily dependent upon agriculture for total production and for export receipts, and a majority of the limited industrial sector was in public ownership. By the late 1980s the value of industrial production was at least seven times that of agriculture, industrial exports exceeded 90 per cent of all exports and private ownership dominated the economy.

Economic policy passed through four stages, as industrial production expanded. The first stage up to 1952 paralleled the Communist efforts at reconstruction to achieve previously attained production levels. The second stage covered the 1950s, when the government supported private investment in labour-intensive light industry, with the aim of import-substitution. The limits of this policy with a small domestic market pushed the government in the 1960s to the third stage, that of production for export, mainly through light industry, but with some development of heavy industry. The first oil crisis in 1973 moved the government to the fourth stage, the promotion of capital-intensive industry, with an increasing emphasis by the 1980s on high technology.

The highest rates of economic growth were attained in the 1960s, but an average rate of more than 10 per cent was sustained for a thirty-five-year period from 1952, transforming the island from a backwater into a major world trader and earning it a place among the 'Four Tigers', the first four Asian countries to achieve economic takeoff in the post-1945 period. The early part of this success occurred against a background of US support, including financial aid up to 1965, and of diplomatic access to the West, but the later part was achieved despite Taiwan's relative diplomatic isolation, indicating the importance of internal factors in the success. One such factor was the high willingness of the population to work and save for family enrichment, an attribute often linked by analysts, somewhat arbitrarily, with Confucianism. Others include the ability of the government to sustain order and safeguard investment and the limited outlays required to provide adequate economic infrastructure within the narrow size of the island, as compared with such equivalent costs on the mainland.

Rapid economic growth has extracted an environmental cost, which has been seen at its worst in the Gaoxiong area in Taiwan's south-west, where there have been severe pollution problems. The rapid growth has also gradually moved Taiwan into a higher wage economy, with the result that its entrepreneurs have sought to expand their production into other geographic areas with lower wage costs. The late 1980s decisions to allow indirect trade with and direct investment in the People's Republic must be partly seen in this context and have provided a mechanism for the continuation of economic growth into the 1990s.

The process of economic growth in Taiwan has gradually increased individual wealth, but, according to most analysts, has not resulted in a widening of an income gap, between a wealthy few and an impoverished many. This has allowed the appearance of a substantial middle class, which has increasingly questioned the lack of political freedoms in Taiwan. The government at first responded cautiously to calls for liberalisation, in part from fears that there would be vigorous calls for the independence of Taiwan, for which end a few individuals campaigned. Nevertheless with the ageing of Jiang Jieshi and with the counter-example of the chaos of the Cultural Revolution on the mainland, it was possible to contemplate limited change, which has been associated with the rise of Jiang's son to effective power.

Jiang Jingguo became the Prime Minister in Taiwan in 1972, just as US policy was turning towards opening contact with the People's Republic. His response was to seek ways to protect and reform Taiwan, so that it would not become unstable if US recognition was withdrawn. He began with a National Construction Conference in 1972 and initiated the increasing appointment of Taiwanese to high posts in government and party. In December 1972 partial elections were held for the National Assembly and the Legislative *Yuan*, and, of the eighty-nine new members elected, seventy-nine were Taiwan-born. 1972 also saw the government's initiation of ten major projects to sustain economic growth. The need for care to ensure stability was increased by the effects of the 1973 oil crisis, which threatened the economic growth strategy upon which the Nationalist Party's right to rule could continue to be justified. After the death of Jiang Jieshi in early 1975, Jiang Jingguo was able to assume the presidency in Taiwan at the next indirect presidential election, but wider liberalization was halted by violence during the 1977 local government elections and by the announcement of the withdrawal of US recognition in mid-December 1978, which caused cancellation of the late December elections.

During the early 1980s there was considerable political activity by individuals in the *dangwai* (literally outside the Party), but rapid change only occurred with three unexpected moves by Jiang Jingguo, in what turned out to be the last eighteen months of his life. The first was to sanction the existence of opposition parties, which allowed the Democratic Progressive Party to be announced in September 1986, based mainly on activists in the *dangwai* movement. The second was to announce in November 1986 the abolition of martial law, which became effective in 1987, although certain aspects of emergency regulations remained in place until 1992. The third in November 1987 was to allow Taiwan residents to visit the People's Republic, even while no formal government-to-government contacts existed. The Democratic Progressive Party won some 25 per cent of the votes in the December 1986 elections, some 35 per cent in 1989, thereby providing a public voice for opposition within the formal political institutions of the Republic, without overwhelming the Guomindang.

Jiang Jingguo died in January 1988 and was succeeded by his Taiwan-born Vice-President, Li Denghui, who was re-elected as President by the National Assembly in 1990. Li has been able to maintain the momentum towards reform, in particular by ensuring that the members elected to political bodies in 1947 and 1948 be finally forced to retire. Dialogue has begun with the People's Republic through the unofficial Straits Exchange Foundation, headed by former government officials, and investment by Taiwan's business community into neighbouring Fujian province has boomed. Total investment in the mainland had reached at least US$ 7 billion by mid-1993. With increased confidence in the economic strength of Taiwan and with Taiwan now active in boosting the mainland's economic growth, Li has pursued a policy of seeking greater diplomatic presence for Taiwan in the wider world, including moves towards a separate Taiwan seat at the United Nations, despite protests from Beijing. Thus while both Beijing and Taibei continue to talk of one China, the moment for formal reunification seems as remote as ever.

In contrast, formal reunification is to take place, by diplomatic agreement, for Hong Kong in 1997 and for Macau in 1999, but under a formula of 'one country, two systems'. This will permit the retention of the existing economic systems of the two territories as Special Administrative Regions within China. Such a formula reflects what has been the key nature of Hong Kong throughout the twentieth century, its geographic and demographic links with China but its ability to remain distinct from China, where political or economic advantage required this.

Hong Kong was established as an entrepôt, a trading centre for foreigners for the safe trans-shipment of goods to and from the China market, but already by 1911 it had developed a considerable Chinese population. This population was to wax and wane, according to the fortunes of China. It rose markedly with the Japanese attack in south China in 1938, fell rapidly upon the occupation by the Japanese in 1941, and rose again during the civil war of the late 1940s, with migrants both from south China and from the Shanghai area. It experienced waves of migration, legal and illegal, from the People's Republic, according to the intensity of distress there, one peak being in 1962 as the effects of the Great Leap Forward hit hardest.

Economic activity was directly tied with China up to 1949, but the imposition of the Western embargo on trade with the People's Republic because of the Korean War hit Hong Kong severely. The local response was to seek to create a manufacturing base in Hong Kong, relying upon the only resources available, Chinese labour drawn largely from south China migrants and Chinese entrepreneurial skills drawn in part from the Shanghai migrants. The results were spectacularly successful, with rapid growth in light industries, despite the absence of the China trade. Again, as in Taiwan, the government provided the framework for stability and ensured opportunities for private investment to be profitable, including a very light tax regime. The reopening of China from the 1970s allowed Hong Kong to resume its role as coordinator for south China's trade, while maintaining its manufacturing and financial operations. The more labour-intensive parts of manufacturing were increasingly transferred in the 1980s to plants operated as joint ventures within China, thereby promoting economic growth in Guangdong. At the same time enterprises from the People's Republic began major investments in Hong Kong, so that economic interdependence of the two increased. These trends might be taken to indicate that the 1997 formal reunification will be a smooth step on an already-established route towards integration. Nevertheless, although Hong Kong has been known as a place to make money with little interest in politics, it is clear that there is some concern over the political arrangements for the reunification, as spelt out in the Basic Law of 1990. The events of 1989 in China stirred a vigorous public response in Hong Kong, with huge demonstrations against the suppression of pro-democracy activists. Some of the Hong Kong middle class have argued for a wider basis for representative democracy than the Basic Law envisaged and Patten, the new Governor in 1992, also proposed changes in the same direction, which have angered the Chinese government. The Chinese government wishes to take over a territory in which it can assert its authority through a chief executive, while Britain through Patten is belatedly arguing for somewhat more democratic accountability, by making the legislative council a more representative body, thereby restricting the executive's authority.

The success or failure of the 1997 reunification and of the smaller 1999 version in Macau will have great importance, not only for the populations of these territories, but for the prospects for eventual reunification with Taiwan. If the current region of high economic growth in south-east China can continue its success after the incorporation of Hong Kong and Macau, this will mean that the Open Door policy in China will retain its attractiveness. In consequence the political distinctions between a south-east China run by local leaders largely beyond Beijing's control and a Taiwan run by its own government will become increasingly blurred. If, however, the incorporation fails to deliver continued economic success, then the central leaders in Beijing may be tempted to seek reunification with Taiwan through threats and direct pressure, in the belief that economic trends will never bring Taiwan back to what Beijing still conceives Taiwan's proper place to be – that is, part of the Chinese motherland to be governed from one centre for the benefit of all Chinese.

Selective Bibliography

General Reference Works

Cheng, Peter, *China* (Oxford/Santa Barbara: Clio Press, 1983) an annotated bibliography of books in English.

Hook, Brian and Twitchett, Denis C. (eds) *The Cambridge Encyclopedia of China* (Cambridge: Cambridge University Press) 2nd ed, 1991; general information by a panel of specialists.

Periodicals

The following are specialist publications on twentieth-century China:

The China Journal (formerly *Australian Journal of Chinese Affairs*), *China Quarterly* and *Modern China*. Articles on China can be found in many scholarly journals on Asia such as the *Journal of Asian Studies*. Contemporary information can be gleaned from the *Far Eastern Economic Review* and from Chinese official publications, especially the *Beijing Review*, formerly *Peking Review*.

Atlases

Blunden, Caroline and Elvin, Mark, *Cultural Atlas of China* (Oxford: Phaidon, 1983).

Geelan, P.J.M. and Twitchett, Denis C. (eds), *The Times Atlas of China* (London: Times Books, 1974).

Biographical Dictionaries

Boorman, Howard L. (ed.) *Biographical Dictionary of Republican China*, 5 volumes (New York: Columbia University Press, 1967–79).

Clark, Anne, B. and Klein, Donald W., *Biographic Dictionary of Chinese Communism 1921–1965* (Cambridge, Mass.: Harvard University Press, 1971).

Bartke, Wolfgang, *Who's Who in the People's Republic of China* (Munich: Saur, 2nd edn 1987, 3rd edn 1991).

290

General Background Histories

Fairbank, John K. and Twitchett, Denis C. (eds) *The Cambridge History of China*, 15 volumes (Cambridge: Cambridge University Press, 1978–); the largest history of China in English: each volume has an extensive bibliography.

Fairbank, John K. and Reischauer, Edwin O., *China: Tradition and Transformation* (Sydney/London: Allen & Unwin, 1989).

Fu Zhengyuan, *Autocratic Tradition and Chinese Politics* (Cambridge: Cambridge University Press, 1993); a pessimistic view of China's prospects for change since 1949.

Gernet, Jacques (tr. J.R. Foster) *A History of Chinese Civilization* (Cambridge: Cambridge University Press, 1982).

Hucker, Charles O., *China's Imperial Past: An introduction to Chinese history and culture* (London: Duckworth, 1975).

Rodzinski, Witold, *The Walled Kingdom: A History of China from 2000 BC to the Present* (London: Fontana, 2nd edn, 1991).

Chapter 1

The following can be usefully consulted on general trends in the Qing period:

Eastman, Lloyd E., *Family, Fields and Ancestors: Constancy and Change in China's Social and Economic History, 1550–1949* (Oxford/New York: Oxford University Press, 1988); a summary of recent writings on Chinese social and economic history.

Hsu, Immanuel C.Y., *The Rise of Modern China* (Oxford/New York: Oxford University Press, 4th edn, 1990); largely political history.

Smith, Richard J., *China's Cultural Heritage: the Ch'ing Dynasty, 1644–1912* (Boulder: Westview Press, 1983).

Wakeman, Frederic, *The Fall of Imperial China* (New York: Free Press, 1975).

There is no single book to cover the build-up towards the 1911 Revolution, but the following can be consulted:

Esherick, Joseph W., *Reform and Revolution in China: The 1911 Revolution in Hunan and Hubei* (Berkeley: University of California Press, 1976).

Rhoads, Edward J.M., *China's Republican Revolution: The Case of Kwangtung, 1895–1913* (Cambridge, Mass.: Harvard University Press, 1975).

Wright, Mary C. (ed.) *China in Revolution: The First Phase 1900–1913* (New Haven: Yale University Press, 1968).

Chapters 2 to 8: General books

Croll, Elizabeth, *Feminism and Socialism in China* (London: Routledge and Kegan Paul, 1978); a general introduction to women's history in modern China.

Feuerwerker, Albert, *Economic Trends in the Republic of China 1912–1949* (Ann Arbor: Center for Chinese Studies, Michigan University, 1977).

Howe, Christopher, *China's Economy: A Basic Guide* (London: Granada, 1978).

Spence, Jonathan D., *The Gate of Heavenly Peace: The Chinese and their Revolution, 1895–1980* (New York: Viking, 1981); a history focusing on intellectuals and their writings.

Tan, Chester C., *Chinese Political Thought in the Twentieth Century* (Garden City, N.Y.: Doubleday, 1971).

Yang, C.K., *Religion in Chinese Society* (Berkeley: University of California Press, 1961).

Chapters 2 to 7: The Chinese Communist Party

Bianco, Lucian (tr. M. Bell). *Origins of the Chinese Revolution 1915–1949* (Stanford: Stanford University Press, 1971).

Harrison, James P., *The Long March to Power: A History of the Chinese Communist Party, 1921–72* (New York: Praeger, 1973).

Schram, Stuart R., *Mao Tse-tung* (Harmondsworth: Penguin, 1966).

Schram, Stuart, R., *The Thought of Mao Tse-tung* (Cambridge: Cambridge University Press, 1989).

Chapters 2 to 8: Foreign Relations

Gittings, John, *The World and China, 1922–1972* (London: Eyre Methuen, 1974).

Quested, Rosemary K.I., *Sino-Russian Relations: A Short History* (Sydney: Allen and Unwin, 1984).

Schaller, Michael, *The United States and China in the Twentieth Century* (Oxford/New York: Oxford University Press, 1990).

Wang Gungwu, *China and the World since 1949: The Impact of Independence, Modernity and Revolution* (London: Macmillan, 1977).

There is no single volume history of Sino-Japanese relations, but one can usefully consult:

Conroy, Hilary and Coox, Alvin D. (eds) *China and Japan: Search for Balance since World War One* (Santa Barbara: ABC–Clio Press, 1978).

Chapter 2

On the political history, consult:

Friedman, Edward, *Backward toward Revolution: The Chinese Revolutionary Party* (Berkeley: University of California Press, 1974).
Li Chien-nung (tr. Teng Ssu-yu and J. Ingalls). *The Political History of China, 1840–1928* (Princeton: Van Nostrand, 1956).
Wilbur, Martin C., *Sun Yat-sen, Frustrated Patriot* (New York: Columbia University Press, 1976).
Young, Ernest P., *The Presidency of Yuan Shih-k'ai: Liberalism and Dictatorship in Early Republican China* (Ann Arbor: University of Michigan Press, 1977).

On the cultural history, consult:

Chow Tse-tsung, *The May Fourth Movement: Intellectual Revolution in Modern China* (Cambridge, Mass.: Harvard University Press, 1960); the seminal study in English on the topic.
Chen, Joseph T., *The May Fourth Movement in Shanghai: The Making of a Social Movement in Modern China* (Leiden: Brill, 1971); a critique of Chow Tse-tsung's view.
Schwarcz, Vera, *Chinese Enlightenment: Intellectuals and the Legacy of the May Fourth Movement of 1919* (Berkeley: University of California Press, 1986).

Chapter 3

On warlords, consult:

Chen, Jerome, *The Military-Gentry Coalition: China under the Warlords* (Toronto: University of Toronto–York University Joint Centre on Modern East Asia, 1979).
Ch'i Hsi-sheng, *Warlord Politics in China, 1916–1928* (Stanford: Stanford University Press, 1976).
McCormack, Gavin, *Chang Tso-lin in Northeast China, 1911–1928* (Folkestone: Dawson, 1977).
Sheridan, James E., *China in Disintegration: the Republican Era in Chinese history, 1912–1949* (New York: Free Press, 1975).
Sheridan, James, E., *Chinese Warlord: the Career of Feng Yü-hsiang* (Stanford: Stanford University Press, 1966).

On the early Chinese Communist Party, consult:

Dirlik, Arif, *The Origins of Chinese Communism* (New York/Oxford: Oxford University Press, 1989).

Van de Ven, Hans, *From Friend to Comrade: The Founding of the Chinese Communist Party, 1920–1927* (Berkeley: University of California Press, 1991).

Chapter 4

On the Nationalist Party, consult:

Bedeski, Robert E., *State-building in Modern China: The Kuomintang in the Prewar Period* (Berkeley: Center for Chinese Studies, 1981).
Eastman, Lloyd E., *The Abortive Revolution: China under Nationalist Rule, 1927–1937* (Cambridge, Mass.: Harvard University Press, 1974) reprinted 1990.
Eastman, Lloyd E., *The Nationalist Era in China, 1927–1949* (Cambridge: Cambridge University Press, 1991).

On the Communist Party, consult:

Rue, John E., *Mao Tse-tung in Opposition, 1927–1935* (Stanford: Stanford University Press, 1966).
Schwartz, Benjamin, *Chinese Communism and the Rise of Mao* (Cambridge, Mass.: Harvard University Press, 1951); the first scholarly discussion in English of the 'Maoist' strategy.
Snow, Edgar, *Red Star over China* (London: Gollancz, 1937) (reprinted with revisions 1968 and 1972); the reports of the first Western journalist to interview Mao.

Chapter 5

On the Nationalist Party at war with Japan, consult:

Ch'i Hsi-sheng, *Nationalist China at War: Military Defeats and Political Collapse, 1937–1945* (Ann Arbor: University of Michigan Press, 1982).
Eastman, Lloyd E., *Seeds of Destruction: Nationalist China in War and Revolution, 1937–1949* (Stanford: Stanford University Press, 1984).
Sih, Paul K.T. (ed.) *Nationalist China during the Sino-Japanese War, 1937–1945* (Hicksville, N.Y.: Exposition Press, 1978).

On the Communist Party at war with Japan, consult:

Chen Yung-fa, *Making Revolution: the Communist Movement in Eastern and Central China, 1937–1945* (Berkeley: University of California Press, 1986).
Goldstein, Steven M. and Hartford, Kathleen (eds) *Single Sparks: China's Rural Revolutions* (Armonk: M.E. Sharpe, 1989).
Johnson, Chalmers, *Peasant Nationalism and Communist Power: The Emerg-

ence of Revolutionary China, 1937–1945 (Stanford, Stanford University Press, 1962).

Selden, Mark, *The Yenan Way in Revolutionary China* (Cambridge, Mass.: Harvard University Press, 1971).

On the civil war period and land reform, consult:

Hinton, William, *Fanshen: A Documentary of Revolution in a Chinese Village* (New York: Monthly Review Press, 1966); the classic account of land reform in a north China village.

Levine, Steven I., *Anvil of Victory: The Communist Revolution in Manchuria, 1945–1948* (New York: Columbia University Press, 1987).

Pepper, Suzanne, *Civil War in China: The Political Struggle, 1945–1949* (Berkeley: University of California Press, 1978).

Chapters 6 to 8: Documents

Hinton, Harold C. (ed.) *The People's Republic of China: A Documentary Survey*, 5 volumes (Wilmington: Scholarly Resources, 1980).

Hinton, Harold C. (ed.) *The People's Republic of China, 1979–1984: A Documentary Survey*, 2 volumes (Wilmington: Scholarly Resources, 1986).

Selden, Mark (ed.) *The People's Republic of China: A Documentary History of Revolutionary Change* (New York: Monthly Review Press, 1979).

Chapters 6 to 8: General Works

Brugger, Bill, *Contemporary China* (London: Croom Helm, 1977).

Harding, Harry, *Organizing China: The Problem of Bureaucracy, 1949–1976* (Stanford: Stanford University Press, 1986).

Meisner, Maurice, *Mao's China and After* (New York: Free Press, 1986).

Parish, William L. and Whyte, Martin K., *Village and Family in Contemporary China* (Chicago: University of Chicago Press, 1978); a study of local life using refugee sources.

Chapter 6

Friedman, Edward, Pickowicz, Paul G. and Selden, Mark, with Johnson, Kay Ann, *Chinese Village, Socialist State* (New Haven: Yale University Press, 1991); life in one of China's 1950s model villages, analysed by Western scholars with privileged access to the village since 1978.

MacFarquhar, Roderick, *The Origins of the Cultural Revolution: Volume one: Contradictions among the People, 1956–7* (New York: Columbia University Press, 1974).

Shue, Vivienne, *Peasant China in Transition: The Dynamics of Development toward Socialism, 1949–1956* (Berkeley: University of California Press, 1980).

Chapter 7

Studies at the time of the Cultural Revolution include:

Dittmer, Lowell, *Liu Shao-ch'i and the Chinese Cultural Revolution: The Politics of Mass Criticism* (Berkeley: University of California Press, 1974).
Esmein, Jean (tr. W.J.F. Jenner) *The Chinese Cultural Revolution* (London: Deutsch, 1975).

More recent studies can be accessed through:

MacFarquhar, Roderick, *The Origins of the Chinese Cultural Revolution: Volume two: The Great Leap Forward 1958–1960* (Oxford: Oxford University Press, 1983).
Joseph, William P., Wong, Christine P.W. and Zweig, David (eds) *New Perspectives on the Cultural Revolution* (Cambridge, Mass.: Council on East Asian Studies, Harvard University, 1991).

Chapter 8

The range of books on recent China is huge, especially in the wake of events in 1989. The following may serve as introductions:

Chan, Anita, Madsen, Richard and Unger, Jonathan, *Chen Village under Mao and Deng* (Berkeley: University of California Press, 1992) 2nd edn.
Chang, David W-w., *China under Deng Xiaoping: Political and Economic Reform* (London: Macmillan, 1988).
Harding, Harry, *China's Second Revolution: Reform after Mao* (Washington D.C.: Brooking Institution, 1987).
Hsu, Immanuel Y.C., *China without Mao: The Search for a New Order* (Oxford/New York: Oxford University Press, 1990), 2nd edn.
Unger, Jonathan (ed.) *The Pro-Democracy Protests in China: Reports from the Provinces* (Sydney: Allen & Unwin, 1991).

Chapter 9

For a general introduction on Taiwan, consult:

Long, Simon, *Taiwan: China's Last Frontier* (New York: St Martin's Press, 1991).

For Taiwan's earlier economic development, consult:

Ho, Samuel P.S., *Economic Development in Taiwan 1860–1970* (New Haven: Yale University Press, 1978).

For recent appraisals of Taiwan, consult:

Tsang, Steve (ed.) *In the Shadow of China: Political Developments in Taiwan since 1949* (London: Hurst, 1993).
Simon, D.K. and Kau, M.Y.M. (eds) *Taiwan: Beyond the Economic Miracle* (Armonk: Sharpe, 1992).
Klintworth, G. (ed.) *Taiwan in the Asia-Pacific in the 1990s* (St Leonards, NSW: Allen & Unwin, 1994).

For a wide-ranging introduction to Hong Kong, consult:

Lo, C.P., *Hong Kong* (London: Belhaven, 1992).

For Hong Kong's earlier history, see:

Endacott, G.B., *A History of Hong Kong* (Oxford: Oxford University Press, 1958) 1st edn; revised edn (Hong Kong: Oxford University Press, 1973).

For Macau, consult:

Cremer, R.D. (ed.) *Macau: City of Commerce and Culture* (Hong Kong: API Press, 1991) 2nd edn.

Index